phonedemic

The unrelenting loss of humanity's ability to *truly* connect

by
Ana Miranda

www.phonedemic.com

Published by:

Cover artwork by Book Brush.
Format and layout by Joanie Wolfe (www.3wolves.org).

This book is a non-fiction work.
All of the events are true to the best of the author's recollection.
Names have been changed to protect the identity of individuals.
The views expressed in this book are those of the author.

ISBN 9780968631263
first edition, first printing

Dear Jay,

Thank you for the positive impact you contribute to the world's people.

With Gratitude,

[illegible]

2025

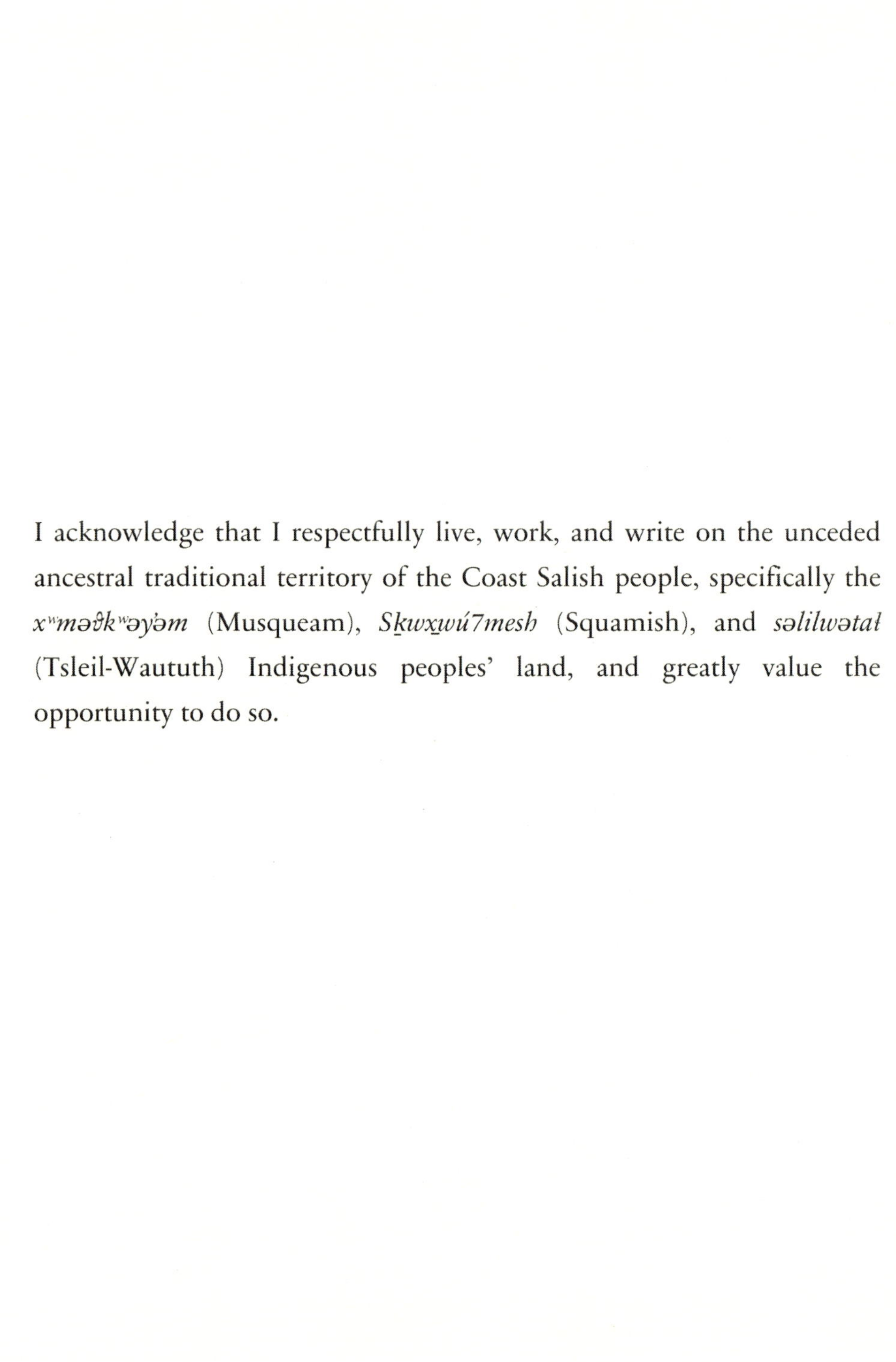

I acknowledge that I respectfully live, work, and write on the unceded ancestral traditional territory of the Coast Salish people, specifically the *xʷməθkʷəy̓əm* (Musqueam), *S<u>k</u>wx<u>w</u>ú7mesh* (Squamish), and *səlilwətaɬ* (Tsleil-Waututh) Indigenous peoples' land, and greatly value the opportunity to do so.

For M.A.R.C.:
May your lives be graced with the gift of presence,
and may you always make the choice to keep your gaze forward and your heads held high.

And to J. L., whose two words "just write"
compelled me to continue forward.

Contents

phonedemic

The unrelenting loss
of humanity's ability
to *truly* connect

The author suggests that this publication be read in a continuous manner, termed *binge-reading*. As it travels through time, this book delivers messages of encouragement and positive change, therefore, it is important the material is not put aside for extended periods.

Just begin and you will understand.

Every choice we make, every thought and feeling we have, is an act of power that has biological, environmental, social, personal, and global consequences. We are everywhere our thoughts are and thus our personal responsibility includes our energy contributions.

Caroline Myss, PhD[1]

1 Myss, C. (1996). *Anatomy of the spirit* (p. 220). New York, NY: Harmony Books.

"Hello...?"

Hello?

Hello—Is anyone there?

Hello?

Buzz, ding, ping, ring...

Is anyone—still—*really*—out there?

I often wonder, contemplate, analyze the current state of our human condition in the Western world, which extends throughout the globe to most of the *civilized* world. Our progress seems to have been swiftly replaced with an anxiety-ridden shell of what we once were, or could be.

A rare sighting in the early 1980s wealthy users could flash from their convertibles, the initial purpose of the mobile phone has morphed into an all-consuming addictive epidemic. Socially normalized and cunning in its presentation, many of us are unaware of how the *smart*phone[2] (referred to as *the thing* throughout) and all its applications (or apps) have swept into our existence with such force. Just drive past a bus stop, watch people walk down the street, witness couples dining-out. From babies, kids, the elderly, and so many in between, what have we become?

2 The first *smart*phone was the Blackberry, developed by Canadian company, Research in Motion (RIM; https://www.cbc.ca/news/entertainment/blackberry-film-baruchel-1.6560875). Johnson, M. (Director, Writer)., & Miller, M. (Writer). (2023). Blackberry [Film] (Producers: Fraser Ash, Niv Fichman, Kevin Krikst, & Mathew Miller). XYZ Films, Rhombus Media, Zapruder Films; Elevation Pictures.

How is it that half of the strollers I walk by have a mobile device propped-up on its tray-table in front of the infant or preschooler? Are so many of us unable to cope that we tune-out what is truly meant to be looked at—that is, each other, ourselves, and the world around us? Yes, I am the first to admit that parenting is damn difficult. I have raised three sons (and for several years four) largely on my own and, I assure you, there was never a device that took from the (at times) constant sock- and shoe-throwing, snack-wanting, bottle-tossing antics of stroller mayhem, and yet this was a part of life—part of the beautiful chaotic mayhem of *all* that parenting is. But a mobile device to dumb it down? How? Why? God forbid the children have some boundaries to face, or their parent or caregiver has to deal with a temper tantrum. How will this generation learn to cope with life? How will they raise the next generation with the battle of *the thing* being the centrepiece of existence itself. What role will it play in healthy attachment?

We have yet to see the long-term damage that *the thing* may produce. Blocked-out, masked, dumbed-down, numbed-out, filtered—essentially causing us to lose ourselves and the beauty in life (amongst times of turmoil) all around us. We haven't even touched-on the images and videos which are viewed, the language and the constant harsh and somewhat toxic opinions and damage they instill.

"Get used to it", "it's not going anywhere," "it's here to stay," "it's the wave of the future" are common responses to all who feel affected yet trapped as to how to be otherwise. Close your eyes, you can see it: The glossy-lit pearl casing of the gold-tone frame with the triple-camera lens, calling you to upgrade and get in on more. More gigs, more data, more likes, more followers. More—More. From bus stops to billboards to popup ads; they are there—calling you. More—More. Like the best-dressed alcohol bottle on the billboard, glistening just so. Its dewy condensation, and back-lit glow. More—More. There. Wanting. More.

Seen to be far less detrimental and mainstream, from the 8-year-old down the street, who was given his dad's *old* phone, to the 11-year-old so-and-so who "really needs it" because 2 days a week she takes care of her youngest sister (insert landline here or—at least—the limiting of device usage to only within the hours of this *needed* time). Everywhere. All the excuses. All the reasons why. Programmed—all the reasons why.

I have a solid "no cell phone until high school" policy in my household. I had to navigate all the pleads: "Billy and Bianca have phones and…and…and…and…." I recall years ago a school field trip to the Museum of Anthropology where a female Grade 4 student had a phone to "take pictures"—a gift from her mom. This device became the focal point of the elementary students on the trip rather than the vast amount to view all around us—such a shame. From doctors' offices to bus benches, restaurants, coffee shops. Everywhere. Not many of us just *sit* anymore. We are constantly preoccupied—obsessed—addicted.

Not many years ago, humans walked down streets with their heads up, eyes forward, looking ahead, looking at each other, or not. They acknowledged, sometimes ignored, at times felt awkward, but this was part of the human exchange. It was part of social learning, growth, and development. Typically peaceful, often inward in thoughts and feelings. Taking-in the world around us, whether light, dark, or otherwise, at that moment. Whatever we were, it was the present, we were present and not being bombarded by outer influences.

How has this happened? Or rather, how have we *allowed* this to happen?

In the following pages, I will describe what I see as having changed—what has been lost over the current course of that which I refer to as the *phonedemic*, and how so many have *lost* their lives and are completely oblivious of this. The silent sweep of the *modern* world has left us walking with our heads down, unaware of our surroundings, each other, and ourselves.

Today, we have lost the simplicity of that which I believe we were created for: movement, free thinking, the pure enjoyment of socialization together as creatures; away from that which keeps us on the constant lookout for something *other*, something else, some*one* else. We have moved away from ourselves, and our purpose.

A canvas hangs on my wall which reads: "Wherever you are, be All there." Simple really. But ask yourself, "Is it simple?" With the sophistication of modern technology companies using calculated angles to prey on our brain centres, targeting us from all sides, it has become increasingly more challenging to separate ourselves from this bombardment. But it is not impossible. I like that saying about life in general, "Difficult, but not impossible." Words I often live by. Yet with the latest generation being raised amidst this culture, they do not know life without *smart*phones. Groomed with the devices in their hands; babies being strolled around with them.... A report[3,4] was released stating that even dogs have become depressed as their owners spend much of their time with their faces directed into their devices, even being glued to them while they are on a dog-walk. Wow.

3 Warning: Your cell phone addiction could be causing 'doggy depression'. *bp Magazine.* Accessed 2024-12-02, https://www.bphope.com/pets/warning-your-cell-phone-addiction-could-be-causing-doggy-depression

4 Petminded.co. (2020, October 3). *How your dog feels about your smartphone.* Accessed 2024-12-02, https://www.petminded.co/blog/your-dog-wants-you-to-put-your-phone-down

We wonder how the mental health crisis has skyrocketed to epic proportions and suicide rates in teenagers have reached an all-time high. Why? Humans are structured to thrive on connections—real connections with other humans, animals, nature. We have an ingrained need to gain information from others through looking into their eyes, seeing their facial expressions, their mannerisms, their gestures which come from their physical bodies, from being in their presence—not from seeing them on a screen. We thrive on *true* human interaction more than many of us recognize, and I can't help but feel this is being sorely missed.

The mobile and media giants have crept in, brainwashing us, bit by bit, piece by piece, they have taken-over our lives, and they will continue to do so as generations grow into this vortex of *loss of oneself*. Whether Gen X, Y, or Z, baby boomer, or otherwise, we are abandoning ourselves.

A few years back, a close family member from the baby-boomer generation whom I love dearly, flew thousands of miles to visit, and I was saddened to see that she had also been sucked into the mobile phone tornado. A former high school teacher and previously engaging conversationalist, she had always been an upbeat and energetic person. Yet on this particular trip with cell phone in hand, she was unable to be present. On more recent trips, I have noticed a positive difference. She has naturally become more aware of the effect the cell phone has had on her existence and has scaled down on her usage.

Years ago, my mother contemplated hosting an international student. Once the decision had been made, my sons were excited about being exposed to life from another country. Though he spoke English quite well, it was quickly apparent that he was unable to connect, converse, or be present without his device in-hand, taking away any potential connections we might have made. At thanksgiving dinner, cell phone in-hand again, all attempts to disconnect him from this all-powerful draw were lost, even on this occasion. Without having personal experience with sending one of my sons away to school in another country, I imagined that one's parents' hope for their child would be to grow in culture, language, and life experience. Yet this too was lost to the downward pull of *the thing*.

I have seen the impact of *the thing* time and time again, and I am deeply concerned about the impact it is having on us all—so much so that it has urged me to write about my opposition with the hope of bringing the seriousness of this situation to light.

Wherever you are, be *All* there.

Check-in

It's time to check back in fellow humans—to check-in to life again, this immense gift. This is the ultimate opportunity to thrive and experience the life we have been given. Look around. Take it in.

The beauty, the strife, the sheer majesty of the daily offering of living and breathing on this planet. Yes, that's right people—planet—this world upon which we *live*. Think of that, in and of itself. Is that not a mind-blowing soul-shaking cell(ular) over-throwing concept to be lost inside? Oh—and the ocean. The same one whose tides and depth of life remains intact as it rotates with gravity keeping all housed inside. The nature, the atmosphere, all the species which co-exist along with our own, the galaxy, the moon, the neighbouring planets. The relationships we experience can offer us the most fulfilling learnings to the least inspiring or abusive encounters, and everything in between—all of it. All of it. It is here. It is now. It is happening—here and now. It's not behind some filtered screen or falsified presentation of self. Can you feel it? Reach out. Touch your skin, grip your hair. Don't have any? Great. Feel it. Breathe. Here. A true gift. Now. Here.

> "To see, to experience, and to honour is to participate in life instead of standing back and judging it."[5]

I acknowledge whole-heartedly that life can also be a gut-wrenching painful rock-you-to-your-core experience—a complete and utter soul-levelling upheaval of oneself. Yes, we need to honour that yet not look to numbing-away through spending countless hours of time *we do not get*

[5] Singer, M. A. (2007). *The untethered soul: The journey beyond yourself* (p. 177). Oakland, CA: New Harbinger Publications.

back in a swiping drift of disconnected escape. This is such loss. Daily loss. An entire culture steered away from being present. *A civilization—lost.*

As an inhabitant of our planet, it is my belief that we do not have time to waste what truly matters. True connection with others. Love. Time spent towards caring-for, standing-up, rallying, for so much that is at stake today. We are so greatly needed. With even a fraction of the time spent on devices applied to causes that truly require our attention, just *Imagine* (insert John Lennon here, "You may say that I'm a dreamer—but I'm not the only one"[6]) how much we could gain collectively in sorting through this mess we have gotten ourselves into, our planet into.

> "Remember to look up at the stars and not down at your feet. Try to make sense of what you see and wonder about what makes the universe exist. Be curious."[7]

I love the story of a famous popstar from England who does not own a cell phone. He has a landline and makes plans with friends to meet-up. Imagine. In this regard, I think of him as a free man. Others adapt. They make allowances. This is what we did previously. There is so much learning in this, in and of itself.

Now, I am not suggesting that this is the way for you. For many, this may seem like an extreme solution (or perhaps not?). But let us check-in on a happier medium which may allow us to gain back our independence and walk more freely, away from the current ties that bind so tightly at times.

6 Lennon, J., & Ono, Y. (Songwriters). (1971). Imagine [Song]. On *Imagine* [Album] (Producers: John Lennon, Yoko Ono, & Phil Spector). Label: Apple.

7 Hawking, S. (2016). *Oxford Union speech* (last para.). Accessed 2024-12-02, https://www.hawking.org.uk/in-words/speeches/speech-5

Flashback 1980

I took my first worldly breaths in the late 1970s (yes, for those Gen Z's and Alphas, this may seem ancient), and my childhood was shaped in the 1980s. Yet what I am about to share are tales of life—before capture.

Walking to school meant sights, sounds, feelings. If we were fortunate to have a walk-mate, conversation; if not, conversation inside oneself. Can you see that? Can you feel it? Life did not exist with the underlying pull to be elsewhere. This was being present. There wasn't an overwhelming external distraction to take one away, or to have to respond to a random outside and (often) uninvited guest.

Growing-up in a suburb of Vancouver, Canada, there was the changing of seasons to feast upon. It was often raining but that, too, was beautiful. Life then was present, natural, and alive. The sound of the rain hitting the umbrella, the glistening puddle under foot. Feeling the connection to the elements. The sun's beating warmth on the top of one's head. The crisp cold on one's nose. Undistracted…real… participatory. A hovering of the external did not exist in one's palm, back pocket, or jacket. One looked forward when walking. Parents attended soccer games, swimming classes, gymnastics. They watched their kids attentively while at times talking with other parents, connecting, and sharing the common space. We were not taken away by anything outside of ourselves. We simply existed together.

Like I have heard from so many already, now as I write this book, I feel the naysayers in my head declaring me as some old fuddy-duddy (do you like that one?) who can't come to terms with the here and now. Someone who is "stuck in the past." No, I am not.

In fact, I am here to bring light back to those who wish to look at what may have happened to them. We humans and those around us have been taken over and many of us are oblivious to this.

Let me ask you this: If you are in your 20s, has the time gone quickly? Do you wonder how you arrived at this place, so suddenly, questioning which direction to go? Tasked with the constant daunting comparison of influencers, others' achievements, the *look* of perfection all around you. I did not have these influences in my 20s—yet we had magazine covers, fashion runways, and all of victory's secrets to still splash across our views. It was different, yes, and still I could have sworn I was just 25, yet now I am closer to double that. Time travels quickly, this life, with fervour, inching-up on us with added speed as time continues onward.

So why would we choose to squander any of these moments, head down, in an endless scroll of meaninglessness? Whether you are 20, 30, 40, 50, 60, 70, or more, who wants to waste a moment? Ask yourself these questions: What is this doing for me? Why the need to escape? Why have I personally allowed myself to become a prisoner to *the thing*? Is there not a far grander plan for my life as a free being? Why have I given my life up so freely, often mindlessly, without realizing it?

"The trouble is, you think you have time."[8]

In 1980, my family and I were living in Toronto Ontario, Pape and Danforth area, which was highly composed of Greek, Italian, and Portuguese (my father's heritage) immigrants. Now, I assure you that this portion will not take-up much time, so please do not hit the snooze button just yet. My dad had immigrated from South Africa after dropping out of

8 Kornfield, J. (1994). *Buddha's little instruction book* (n.p.). New York, NY: Bantam Books.

school in Standard 6, when he was put back repeatedly for not adhering to the strict Catholic upbringing his mother stringently conformed to (she attended mass at 6:00 a.m. daily). Their family with two sons had little money, and my grandfather was away on fishing boats between Madeira (Portugal) and Western Cape (South Africa) for years at a time. My father shared sordid stories of wearing his 4-year-senior brother's shoes with a wad of newspaper stuffed in each toe. Their dog, Funchal, was fed broth and fish bones which were skimmed from their soup on the front stoop. Canned dog food was not a thing back then, and that was just fine.

The whippings and beatings from the Catholic sisters at the school left my father taking to playing hooky from school. Instead, he would opt for the movie house or the library to feast his senses with learning. A voracious reader, he became self-schooled. He was an astute debater and well-versed on a wide variety of topics including current events, politics, spirituality, global geographical and historical interests, among others. He poured over film and book images of the "freedom land"—his first glimpses of America, which highly contrasted his homeland South Africa.

Our home was full of books on photography, art, improved health, self expansion, alternative God consciousness, training manuals, and body building. I remember one of his self-help books was titled, *How to Throw Away Your* [eye]*Glasses*. He even had the whole family performing eye exercises to help prevent us from needing to wear glasses. One of my dad's greatest challenges was not having enough time to learn, achieve, feel, and experience as much as he would have liked in his lifetime. He was a friend to many, regardless of their backgrounds or skin pigments—a dark Caucasian product of Portuguese immigrants who felt uncomfortable with discrimination and apartheid policies. Racial tensions ran high; religious, political, and economic insecurities were at the forefront. He wanted out, and so he did. Somehow those images of America brought him to *North* America where he touched-down in Canada. He arrived in Toronto to attend Ryerson University as a mature student while also apprenticing as a hairdresser.

In contrast, my mom had grown-up on a farm in southern Ontario, the eldest daughter of four children, green-eyed and flaxen-haired with kittens in their hands and trees to climb. My mom had only a single dress. They all bathed in the same bath water, my grandfather being last in line when retiring from the day's farm chores. They also knew poverty, going without, the deficits of crop yields, animal welfare, post-postpartum depression, and what alcoholism could cast upon one's well-being while growing-up. Their father worked hard to manage the farm, while also managing their mother, who had gone within after the birth of their last daughter. Never truly emerging back as, in those days, there was little assistance for such a condition. She spent much time sitting upright in a chair with a blanket over her head, covering her entire body while moans came from her mouth. One of the stand-out phrases she flung my way was that of me being "the devil," which was brought on by the platform patent heels I chose to wear in her presence once. Not the sort of adoration a young girl seeks from her only living grandparent. My mom's father passed early from alcohol-related illnesses. My father's parents had both passed before I was born. I was often told they would have loved me.

My parents met in 1969 when my father was "doing hair" in a humble salon in Toronto. My mom-to-be rented a flat upstairs and he began cutting her hair. She mentioned how he had cooked her a meal, and she was so impressed with how domesticated he was. "He even swept-up after dinner!" she exclaimed. They eloped 7 months later and were married for 43 years until his passing from cancer in late 2012.

How does this relate to the 1980s you might ask? And HTF,[9] does this relate to the extreme device overuse our world is facing...? Well, I am getting to that.[10]

My parents won $10,000 in the lottery in 1980 (which was a significant amount of money at that time) and with their winnings my dad bought a Chevy ¾-ton van. They told my mom's siblings and parents that we were going out west and would be back in a year. I was 4 years old. My brother was almost 9. We packed-up all our earthly belongings, which consisted of many tropical house plants (most of which my dad had brought here from Africa, prior to that being illegal), milk crates, my dog Fonzie, copious amounts of paperwork, and basic personal belongings. We travelled in two vehicles and communicated between the two with a CB radio. My radio name was "pink blankie."

Feeling Fonzie's nose on my shoulder along with the tickle of the tropical plants' leaves, my ears filled with tunes from ABBA, Cat Stevens, and Bob Dylan on our 8-track tape player[11]—it was all any kid could ask for, aside from my family's love, which I had. I looked-out the window and soaked-in the vast scenery of the varying landscapes. It was pure, natural, and a road full of education. I remember the trip, even at that young age. I was present.

9 Acronym for "how the fuck."

10 By the way, I do not normally swear. This was just an attempt to get your attention. There are many words we can choose to use that are much more effective, and you will see that I often refer to "choice" in various circumstances. We do have choice, and we *are* able to make another choice.

11 8-track tapes were a music format that were "created so people could play music in their cars. Unlike cassettes, 8 tracks are a continuous loop of tape. They did not need to be turned over to keep playing. There were four programs of music on each tape with two tracks on each program to create stereo sound." *Wikipedia: The Free Encyclopedia.* (n.d.). 8 track tape. Accessed 2024-06-30, https://simple.wikipedia.org/wiki/8_track_tape, para. 1.)

We landed in an area north of Vancouver. Years later when I asked my mom how we arrived in that specific location she said, "We just drove until it looked like a good place to get off the highway." Beautiful. They continued until they saw a sign on a lawn for a place "For rent." This would become our first home on the West Coast. Little planning; no devices. Simple. I attended the same elementary school from kindergarten until the end of Grade 7. We rode bikes, sat on the sidewalk eating Milk-Bones® out of a box, frequented the corner store in bare feet, and rolled down the hill in the park across the street.

Early on, I became attuned to the difference between picture-perfect and that which truly is.[12] Our little dog Fonzie came complete with papers of champion stock parents and markings that set him aside from his competitors with a perfect brown saddle marking on his back. One day, a highfalutin English lady came to our home, placed him on the table and seeing the tip of his long snout in exact alignment with the top of his tail, slated him for greatness. He was to compete with some of the world's best.

Upon awakening one morning soon after, I recall our beloved canine could not get up. He seemed paralyzed and with no apparent reason. Veterinarians were unable to pinpoint what had happened or why, and with a battery of tests they attributed his paralysis to the possibility of ingesting slug bait. Later, it was later determined that he had suffered a stroke.

Being avid animal lovers, my family cared for him, his rehabilitation, and living the remainder of his life with the use of three legs. His colour paled; his stature shrunk. Passersby would rarely walk by past without making mention of him, and the concern they had for his

[12] The concept of perception versus reality resurfaces throughout this book.

well-being. I grew up with this experience and, within it, the lessons of preconceptions versus the reality of a situation. We adored Fonzie and, throughout his many years (until I was 16), he expanded the love in our lives. He had another companion during the years ahead, a Neufie/black-labX.[13] He enjoyed the remainder of his life despite his disability.

From age 5 onwards, I had a successful modelling career and made a good wage. I had a catalogue contract with a national company that provided a choreographer, hairstylist, makeup artist, and photographer with whom I worked closely. I was also a competitive baton twirler and travelled throughout the States competing, which also led me into pageantry at a young age. Various forms of dance called to me and also filled my soul. Early on, physical appearances were at the forefront yet being down to earth was also in my nature.

I was adamant about not taking money from my parents—rather, I wanted to make my own. When I was 13, I began my first part-time job in the fast-food service industry. The first evening my parents picked me up, I was crying. I still remember the rain coming down in the parking lot as they both waited for me in their burgundy station wagon. I wiped my tears and told them the weight of the mop that I used to clean the floors felt like more than my own bodyweight. At night we would disassemble and sanitize the dairy machines and fryers. I can still smell the chemicals in the bucket and the grease we needed to apply to the O-rings before reassembling the machines. I am not being sexist, but it was not work for a young girl, nor anyone of my slight frame or build. But I did it anyway.

[13] Newfoundland/Black Labrador cross.

Soon after, I worked three jobs at the same time and managed to qualify for multiple credit cards. A consumer at last, I was the successful target of large sales companies' ploy to suck us in early. I worked hard and spent plenty. It wasn't long before I racked-up $10,000 in debt, which I found tedious to pay-off. Being that my start in life was often focused on outward appearances, I struggled to find balance with any *inside* self-improvement that was needed, particularly at this age. Brought on by my father's experience, my upbringing held tightly to turning away from any organized religion and left me with little faith of anything higher. Yet by this time, my dad had developed his own spirituality in that he practised meditation and spoke freely of God. When he meditated downstairs all I really took from it was that us kids needed to be quiet when walking above. We were already accustomed for the need to be quiet since my mother was a nurse and worked long shifts on the intensive care ward. Being quiet was not my nature, but I did it anyway.

I was fortunate in not having to change schools in my childhood and felt this as welcomed stability in my life. I attended the same high school from beginning to end though my family moved twice during this time. My parents believed it was important to maintain stability for us kids, which I still appreciate.

Life began to turn sideways at this point after I went to a friend's older sibling's wedding and drank alcohol for the first time. The next 16 years of my life would test the depths of my strength to claw my way out of the intensifying grip alcohol had over me, and to push me to find a faith I did not know possible.

Flashback 1991

I was driving my dad's beat-up van, which had been T-boned[14] in earlier years. Still driveable, yet several years passed and the West Coast rain had rusted the side panel extensively. Being the thrift-conscious man that he was, dad had some extra white house paint that he threw from a bucket onto the rusty dent. The rest of the van had been off-white when first purchased in 1980, so you might be able visualize how this looked. The odometer had long-before stopped working—it had already rolled-over a couple of times—so he used a clipboard to record the miles he clocked. When the heat or air was turned on, somehow the smell of curry blew through the cabin, even though I am certain he had never eaten a bowl of curry in the van throughout his travels.

Those were the days of home-cooked meals, when a fried egg sandwich in a Tupperware container would be more standard than Skip's[15] or an ethnic take out in a soon-to-be-banned foam container (don't start me on that one). So, again, no curry had been consumed in the vehicle. There were certain areas under the vinyl floor mats, which one knew not to step on as they may go through the floor. Were we poor? No, as we also had a Ford station wagon in the driveway of the home my family owned. Yet things were held onto during those days in a different way. Life was not disposable as many, today, will likely argue it has become.

I ran with the popular group in school (whatever that means), a cheerleader and soon-to-be-alcoholic living life in the fast lane. Driving my dad's tan van, my Motorola flip-phone with piggy-back battery in tow, had I made it? Not at all. While having the ability to communicate with

[14] Crashed into the side, head-on, by another vehicle.

[15] Skip's is lingo for "skip the dishes" or a mobile food delivery service.

others on the go was useful at that time, it was worlds' apart from what it has now become.

There were no pings, dings, alerts or internet capability. Just a phone, which from time-to-time rang. Simple. I would get my bag with that puppy inside it, grab the towel on the dash, a quick swipe of the windshield (the defrost functioned poorly), and we hit the road. Where we went, I really don't recall but, wherever it was, I was going to show-up and have conversations with some people and look at them in the eyes—that much I knew. If there was ever a reason, and there usually wasn't, we could reach into that bag and use that phone to call someone to join us, to come and spend time, connect, have eye contact, laugh, listen, and talk to each other.

Back at home on the landline, we would have hours of calls as teenagers, my highest-documented time clocked-in at 7 hours. Yes, we talked: in person, over the phone, and face-to-face when we saw one another. No distractions from outer sources. We were there. It was grand. Also, I can say "It *is* grand" because this is largely how I continue to operate.

You see, the way I see it is living in this device-centred time requires discipline. Yes, you heard it. Discipline. "Discipline is a well-organized expression of love."[16] Related to our topic, discipline means not falling victim to *smart*phone companies' designs that have been carefully crafted for all to drift blankly inside-of. Or, if already a casualty, to work diligently to pull yourself out from under it. A parachute is not provided, and a safety-net is not supplied for bouncing back into reality. Self-discipline *is* required.

[16] Behan, K. (2011). *Your dog is your mirror: The emotional capacity of our dogs and ourselves* (p. 47). Novato, CA: New World Library.

We have fallen under an intricately detailed cyber-attack, which deceives us—that lures us away from the truth and meaning of human life, what we are meant for, and how we truly connect. All while these corporations gain mega-high revenues, which pad their collective pockets and leave holes in our souls.

Dramatic you think? Just look around. Spend 1 day (and I am not talking about at some unplugged retreat you have fashioned just for this purpose)—just 1 day—looking around, ingesting, people-watching. Leave your device at home—that's right—you've got this. What do you see? How has this shaped us as a society? You may notice someone sitting on a coffee-shop patio, who has not succumbed to the pull of *the thing*. How do they look different? Does it feel to you like they are *truly* there?

Don't get me wrong, my head is just as often a mess with a flood of thoughts that are difficult to manage at the best of times. But that, too, is okay—I honour that by feeling this state, going deeper into it, working towards accepting, and being better for having done so. I have created the time to do so. And in this publication, I will share with you how I have done this.

Now back to your assignment: Notice the teenagers, the young people. Are they together? What is keeping their attention? Go by a bus stop. How many of the standees are glued to a device? Restaurants, patios, malls, dog walkers, strollers. Take it in. What do you see? What do you deduce? Had you noticed this previously? How is it for you to be without *the thing*? Is this the first time you've noticed these things? What thoughts come to mind?

When you arrive back from this assignment, we will continue.

(Everyone Has) A Story

Everyone has a story—Everyone. Yet so often, and particularly now, humans are living on autopilot—trapped in the shuffle of the race of it all—without stopping to ask or converse, to take time, to sit, to be attentive, to pay attention. Why?

Ding—beep—ping.

Ding.
Ping.
Ring.
Lip pucker, eyelash bat, selfie-shoot—Click.
Ping.

"Why?" you ask me.

"Why? Well...there's this *thing*, which has gotten in the way.
Taken us—away...."

It is shaping—has shaped—a whole new generation. And yet, most are unaware of it. Carefully orchestrated, curated and crafted to slip quietly under the radar—shhhh—bit-by-bit, piece-by-piece, soul-by-soul, brain-by-brain—Poof—the master-marketing of *more*.

While I was on volunteer lunch duty at my sons' school, a boy in Grade 2 came running towards me as though he was going to announce something *big* to me! The tension in his clenched fists at his sides and his opened mouth uttered, "Oh, *I wish I had my iPhone 10 with me!!!!*" *Gah*—wow—yes—there it is. So truly sad to hear. A beautiful day, far warmer than seasonal temperatures, children playing and running, excitement of hot lunch day. Yet there it was, underlying, sucking elsewhere, wanting, craving, taking him elsewhere. There. It was.

Earlier, I was in an elevator. We have become so paralyzed that even the 30 seconds spent in an elevator cannot be freed from *the thing*. Every rider, *the thing* in hand, heads down, elsewhere. Walking down the street the other day, I came within 10 steps of a young man. As soon as we were within that range, I could almost feel how uncomfortable he was having to walk past me, to possibly make eye contact, to possibly say "Hello," or simply smile. He quickly lifted his *smart*phone (which was already in his hand), as if to avoid the possible catastrophe of this walk-by encounter. I have noticed this countless times.

What have we become? The simplest of exchanges, such as passing by another of our human counterparts, can be so uncomfortable for some that we must resort to blocking such interactions at all costs? How have we been robbed of these simplistic daily acts which, for our entire evolution, prior to invasion, had been part of our existence?

I refer to this as the *Heads-Down Generation* (H.D.G.). Several generations now qualify. Anyone can become entrapped—or choose differently. The H.D.G. now claims billions of captives. It is not based on ethnicity, sexual orientation, denomination, age, religious affiliation, or otherwise. Anyone can find oneself enslaved away, unable to be present, for themselves or others. Unable to fully land where-ever they are. Unable to experience life—actually. The term FoMO[17] was coined in 2004 and its definition describes a unique "phenomenon observed on social networking sites. FoMO includes two processes; firstly, [the] *perception* of missing out, followed up with a *compulsive behaviour to maintain these social*

[17] Acronym for "fear of missing out."

connections" (author's italics).[18] My take on this research is that people need to be far less concerned about FoMO and more concerned with missing living a *real* life—and I suspect many may be unaware that this is happening. Rather, we ought to concern ourselves with *fear of missing a real life* (FoMaRL).

The thing interferes with personal relationships and, at alarming rates, has been shown to affect intimacy.[19] It can get in the way of parenting.[20,21,22] There are signs at my kids' local pool where it shows a mobile device and reads: "It only take 3 seconds for a child to drown. Put your device down."

Yet, look around. What are all the spectators doing? A large portion of them are *gone* while their children wave enthusiastically from the pool to gain their attention. But no—they are gone. A mother sits behind her young son in the stroller with *smart*phone in hand in a visible IG[23] scroll of seemingly utmost importance. He writhes uncontrollably, wanting to be set free from the buckles that hold him down, to be picked-up and paid

[18] Gupta, M., & Sharma, A. (2021, July). *Fear of missing out: A brief overview of origin, theoretical underpinnings and relationship with mental health.* doi:10.12998/wjcc.v9.i19.4881

[19] *BYU Forever Families.* (n.d.). How mobile devices can interrupt romantic relationships. Brigham Young University. Accessed 2024-12-02, https://foreverfamilies.byu.edu/how-mobile-devices-can-interrupt-romantic-relationships#:~:text=Even%20though%20smartphones%20can%20help, meaningful%20interactions%20may%20go%20down

[20] Hunt, S. (2018, July 16). Cellphone use by parents determines children's behaviour, study suggests. *CBC News.* Accessed 2024-12-02, https://www.cbc.ca/news/canada/calgary/cell-phone-addiction-parents-negatively-impacting-kids-1.4749389

[21] Hamm, K. (2023, June 2). What happens when you use your phone around your kids. *Greater Good Magazine.* Accessed 2024-12-10, https://greatergood.berkeley.edu/article/item/what_happens_when_you_use_your_phone_around_your_kids

[22] Halton, C. (2024, August 9). Yes, your smartphone habit is affecting your kid—here's how. *Today's Parent.* Accessed 2024-12-02, https://www.todaysparent.com/family/parenting/yes-your-smartphone-habit-is-affecting-your-kid-heres-how

[23] An acronym for Instagram.

some attention. But sorry son, your mom is gone; gone elsewhere; this scroll is *so* important. She has been programmed. Your brother in the pool; attention, gone, gone. This has taken precedence. Gone, sorry dear boy, mama is gone right now.

> It only takes 3 seconds for a child to drown.
> Put your device down.

We will wonder in future years what happened. We will wonder.

Has our attempt to *connect* to the worldwide web, to social media, to our work, proven to be the largest disconnection between ourselves and others? When questioned, many people will claim, "Oh, well, I like keeping in touch with people and seeing their photos." But if you dissect that for yourself, how much of your time is spent doing that and how much is spent on other paths? For those truly in your circle, could you personally send those special photos to one another instead and cast aside the rest?

Research shows that, in 2021, the average American spends between 5 and 6 hours on their mobile phone each day.[24] This translates to *2,190 hours per year*. And this is only the average—in 2021—and many now would be far above this amount. Let me ask you, when you signed your first mobile phone contract, is this what you signed-up for? Now, I know I may be losing some of you, or you may be dropping into defence mode right now with "Oh—that's not me" or "I'm only on mine a few times a day" or "Oh, I really try to limit myself." But let's put that aside for a moment and just contemplate the force—the pull, in and of itself. Even if that is not you, how many times would you say that *the thing* pulls your

[24] Ceci, L. (2022, June 14). *Average time spent daily on a smartphone in the United States 2021.* Accessed 2024-06-31, https://www.statista.com/statistics/1224510/time-spent-per-day-on-smartphone-us

mind to it? To just tap it, to swipe—just once—and check. To just look at *all the things* for a few minutes...repeat this several times daily and what you have is an unnatural tipping point that sways us away from ourselves, from each other, from our source.

> ...is this what we want? To let them get away with it—and to sit back and play with our phones as this darkness falls?[25]

When interviewed, even the top executives of the major *social* media platforms have admitted that, when developing these tools, they really did not anticipate the all-consuming often-negative impacts that could have occurred—and *have* occurred.[26]

> ...you set out to connect people—and you are refusing to acknowledge that the same technology is now driving us apart.[27]
>
> Our dignity as humans is at stake....crippling divisions...begin with the manipulation of one individual. Then another. And another....[28]

The top execs[29] admit it themselves! Now let me ask you, do you really think they will hold a press conference stating that they are sorry, they had no idea when first developing this technology and jumping on the bandwagon that it would suck you away from living your life—that it

[25] Cadwalladr, C. (2019, April). Facebook's role in Brexit—and the threat to democracy [video]. *TED talk.* Accessed 2024-11-15, https://www.ted.com/speakers/carole_cadwalladr

[26] Carole Cadwalladr (British author and investigative journalist) interview in Orlowski, J. (2020). *The social dilemma* [Documentary film] (Writers: Davis Coombe, Vickie Curtis, Jeff Orlowski; Producer: Larissa Rhodes). Exposure Labs, Argent Pictures, The Space Program; Netflix.

[27] Cadwalladr, C. (2019, April). Facebook's role in Brexit—and the threat to democracy [video]. *TED talk.* Accessed 2024-11-15, https://www.ted.com/speakers/carole_cadwalladr

[28] Professor David Carroll interview in Amer, K., & Noujaim, J. (Directors). (2019). *The great hack* [Documentary film] (Producers: Karim Amer, Geralyn White Dreyfous, Judy Korin, & Pedro Kos; Writers: Karim Amer, Erin Barnett, & Pedro Kos). The Othrs; Netflix.

[29] Short for "executives."

would be an avenue for toxic trolls to thrive, separatist groups to recruit, hate speech to gain momentum at alarming rates, sexualized vultures to prey on their victims, illegal drugs to be traded, weapons to be glorified, and plans for mass shootings to band with others who share their (isolated) pains? And that with billions of dollars in their pockets (and the likelihood of billions of dollars more), they now *choose* to shutdown that which was previously otherwise intended.

Are you *waiting* for this to happen? Do not wait—let the change begin with you.

> "Be the change you want to see in the world."[30]
> ~ Ghandi ~

Shareholders and stock portfolios intricately requiring ad[31] space to gain revenues which are on the constant increase. Mergers from other platforms joining the verse which has gained further momentum in the outright capture. Are you waiting for this announcement and this press conference? Why? Is there not enough evidence for you yet?

Look around you on the streets, bus benches and park benches, in stores, restaurants, coffee shops, everywhere. Carry-out your own social awareness experiment. Do some research. Have you viewed the films *The*

30 Though Ghandi is often given credit for this saying, there may be evidence to the contrary.

31 Short for "advertisement."

Social Dilemma,[32] *The Great Hack*,[33] and *The Social Network*,[34] which address these issues? If you haven't seen these movies, why wait? Watch them a few times to soak-in the information,[35] or perhaps intuitively you already know. Simply put, being exposed to hundreds (or for some, thousands) of digital images daily is unnatural for our brains.

We were not meant for this. Remember, even the developers admit that they did not know that it was going to go this way. Yet, they continue to develop the technology to advance the hit, the rush, the signal to your (once) beautiful brain to permeate it more wholly.[36] The time to save our species from the brain-drain of modern society's dribble into oblivion is now.

As previously indicated, anyone who chooses to be in the H.D.G. can qualify. They have given themselves to walking head-down through life, avoiding interacting with others, staying away from being fully aware of their surroundings. Being steered and pulled downward into the digital vortex. Tech-neck aside, how is this shaping humanity as a whole? Regularly I witness people walking head-down into traffic. Daily I see

---

[32] *The Social Dilemma* (2020) documentary "covers the negative social effects of social media and is interspersed by a dramatized narrative surrounding a family of five who are increasingly affected by problematic social media use." *Wikipedia: The Free Encyclopedia.* Accessed 2024-12-02, https://en.wikipedia.org/wiki/The_Social_Dilemma

[33] *The Great Hack* "is a 2019 documentary film about the Facebook–Cambridge Analytica data scandal." *Wikipedia: The Free Encyclopedia.* (n.d.). *The Great Hack.* Accessed 2024-12-02, https://en.wikipedia.org/wiki/The_Great_Hack

[34] *The Social Network* (2010) "is a 2010 American biographical drama film directed…based on the 2009 book *The Accidental Billionaires* by Ben Mezrich. It portrays the founding of social networking website Facebook." *Wikipedia: The Free Encyclopedia.* (n.d.). *The Social Network.* Accessed 2024-12-02, https://en.wikipedia.org/wiki/The_Social_Network

[35] In particular, it's worth reviewing *The Social Dilemma* (2020) [Documentary film] a number of times as it addresses the targeting of users from a variety of developers' perspectives.

[36] Amer, K., & Noujaim, J. (Directors). (2019). *The great hack* [Documentary film] (Producers: Karim Amer, Geralyn White Dreyfous, Judy Korin, & Pedro Kos; Writers: Karim Amer, Erin Barnett, & Pedro Kos). The Othrs; Netflix.

drivers using their phones while driving, apparently unable to complete their journey without giving-in to the pull. Wow. The draw is forceful.

> The time to save our species from the brain-drain of modern society's dribble into oblivion is now.

I sat in my vehicle the other day waiting to make a right turn. The walk-signal lit-up and the young lady standing there was immersed in *the thing* until the walk signal expired and changed to the flashing don't-walk hand. At this point she came-to, then, eyes up, sent me a death stare as if to say, "How dare you sit there. This is *my* right of way." Gone. Gone into oblivion. The basic etiquettes of days gone by. Gone. Yet optimistically, all is not lost—it is never too late to arrive again.

It seems so many are completely unaware of being sucked down into the endless abyss of feeds, burrowing down tunnels of instantaneousness to a seemingly endless stream away from oneself. A fascinating phenomenon really. Kudos to the spearheads who made it all possible and the masterminds of manipulating our senses while triggering our addiction pathways to make their personal financial dreams come true.

This didn't arrive overnight and, furthermore, the complete pull downward has not fully taken effect—yet. This, like all else presented to our species, is an evolution. An evolution that the algorithm analysts are fine-tuning to further the pull in their favour at an alarming rate. All while most of us have little awareness that it is occurring.

After several years from my marriage having ended, I decided to give online dating a try. I was committed to try for 1 month on one site. I found myself forming a profile and listing my attributes, hobbies, likes, among others. When arriving at the "my ideal partner" section and having 90 characters to do so, I found myself entering: "has a disciplined relationship with his handheld device." What?!? Seriously. With so many possible alternatives, has this now become so glaringly noticeable that it makes the top 90-character cut? Again, telling in my opinion. Like saying, "Please do not include me in your equation to sit across the table at dinner while you stare into your phone as this will not happen on my clock."

I have seen memes (eeeww!) that state "I'm having people over tonight to stare at their phones if you want to come along."[37] Really? Yuck! Have we all lost it?

Others have tried to get on top of this feeling of imbalance or disconnection they have with others by having a box at the front door into which others leave their devices when they enter. Not a bad idea I suppose but, at the same time, indicative of the state into which we have entered.

This again illustrates how far removed we have become. Also worth mentioning is, at some point prior to the evening's completion, certainly someone is going to state the highly important reason they need access to their phone. Aside from that, one or two people who forgot to silence their chime and—oops—*the thing* weaseled its commanding presence into the room again.

From the gym to church to schools to one's workplace, doing something with one hand while *the thing* is in the other. For example, flag person with stop-sign in one hand and cell phone in another. I once asked a man at the gym who had been sitting on the end of a bench for 10 mins without touching a weight in a seemingly heated phone call. "Excuse me, are you [actually] using this bench?" I asked in a sweet tone. He said, "Yes." I said, "Oh, because I have been waiting and it seems that you are

[37] A meme is "an image, video, piece of text, etc., typically humorous in nature, that is copied and spread rapidly by internet users, often with slight variations" (*Oxford Online Dictionary*, 2018).

on the phone." He then said to the person he was talking to, "Hold on, some bitch is trying to talk to me."

We have arrived at a crossroads: The disrespect for one another and the overturn of our well-being in a fight against common morals and considerate attention—the basic fundamentals for peaceful cohabitation. These are important elements in the *gift of life*. Now this is my opinion, and it's possible none of it resonates with you. Perhaps "the way *it* is" works for you. As for me, I feel the *phonedemic* that has spread exponentially. It may very well continue to deteriorate our human race until enough of us shift our perspective from the H.D.G. to the *Heads-Up Generation* (H.U.G.).

Are we not important enough to ourselves to have the space to walk freely, heads up, soaking-in all that is around us? This is not, whatsoever, an ego-based statement. Whether pleasant to the senses or otherwise, it all adds to the complexity of our experience. To think, to feel, to wonder, to contemplate. To address one another, or not. There is meaning in all of this, however simple or tangled it may be. Are we able to show-up once again? The hope is not to get back to how things once were as it is likely foolish to think this attainable, but rather to make adjustments, which for some might be major. To stop making all the excuses around usage of *the thing*. To look closely at the *relationship*, we have with our mobile devices and clearly understand the technology involved in driving it further into our lives without us being fully-informed as to how this has occurred.

From students who "*need* their devices to look things up," yet instead spending immeasurable time snapping[38] one another, texting, ticking-and-tocking to their hearts' content (though this will never *truly*

[38] Snapchat is a readily used social app used particularly by the younger generations. Users need to maintain their *streaks*, a tactic to keep them active.

content their hearts), scrolling Insta[39] *ad infinitum*.[40] Are there no rules anymore? If the lady on the elliptical machine beside me is trash-talking on the phone for 30 mins, does *my* enjoyment not fall into the equation? Oh, but she *needs* to "listen to music, while she works out so...."

One hour—that is the average workout for most individuals. One hour. Yet it is seemingly impossible for some to leave their devices in the locker, glove box, or pocket—zipped away for just 1 hour. Hmmm. Fascinating—truly.

We are here now, but where are we headed? With the current young generations being raised with a *smart*phone on their strollers' tray-table and both parents glued to their devices, how will they positively function in the future? If we continue on this trajectory, true human contact and relations will become a lost art.

> We're training and conditioning a whole new generation of people that, when we are uncomfortable or lonely or uncertain or afraid, we have a digital pacifier for ourselves that is kind of atrophying our own ability to deal with that [those feelings and experiences].[41]

I say "Wake-up! Wake-up and see what is happening. Wake-up and look at life around you. Feel—breathe—be. Remember? We are here." This is it. There is no dress rehearsal, and we are squandering this experience—our lives. We have become entrapped. Take a stand—take the opportunity and fully experience your life.

39 Insta means Instagram.

40 *Merriam-Webster Dictionary.* (n.d.). Ad infinitum. Accessed 2024-10-15, https://www.merriam-webster.com/dictionary/ad%20infinitum

41 Quote from Tristan Harris, former design ethicist at Google and co-founder of Centre for Humane Technologies in White, E. (2020, November 23). Six chilling quotes from 'The Social Dilemma' (Item 5). *The Utah Statesman.* Accessed 2024-12-03, https://usustatesman.com/six-chilling-quotes-from-the-social-dilemma

We have arrived at a crossroads: the disrespect for one another and the overturn of our well-being in a fight against common morals and considerate attention—the basic fundamentals for peaceful cohabitation. These are important elements in the *gift of life*.

Back to My Story

Everyone has a story, and this is a part of mine. It is vague as to when I took my first alcoholic drink but, as I mentioned, the thought of the wedding of my best friend's far older brother seems to be the time. I do not recall what liquor it was, with whom, or how we attained it. I do recall the spinning of my head, nausea, lying back down on the sidewalk outside the house, and the feeling of the strength of the sunshine. Spinning. It would be the first of many times to follow, a pattern yet to emerge. There were 2-litre bottles of "Rockaberry Red," the salt-shaker, and biting-in-half the worm at the bottom of the bottle between two of us. Parties a-plenty, excess from early-on, and being voted the drunkest at the wedding (sometimes before I had even arrived). How had this become me? I had come from a loving home, two parents, a "tan van," a station wagon, an older brother, childhood pets, the feeling of love, and stability in my schools.

I would soon learn that the brown paper-bag stigma I had grown-up with was not only reserved for males. It was me, too—and this realization was crushing. By the time others had reached legal age in the United States (US), I had a firm awareness that I had a problem with alcohol, and I did not see a way out. My mother was a teetotaller, and my dad seemed to have a fairly normal grasp of his consumption. Although I do recall the words, "If I had the money, I would drink every day" coming from his mouth. Though early in my life retching sounds echoed from the bathroom following over-consumption at a Christmas party, occurrences were isolated enough for me to count the incidents on both hands. It was more likely that my mother's father carried some of the genetic characteristics associated with alcoholism and that I had inherited it from him.

As far as I was aware, childhood models, pageant winners, masters of ceremonies at high school graduation class banquets were not alcoholics. I would spend the next few years trying to ensure that I did not qualify—that I could get a handle on the situation. I was convinced I would muster an exception out of this impending doom. I graduated high school and, though the term "gap year" was not yet coined, I felt I deserved a well-earned year off. The year had me gravitating towards less wholesome company and, before I knew it, I had chosen a fellow with less-than positive attributes to spend most of my time.

The next level of life in the fast lane—loud music, fast cars, and drinks a-plenty. The time with my boyfriend would culminate one April 20th (of unknown year) when again I was in the wrong place at the wrong time. In general, being with him, proved to be in all the wrong places at all the wrong times. My life would be altered on this day when, as we walked-up the pathway to the side of his house, the sun casting its warmth upon us, ahead of me I heard a male voice say, "Can I help you?" That is when I saw them—men—several of them. They responded, "That's him!" and the chase ensued. He went towards the back of the lane-way, running, being chased, and me, running in the opposite direction, until downed. The pavement hitting hard against the side of my face, like running full-speed into a brick wall. Three grown men, beating, punching, kicking me square in the right side of my face, one holding my hair from the back of my head, while the other hammered my jaw with his steel-toed boot. A younger female with ashen pale skin dressed in all-black leaned-up against a tree, smoking a cigarette, watching, blankly.

My head rushed with extreme heat, I tried to cover my face and then, again, the blow struck me in the side of the ribs, the head, the face again. At some point, I escaped out from under it, as if propelled, running with the speed I had honed from track practice and my dad's training. "Do not stop until you are past the finish line," he would say. With all my strength, I jumped a high fence, tearing my pants on the top. Reaching the other side, running. Away. I had to stop to catch my breath. My head was smouldering. I was stumbling, falling-off the curb. I fell into a bush and waited. Entering a nearby corner store, I asked if I could use the phonebook. (Yes, we had these.) Who was I planning to call? I flipped and flipped its pages, delirious, accidentally ripping one of the pages before exiting the store. What would I do next? I could not go home. I could not be seen like this. It was my greatest worry. How would I explain? Dizzying molten lava flowing through my concussed head, I sat on the sidewalk. The sun beating down on my brain. A police car pulled-up. The officer got out of the car and said my name. I denied it. He said he believed I was who they were looking for, perhaps from an onlooker's sight of me or from the incident. He said I needed to go to the hospital. I didn't disagree. It was my first and only ride in the back of a police car.

If ever recounting this story in the past, I am usually asked if I was sexually assaulted during that victimization. I was not and, given the ways some of the world's people operate, in hindsight I was both staggered and extremely grateful for this fact. The purpose, as I see it, was to deter me from witnessing the attack on my boyfriend and the vicious beating he was receiving.

In the hours ahead, I was diagnosed with a concussion. I also had facial bruising and swelling, road-rash, damage to other areas of my body, and a ¼-inch bald-patch where my hair had been ripped from my skull, dreadlocked onto other strands of my hair, and dangling down my back. It would be difficult to look at men the same again from this day forward. I was changed.

My then boyfriend had ended-up on the same ward after his beating with baseball bats and padlocks in the end of tube-socks. We met by chance in the hospital hallway, and he said, "I will never, ever, forgive myself for letting this happen to you." Maybe so. All I knew was this was the end of my involvement with him. A few years ago, I was informed he died of a fentanyl drug overdose.

Shortly after, I was subpoenaed to go to court to testify as a witness in his case. As far as my case went, it was stated that there were no witnesses so, therefore, I had no case. I recall telling the bailiff over the phone that I would not testify for fear of seeing my assailants again. "This has taken enough away from my life already. It is not going to take anymore."

I landed a contract to do television (TV) commercials and a part in a series in Tokyo. I felt it was time to go. With the credit card debt, three jobs at home and this toxic lifestyle, I felt there was no other way out. Much to the harsh warnings of friends and family ("They are going to take away your passport!" "They will turn you into a prostitute!"), I simply went and did not look back—not even to my father when he grasped my shoulder as, facing forward, I walked down the stairs—the first time I had ever heard him sob.

I had very little money. I did not know the language. I didn't know *anyone*. I simply went. Away from the trauma. Away from the men. Away from what I had known.

I first stopped in Seoul, Korea, for a few days *en route*, and the busy loud contrast of the city along with a sick roommate, who made sleeping difficult. She coughed and hacked and blew her nose all night as she piled-up tissues in a mound on our shared nightstand. I pulled the covers over my head and tried not to breath.

Having travelled for a month to South Africa with my father during adolescence, it opened my eyes to a completely different cultures, lifestyles, climates, and environments. With a 3-day layover in New York City, a refuelling stop on Isla del Sol, a tiny island in Bolivian Lake Titicaca. From there we travelled to Cape Town, Johannesburg, Pretoria, and Durban, and went on safari in Kruger National Park. It was a fascinating expedition.

However, life in Tokyo opened-up a whole new lens I had not yet experienced. Of all the people on the plane to Tokyo, I was seated beside two young cool foreign-exchange students, who had lived for some months in Vancouver. They cheerfully took me 3 hours out of their way to ensure I arrived at the ANA Hotel.[42] I still hold this act of kindness dearly in my heart.

Then 19 years old, I would spend my 20th birthday there, away from my family, alone at a bar, meeting-up with new friends later that evening. My drinking was about to take on a whole new level, but I was unaware of this then. My friends were from Australia, New Zealand, Israel, and my roommate from Sweden, who was on a modelling contract, ate a steady diet of solely mandarin oranges, and took daily ice-cold showers in an effort to keep her weight down. Her infectious laugh and forever energy (oranges anyone?) made for fun, excitement, and laughter. House parties

42 This was prior to any English signage for travellers at Narita National Airport and on the Shinkansen (Bullet Train).

with 16,000 people at the base of Mount Fuji and hitchhiking the countryside to get to where the bullet train didn't go provided a welcomed release from the stresses at home, which were gaining in distance. Japanese people became my first true love as a culture—their hospitable nature and kind ways. Everything which my friends and family had warned me against was the furthest thing from the truth. In contrast, my homeland scared me more than the place I would call home for the next 6 months.

Shortly after arriving in Tokyo, I became very sick. With a high fever, sinusitis, otitis media,[43] bronchitis (among other itises), I had roommates with whom I had just met bathing me in ice. This did not stop me, however. I knew I had this debt to clear-up and I was not leaving until that was done. I called my parents from the lane with a funny-looking neon Japanese calling-card phone (a reminder, no devices back then). They were distraught with the sound of my voice, and convinced I was being held against my will or something of that nature. Really—I just had these ailments, and now laryngitis. The antibiotics were not effective (I've learned that when being raised in different countries, we have different microorganisms in our systems), so the Japanese medications did not touch whatever I had picked-up. This was all part of it. I was sick for my first few months in Japan, kept working, and eventually saved enough money to clear my debt and then some.

Daily I visited a large fish tank and came to know the fish swimming inside. I felt as though they recognized me and perked-up upon my arrival. Present and watching, these exquisite creatures showed me their beauty and abilities in contrast to mine. I revelled in going to temples. The musky smell of incense urns moved me to breathe-in their potent

[43] Infection of the inner ear.

diffusions deeply within. The giant Buddha of Kamakura, whose powerful force beckoned me to begin healing in its presence. I felt God here. The beauty and vastness cradled me. My sickened body and weary mind were sheltered towards a peaceful solace, floating forward across Koi[44]-filled ponds amidst gentle visions of peaceful processing.

I quickly learned that Tokyo's nightlife had plenty to offer—the people, the lights, the music. The international visitors who appeared to be free from the lives they too left behind offered excitement and common ground between us. We were young and because I was now getting to the other side of my illnesses, my alcoholism was poised to gain momentum once again. I was introduced to a gorgeous woman, Angelique and, upon seeing her in the mirror at the end of the dressing room curling wand in hand, she near took my breath away with her beauty and presence. I would come to learn that she and her boyfriend Sean (a handsome dark-haired Australian) were a strong presence in the club scene and moonlighting with them while working during the day would become commonplace.

From day-time photo shoots to night-time after hours, the days were long and the sleep, little. I lived in the most expensive area of Japan (and the world at that time), Nishi-Azabu, in a small flat where, upon opening the cutlery drawer, cockroaches scurried-out. They clicked and clattered along the walls as I slept on the *tatami* mat on the floor. Life was different. I had escaped from what was at home in Vancouver. But had I?

Living in Japan exposed my soul to tradition, culture, and new experiences I did not know existed. George Michael's *Older*[45] album's

44 Koi are Japanese fish.

45 Michael, G. (1996). *Older* [Album] (Producers: George Michael, Jon Douglas). Labels: Virgin, Aegean, DreamWorks, Sony Music.

songs were my anthems. "Jesus to a Child" was on replay on my CD, "Fastlove," "Older," "Spinning the Wheel," "Move on," "Star People," "You Have Been Loved,"…. I highly recommend this album.[46] Deep, meaningful and, at times, melancholy, questioning, versatile. It's interesting to look at the titles of those songs now with having needed them immensely at that time. There was so much music in my life, and there still is: Everything but the Girl, Mariah Carey, Keith Sweat (it was a phase at that time) were artists I held onto among too many other to mention. I'd turn them up to get the full sound through the speakers. Though I have never been into headphones, nowadays headphones present a further *phonedemic* issue—a safety hazard when out in public and a block to communication.

The independence and growth I experienced as an adult in Japan was pivotal to my world becoming widened. Though the trauma of the prior violent incidents kept me guarded, Tokyo showed me that the world and its people are fundamentally kind and caring, even though each and every one of them had also struggled at some time in their lives. I was able to find peace within nature; to bond, to talk, and to share through experiences. I walked through a majestic bamboo forest, trunks wider than I knew possible, their power, the vastness of the landscape, the humid beauty of it all. In this forest, I also witnessed a large group of nuns in peaceful procession, their garments flowing.

This scene highly contrasted my father's recollections of nuns that he had shared with us as children. He spoke of the physical abuse he faced in the 1940s at the hands of the nuns in his South African Catholic school. This set the tone for the lack of organized religion throughout our childhoods. This experience likely prompted his desire to escape to North

46 An aside here: George Michael, you are dearly missed—your music helped me immensely.

America. And justifiably so. Searching for better, for fulfillment, for togetherness, for freedom. Isn't that what most of us strive for, regardless of our individual experiences?

Although he encouraged us to one day find a religion that suited us if we so desired, the residual guilt and shame together with shades of a *punishing* God ran through me.

Finding *my* God has been a complex journey. As time went on, I experienced further trauma, which ultimately prepared me for the levelling that was still to come. Though the experiences in my life had shaped me, I felt protected and guided[47] along the way. And when I had no where else to turn, I surrendered completely.

[47] My experience has been that the guidance and protection I have received comes from source and the etherical. It comes from a power, a force, which is greater than me, greater than us. Though it is not us, it is a part of us.

I Can See It Now

I can see it now in my vision: Sales of the newest models to flood the market—The O Phone[48] Basic 00—with *your* needs in mind—with standard calling features and text ability; with mapping and scan-card features as the only options. As with vinyl records, sales of cameras again take flight; cameras that use film which we take to the store to develop prints rather than have them sit untouched, forever-stored in our devices. Do you feel a load lifted already? Did you hear the cling of the chains drop? Or the Uphone, carefully designed with *U* in mind. By using the Uphone basic, U can actually get *your* life back—and your brain function!

When necessary, people politely excuse themselves to a private area or leave the pathway rather than discuss their cousin's recurring yeast infection issues in front of complete strangers on the street. Yes. People being considerate of others while being mindful of themselves.

I mean seriously, if the world is our playground have we lost all couth where "the sky is the limit" applies to the discussion of *all things* with seemingly no concept of how others may not want to be privy to them (not to mention the person with whom you're in-conversation with thinking they're having a private discussion with you)? But, alas, no. Beside me on the elliptical trainer at the gym, another woman has a 30-minute conversation, carrying-on about her sister-in-law and all the complications with her. Why is it that I have to be exposed to this? Why are there not rules put in place to deter this behaviour? Do I choose to watch the eight televisions in front of me with no sound? Not usually but, then again, I don't have to listen to them. I don't mind the cooking show,

[48] I called it the O Phone because it's your O(wn) phone.

or a talk show or news feed with captions at times, or nature documentaries, but typically I look out the windows. The bustling below. The beauty of the ocean in the distance—Wow. The city and all that it portrays. The mountains to one side, and the majesty of their magnitude. The trees. So many trees—too lush to count. And still the lady beside me, continuing on. And I smile while sending a prayer that she may be given some moments to pause, to be able to realize that others around her may not want to hear her woes, to just have an hour to herself, to feel her body move, to be present. The rhythm of the gift to move, to feel, to build. To allow others around her to do the same.

The gym is full of people staring into their phones. Strange to me that this is permitted. "Hi, sorry, just wondering how many more sets you have?" Eyes down, pause, click-off headphone, and I get the "you-have-disturbed-my-scroll" glare. "Oh, I am just starting." Me thinking, "Oh really? Well, it doesn't look like you are doing anything and, if I have to be brutally honest, it feels like you have mistaken this for your personal office space." But, then again, with no "rules" around it…, why not, right? These are only two examples, but think of all the times you've experienced someone else's phone-time encroaching on your space, taking your time, disrupting your energy field?

You want to get to know me? Great, lets talk. I have a lot to share, as I'm sure you do as well. I am interested in others and consciously look them in the eye. I smile at people and say "Hello." I parent my children, and it is difficult at times. This is okay though—I feel blessed to be given the opportunity to do so. I also do it on my own, and that can be harder still. Yet what a gift—the opportunity to do so *and* at times it is difficult. Whatever cards we are dealt in life, we have gifts to savour each and every day. Do not allow them to be wasted or cast aside towards another moment of disconnect. Re-engage in your existence, in others existence, in the planet (yes, again—Wow), this amazing planet that we call home. Oh, and our planet is in grave trouble, but the Earth will survive as it has for millions of years—it is the human race, other species, and the vegetation that are in danger.

And here we are, scrolling-away on our phones rather than putting our energy into reconnecting with and restoring life on Earth. If there is any hope for our future, we need to re-engage and learn to come together in unity. We are on the brink of destruction, which seems to be beyond our ability to comprehend and perhaps to even recover. Dropping the chains that have been placed upon us by technology giants (more accurately, by ourselves) to which so many of us have fallen prey. *We* have given-in to this being the norm, a part of life that we must accept and adopt.

Let's pause and think for a moment about our systems—the thoroughly-crafted mind and body centres that we humans have. Whether, old, young, abled or differently-abled, disease-ravaged, short, tall, large, small, regardless of pigment—the meticulously-engineered mechanisms that work for us without us even being aware. From the first breath of oxygen, we are crying-out. Crying at the sheer shock of leaving the warm environment of the God-gifted womb each of us grew inside. Wow—such a miracle. Then to be brought to your mother's breast, to be *connected* right away. Then for others, the devastating experience of baby not crying-out, or perhaps your story began with being plucked from your mother's side and placed in the care of another. If either of these, or others, were your experience, I honour you. I encourage you to share your story, be real, feel the pain, *honour* the loss. How has this shaped you?

From our first moments, our carnal instinct is to connect, to be held, to eye-gaze.[49] In time, we become aware of the sounds coming from our mouths, the babbling that leads into words, and what these sensations feel like. Our learning progresses into the freedom of taking our first steps. I remember my oldest taking his first stumbling steps through the hallway. I still remember—with clarity. The bliss and glee on his little face with clenched fists out to stabilize. Six steps. So beautiful. There. Present. Locked in my brain—not on a device. Even though it happened over 15 years ago, those moments were captured in my mind. If I had run for my phone to catch that moment, I would have missed the experience completely. And having my phone in front of my face would have blocked my expression of excitement from him. What kind of impact would this have had on him? How does this affect the connection between child and parent? Do we stop to take this into account?

And from there, do you *truly* feel that toddlers are meant to have a device attached to their stroller-tables or high-chairs? If this is happening now, what does the next downward-pull generation expect the standard will be at that time? Meticulously-crafted systems—our bodies, our minds. Do you really believe this is what was meant for us? Really? I encourage you to dig deep to arrive at your answer.

Communication companies create devices carefully-designed to pull you into their systems—for *their* benefit I might add. Pulled away from true connection to ourselves, each other, and the many gifts around us, whether pleasant or painful. Social media giants capitalizing on our

[49] My first son did not close his eyes for 6 hours.

*algorithm*ed[50] patterns in order to have us feeling like we are missing-out when *they* have actually led us into this way of thinking and feeling. Ping, ding—notification. Check me. Come get me. You need me. Pick me up. Hold me. Leave reality behind. You *need* me. Carry me around. More.

50 "Having your comments, art or videos hidden from view by an automatic process employed by a tech company, often as a result of a form of soft censorship that is built into the algorithm employed by the tech company to suggest or deliver content to a viewer." *Urban Dictionary.* (n.d.). Algorithmed (para. 1). Accessed 2024-06-30, https://www.urbandictionary.com/define.php?term=Algorithmed

Please Hold

Having first-hand experience and knowledge of alcoholism and addiction, I can see that this modern and (somehow) widely-accepted dependence is plaguing us, yet it is not recognized as being problematic to the degree that is warranted. If we are able to step back and look at *the thing*, it constantly takes us away from ourselves and each other. The fact that many of us cannot leave home without it, we always carry it around, or we cannot put it down for a significant amount of time. It chimes to take us back to it. Do you look for it, feel the *need* for it? Do you feel lost without its presence? Doesn't this sound like addiction? For many, it's the first thing they look at in the morning, the last thing they look at before bed, and they incessantly look at it throughout the day. All the check-ins, for *all the things*. Again, does this sound like a dependency? Are you able to admit you have *Obsessive Device Compulsion* (ODC) behaviour? Will you take action—now—to reclaim your life ?

Ring-ring.

"This is your life calling—I want *you* back."

Are you truly okay with having given your life over to *the thing*? Does this apply to you, or how does it not? For example, the last time a friend or family member stopped by, did they come to visit and place their phone on your countertop, or did they sit with *the thing* cradled in their hand? How was that for you? Perhaps you were right there with them with yours in hand. How did that change the dynamic of your time together? Have you given this any thought? Or did you just fall into "This is the way things are—can't do anything about it?" When *little buddy* joins you out for dinner on the tabletop, does it feel to you as though another guest is there? Perhaps an unwanted guest? Table for two? Or is it actually table for four?

The 4 C's of addiction are stated as: compulsion, craving, consequences, and control.[51] So many of us feel a compulsion to reach for our devices all the time—from when we first awaken to the time we go to sleep. Has the check-in and the look-through become a craving? How does it *feel* to think of life without *the thing*. Could we re-adjust our lives to a healthier discipline around its usage? And what are the consequences of such extensive device use in our lives—in the lives of our children?—in society as a whole? Do we have control over this and, if so, do we actually exercise that control?

I am not saying that there isn't any use for these gadgets but, rather, that our usage of them has grown to the extent that it is now manipulating our lives in ways we seldom recognize or choose to do anything about. *The thing* has taken-over our daily interactions and conversations with others in ways which say, "You are less important to me than my *smart*phone." Even my own connection with myself had become less important to me than my constant recurring exchanges with *the thing*.

Though I discuss the social media apps that influence us later, I will briefly touch on the topic here. I refer to these as "Social NeedyAh." With the predatory nature that can exist, the risks to self-esteem levels, the false representations, the comparisons, and always having others' experiences in our view, there really isn't much "social" about social media. Don't get me wrong, I love seeing a friend's wedding photos from years-gone-by on this day and I revel in seeing the growth of children I know on their first day back to school. In other media, I can fall into listening to the

[51] The Centre for Addiction and Mental Health [camh]. (n.d.). *Addiction*. Accessed 2024-06-30, https://www.camh.ca/en/health-info/mental-illness-and-addiction-index/addiction

"corn song" on repeat via my online music, which I would not have discovered without my son exposing me to this via the internet. But if I am a friend of yours and I posted something that then led you down a rabbit hole of mostly nothingness, ads, and other unrelated views and you wasted an hour or two of your time because of my post, would I *truly* want this for you? If you posted something, would you want this for me? At what cost to ourselves—and at what cost to each other? Is it to share our recently sprained-ankle photos and now being laid-up in a hospital bed? Is this social? How many people really limit their daily usage to the hour of rabbit-hole dwelling I mentioned above? Is *social* media truly social? Does it contribute to one's well-being—especially when considering the associated risks?

If you wish your mom or BFF[52] to see your swollen ankle, then send it on to them and wait for the phone to ring or ding with their sympathy. Gosh knows, hospital stays can be lengthy and usually don't include a ton of inspirational wall art that commands the patient's lasting attention. Close your eyes while waiting, drift-off, connect with Source. Take the time to connect with yourself. Breathe into the pain. What a gift to be able to *feel*, to learn what the pain is telling you, to know yourself better. Be curious, grow, expand.

You are a friend of mine? Amazing. I would love you to send me your kids graduation photo. Went on vacation recently? It would be great to sit and look at those photos together in person. I would love that! Real. Authentic. Togetherness. Oh, yes....and I can hear all those with differing viewpoints ridiculing my views around all of this, or maybe not? Feel free

52 Acronym for "best friend forever."

to critique my perspective. Then again, why not just get back to living your own life in the most positive and productive way possible?

This morning walking out of the gym, I viewed four people on equipment not working-out but looking at their phones. A man sat on the sofa in the lobby—you guessed it, another from the H.D.G. Even the two people blessed to be on the aqua massage units, fully contoured to their bodies stretched-out to have 10- to 20-minute sessions. Did they lay back and enjoy the sensations, eyes closed? No, *the thing* got in the way again. Just 10 minutes—for them, not possible. Hooked. Taken elsewhere. Typically, 1-hour workouts. Somehow *the thing* has disallowed that time, too. Not possible now for most to release the chains for this hour ("but I *need* my music"). Once leaving, I spotted a H.U.G. comrade. The look of peace blanketed across my face seemed to be shared by her. The unspoken words between seemed to say, "It's too bad, somewhat humorous, and so very sad that they have all been lost to this." "God give them the strength to make it back." We walked through the door together, only for her to then reach into the side pocket of her purse and float away, too. "That's okay," I thought. In solitude with my internal smile, I somehow got the memo that there is so much more in our life's plan, so much deeper than any of that.

From the parking lot to "on the road," people do not seem to fully land where they are anymore. Driving requires focus, attention, and concentration. Device in the glove box, "Now I can drive"—straightforward, right? Seemingly, not for many. Using a cell phone while driving is extremely hazardous and has not been addressed with the strength that is needed to deter drivers from continuing this behaviour. Fines could be increased with repeat offenders paying more for each subsequent infraction. For example, the first offense could be $500, doubling with each additional infraction. This would provide a much-needed revenue stream for police departments.

> Using cell phones while driving is extremely hazardous, and it hasn't been addressed with the strength that is needed to deter drivers from continuing this behaviour.

This aside, I am now in a parking lot and have gotten into my car. I need to leave my spot as someone else may need it—or is actually waiting for it. I am going to leave my parking space now. Nope. I am going to sit here rabbit-holing into la-la-land and you, Ms. Looking-for-a-Spot, can stuff it. *The thing* seems to make people oblivious to others and their needs. In consideration of others, one could *choose* to move their vehicle to a less prime location.

The question again is: "How has *the thing* shaped how we behave?" The common sense and courtesies of yesteryear have gone *poof*. Does that word make you angry? Courtesy? Does it make you feel like, "Why should I"; "I'm not ready yet"; "They can wait." Yet, *the thing* also teaches us that *it* cannot wait. It *has* to be looked at—*now*.

So, I guess it is time, time to ask yourself, "Is it okay with me to have unknowingly given myself to *the thing*?" Contract signed; monies paid. Are you a daily user, hourly user, moment-to-moment user, shackled checker, under-the-table swiper, all of the above, none of the above? Does this apply entirely, does it not apply at all, or everything in-between?

Had we only read the contract's fine print.

THE CELL-for-LIFE CONTRACT

I pledge my life to you, to pay close attention to your expectations, putting your needs first and foremost, before mine and all others. To walk with you and devote my attention to you always. I promise from this day forward to see you first thing in the morning and last thing at night. You are mine, and I am yours. Forever and always, we will be together. I pledge that you, my dear device, are my focus, and I am yours. I know you will always come to me. If I lose sight with making contact, you will always ensure you cast your attentive reminders toward me. I am yours, and you are mine. Even in times of detriment when I feel like you are too much for me, when what I have seen in you is depleting, I will not loose faith in you. When my esteem is shaken by you, I will not falter. Instead, I shall run to you once again, to search, to stay together, to seek the attachment we one had. I will be relentless to go deeper with you, my dear device. For ever and always, I will hold you tight. I promise to put you ahead of everything else. There will be nothing that gets between us. To you I pledge my life.

______________________________ ____________________.

Signature[1] (in blood, preferably) Date

Disclaimer and Cautions

Overuse of this device may result in socially inept behaviour in real-life situations.

Under-age exposure may inhibit one's ability to make and/or maintain eye contact with others, to converse, and to form real-life connections with others.

Parental usage while caring for or in the presence of children may result in subpar parenting and/or harmful modelling, which can be passed through subsequent generations.

Excessive usage may result in a decreased body image and diminished self image. Suicidal thoughts may occur. Excessive exposure to images viewed may result in biochemical changes occurring in the brain.

Use device with caution. Extreme caution should be taken with children. Limiting exposure prior to the age of 18 with continued limitation prior to pre-frontal cortex development (age 25).

Failure to follow these warnings may likely limit one's enjoyment in life.

This device has the potential to cause acute addictive behaviours.

[1] The signee assumes complete responsibility for the device and its repercussions.

How do we come back from *this*?

If this is your current reality, remember, *the thing* and all it's apps are intricately designed. Developed (perhaps?) with the ultimate goal to connect, its purpose has been perverted into a deviant that plays on our desires, our emotions, our drives, which are then used against us.

Yet you do have a choice to take a stand and live the life you would like to have. This is enlightening. *You* have the ability to reclaim your power!

I looked-up and paused from writing. I looked at the wall, and I noticed that all was silent around me. I could actually hear my own pulse, beating through my ear drums. It was beautiful. Have you heard this lately? Have you been so still and present that you noticed these small and magnificent gifts this human life has to offer?

I encourage you to come back. As part of this human experience, your worth is immeasurable. Do not allow yourself to be distracted away from your mind and surroundings for another moment.

Be alive—with feeling, with energy—with living.

Porny Toads

I battle with the term, "*smart*phone," in a similar way that I did with my last TV purchase, yet on a vastly different scale. My most recent TV came fully equipped with all the *smart*apps already loaded. And what if I did not want them?[53] In the US, thousands of innocent civilians, students, teachers, and children have been killed with their government's "right to bear arms" policy.[54] Even in this most dire example, US citizens have a choice. However, the world seems to have less choice when it comes to new *smart* technologies infiltrating our existence.

For example, when a TV arrives equipped with *smart* technology, there isn't a quick fix to removing these features. Hmmm. It took several painstaking sessions with an over-the-phone technical support agent to assist me with uninstalling some of these apps; there were a few that could not be uninstalled. The same goes with lack of choice with our cellular devices. As a matter of fact, a few of my *smart*phone apps have given me warnings that, if I uninstall them, my phone may not function properly. Instillation of fear is another widely used technique to continue to hold us captive.

One can search anything on a *smart*phone and come-up with a plethora of information and imagery in any category, including porn. Why? Sure, we parents can attempt to go in and set the parental controls to limit such viewing—*if* we have the capability to do so. I am no prude (which I hope you have been able to deduce from the experiences I have

53 With great effort, I discovered there is a "Dumb TV" available in the marketplace, which is excellent. But why not refer to this as a "Basic TV" instead? The language that we use to communicate is vitally important.

54 In my opinion, an archaic policy and a gross inadequacy of a government to protect their citizens.

shared herein). However, am I really off the mark to feel that this is an area that should be restricted in its viewing—that there ought to be an intense screening process and possible separate subscription required *before* users are able to gain access?

For those young adults reading this book, let me ask you: If, in the future, when the children in your lives become the age of using a *smart*phone, how would you feel about them accessing the litany of vile images that is currently available at the click of a button? Can you feel how damaging this is? How does this shape their view of women (and of men)? How does this affect their sexuality? And what happens to their experience of true intimacy and love? The effects may very well continue into adulthood and future generations. One example is Intimate Partner Violence (IPV), which has increased exponentially.[55,56]

I repeatedly hear a Pollock Clinic radio ad stating that approximately 50% of men aged 40+ now have erectile dysfunction (ED),[57] and there are statistics that reveal ED has been on the rise and is a becoming a significant

[55] Brem, M. J., Garner, A. R., Grigorian, H., Florimbio, A. R., Wolford-Clevenger, C., Shorey, R. C, & Stuart, G. L. (2021, June). Problematic pornography use and physical and sexual intimate partner violence perpetration among men in batterer intervention programs. *Journal of Interpersonal Violence, 36*(11-12), NP6085-NP6105. PMID:30461344; PMCID:PMC6942232. doi:10.1177/0886260518812806 Accessed 2023-11-29, https://pubmed.ncbi.nlm.nih.gov/30461344

[56] “IPV often stems from one person seeking to gain power or control over their partner, according to the RCMP, threatening their safety and security in various ways.” Hanick, M. (2023, July 8). What to know about intimate partner violence in Canada after Ontario mom and kids shot dead. *National Post.* Accessed 2024-07-10 https://nationalpost.com/news/intimate-partner-violence-ipv-canada

[57] Pollock Clinics. (n.d.). *Erectile dysfunction.* Accessed 2024-10-04, https://www.pollockclinics.com/erectile-dysfunction/?lnsg=47afcac0-b47e-42d8-943e-4c2cce4e56fd

concern.[58,59] Prior to online porn being accessible this was recognized as a late-adulthood ailment.

To think that we have also fully-allowed the images of violence against women and (sometimes) men or any other specified or non-specified genders to be viewable on these *smart* devices by any age group (without screening) is beyond disturbing.

American journalist and social-political activist, Gloria Steinem, stated that:

> The single biggest determinant of whether a country is violent or will use military violence against another country, is not poverty, natural resources, religion or even degree of democracy; it is violence against women.[60]
>
> If we raised one generation of kids [children] without violence and shaming[/humiliation], we don't know what might be possible.[61]

Another point, with this level of access to such imagery, we are losing so much of what has been accomplished with women's rights. It seemed we had come a long way in terms of gender and equality issues.

58 Park, B. Y., Wilson, G., Berger, J., Christman, M., Reina, B., Bishop, F., et al. (2016, August 5). Is internet pornography causing sexual dysfunctions? A review with clinical reports. *Behavioral Sciences* (Basel), *6*(3), 17. PMCID: PMC5039517; PMID: 27527226. doi:10.3390/bs6030017

59 Rastrelli, G., & Maggi, M. (2017, February). Erectile dysfunction in fit and healthy young men: Psychological or pathological? *Translational Andrology and Urology, 6*(1), 79–90. PMCID: PMC5313296; PMID: 28217453. doi:10.21037/tau.2016.09.06

60 Steinem, G. (2020, March 5). 50 years ago, Gloria Steinem wrote an essay for TIME about her hopes for women's futures. Here's what she'd add today. *TIME.* Accessed 2024-03-24, https://time.com/5795657/gloria-steinem-womens-liberation-progress

61 Blackwell, G. (Director). (2022). Episode 6: Gloria Steinem. In *Live to lead* [Documentary series] (Executive Producers: Prince Harry Duke of Sussex, Meghan Duchess of Sussex, Ben Browning, Chanel Pysnik, Geoff Blackwell, Ruth Hobday John Sloss; Producer: Ruth Hobday). Blackwell & Ruth, Nelson Mandela Foundation, Archewell Productions, Cinetic Media. Accessed 2026-06-30, https://quotefancy.com/quote/819185/Gloria-Steinem-I-think-if-we-could-raise-one-generation-of-kids-without-violence-and

Now with an uncensored click of a button, we degrade and devalue people (women in particular) in ways our society has never experienced before. Without addressing this serious issue, have we *truly* advanced? In my opinion, much of the ground we have gained on equality and rights is perverted, yet again, by this ungoverned wretch, which continues with ferocity.

This is beyond comprehension. Brutality *included* on a *smart*phone without any restrictions is unacceptable. Furthermore, the onus is on caregivers to rectify this issue. Some are not even aware of this possibility; others don't have the means to address it.

There is a simple solution to this mess that appears to have been overlooked. Users must provide a credit card in order to access such material, which would ensure that they have reached the age of majority. All companies would be required to use their full company name and website addresses on credit card statements and to be held accountable in the event that a parent discovers that their child has used their card without their knowledge. (This stipulation might assist with other online deceptions at the same time.)

I do not support the funding of such corruption; however, this serves as a straightforward and immediate screening tool for those who are minors. It also safeguards against skilled under-aged users from by-passing parental controls. Beyond these requirements, governments could order adult-xxx companies to exist solely on subscription funding and discontinue all advertising to fund their platforms.

I know that this is an uncomfortable topic for many, and others may prefer to pretend it does not exist. A whole generation being brought into adulthood thinking that this is the way human interactions look, that this is what people like—and *are* like.

Human and child sex-trafficking brought straight to you and included in your data plan. Sure, you may not view such videos but, they are there for you if you wish, all courtesy of your *smart*phone.

> Unfortunately, in our modern society, many have taken the view that "sex work is work" and do not recognize the vulnerability of those who are exploited through trafficking and prostitution, many of whom are marginalized through poverty or homelessness, among other factors. Children in care are particularly vulnerable to manipulation and exploitation.[62]

We haven't even begun to expose the detrimental impact *the thing* is having on our health and well-being, or the environmental implications that are rarely, if ever, discussed.[63] Again—we will wonder. Scratching our downturned heads, we will wonder how we, the human race, has arrived here. A new zombie species devoting much of their lives to a constant scroll of falsification and mindlessness despite some of the more serious implications I have just revealed.

Shall I continue on this topic or is this enough to have you think, "Right. How and why has this been allowed?"

Now would be a good time to write your member of parliament or government representatives and express your concerns.

[62] Renaud, B. (2024, July 30). *Leave no child behind: The fight against human trafficking.* Accessed 2024-12-02, https://churchforvancouver.ca/author/barbara-renaud

[63] We need a serious re-assessment of so many issues before our environment pulls it all out from under us. But I digress, as this is not the subject of this book (nevertheless perhaps a publication for the future as I have a lot to share on this topic as well).

Back Again

I had completed my stint in Tokyo and had accomplished what I set out to do. I earned and saved enough money to pay-off my debts in full, and then some. I gained a fresh perspective and had grown in ways further than I could have anticipated. The billboards around me signalled that the holiday season was fast approaching and that it would soon be time to go home for Christmas. This made me smile.

With my massive suitcase bulging (prior to suitcase weight or size restrictions), I donned my knee-high wooden-heeled platform boots with lace-up front and zippered backs (a buy from someone who had acquired them during a Thailand "visa run"). With the thought of folding the leather and the space they took-up in my case, it seemed only logical to wear them home. Teamed together with my Dalmatian-print scarf (matching fluffy platforms in the suitcase) and black terrycloth button-up shirt created quite the look for customs officials to target me on my way-out. They pulled me into the back room for 4 hours of questioning, ransacked my belongings, and detained me until they saw fit to let me go.

As I was writing this, I received flashes of the man from Mexico City I was seated beside at the back of the plane. The man who shared with me that he was excited to see his wife and young children back home. He even showed me (print) photos of them and gave me his address in case I was ever in Mexico so I could look him up. During our long flight together, I awoke to that same man with his hand down my shirt, groping my breast inside my bra. I supposed he figured I was sleeping so this would be his chance. The possibility that I would not wake-up as I did, or if I did wake-up I would freeze and be unable to move or do anything about it for the sheer terror of what may come after. And these many years later, I still cringe from the feeling upon hearing the words "Mexico City." Staying silent did not serve me.

It's interesting to think that I had made it unscathed against the warnings of all who feared what would become of me in Japan, only to be sexually violated on my way home at the hand of a man from another country.

Once back on home soil, it was rumoured that I had gotten a "boob job" and had been an exotic dancer while away. Neither applied. In fact, I had taken to eating "spaghetti carbonara" from ampm convenience store almost nightly. So not only had my breasts grown, but all of me had taken on a more womanly appearance. I was accustomed to people talking about me, whether negative, gossipy, catty, or otherwise. Talking.

I knew the truth though. Breasts grow, some more than others.[64] The same ones that had put an end to my ballet career at 16, since I no longer fit into the box of what ballerinas *look* like, so I let them talk and I continued on with my life, now connecting with a whole new group of Angelique's friends. (Remember the stunning Canadian in the mirror with the curling iron? Intuitively, she knew I would get along with her friends once back home, so she passed on a number.) This led to the next year's opening-up in terms of people and places while, at the same time, closing-in on any semblance of who I was as alcohol's power over me grew significantly.

One new friend, Kiki, was an upbeat positive ray of light with an infectious smile. We shared a European upbringing, which had us looking for ways to get away from a stifling home life in adulthood. On our first meeting, we ended-up being snowed-in at a hotel in downtown

64 In order not to exclude anyone, breasts can also shrink.

Vancouver, while the city shutdown in a blizzard not seen in many years. I did not know this woman, but bringing stories of Angelique was enough to bond us initially. The rest was a natural meld of good vibes that had us feeling as though we had known each other for years before, if not lifetimes. It was set. Kiki, her Chinese Fijian boyfriend Kris and his closest sister Malory,[65] my soon-to-be new best friend along with her husband Andre and his good buddy Ban, would introduce me to the group of soul-filled people I would travel with for several years. With immediate family get-togethers in the backyard of 50+ people, who were cooking, sharing, talking, laughing, I opened-up to an entirely different culture and way of being than I had previously experienced. We danced endlessly. We felt free.

Without recognizing it at the time, this was also an opportunity to continue distancing myself from the people and circumstances I had left behind before I went away. My new-found friends were of Korean, Vietnamese, Filipino, Chinese, Fijian, British, and Greek backgrounds and all of them were older than me. Everyone was so gracious and welcomed me as a family member. Thankfully, I was unaware I was the minority.

Through Kiki and Kris, I met my new boyfriend, a party promoter, which meant that…well…we didn't miss one. The pre-rave era of house music and underground vibes was in full effect. We had access to world class DJs[66] and the most inspiring freeing music that had ever touched me—early Tiesto, Aoki, Danny Howell, Pete Tong, DJ Amtrak, DJ Pascal, Mistress Barbara, and so many others. Draped in one of many colourful feather boas and wearing a newly-acquired pair of platform heels amongst

[65] Malory was the youngest of 12 children who, along with their parents, immigrated to Canada from Fiji, which I always felt was an impressive accomplishment.

[66] Acronym for "disc jockeys."

(one of) several faux fur jackets—I was set—set for my first ride on a stretcher out of a nightclub; set to get my first 24-hour suspension. Set.

In hindsight, my drinking consumption had escalated to an entirely new level. I was becoming more aware of the magnitude of my problem. I continued in denial and fought the battle for several more years.

On occasion, my high school friends would travel the distance through bridges and tunnels to visit me with my "new friends," one saying afterwards, "You were gone. Your eyes were gone. You were just gone." "Envy," I thought, as she must have wished she could get that wasted—and the delusion in me set-in further, away from the glistening ads with the well-dressed outwardly-joyous sequined figures shining in the "just-so" positioning of it all. Designed to have us feel this is what people do—the multimillion-dollar ad campaigns that set us up for poisoning ourselves—and the normalcy of it all.

I did not look like the ads. I thought I did...possibly...I really wanted to. But my body and mind chemistry did not allow for it. I dressed the part and so did those I travelled with, yet with each additional sip my eyes would further leave the building taking with them the windows of the soul that they housed.

I moved into the lower level of another home in which a young family was living upstairs. By this time, I had gone on the (water)wagon as one of my latest attempts at drinking proved much less than successful to say the least. After a couple months of abstinence, I opened my new fridge and found a single item inside—a fresh box of white wine—my favourite. I figured it was an omen, and my ship set sail once again. T'was not in me to give it up just yet. Many others of a similar age were just getting started, and those I travelled with consumed large quantities to further the example of normality.

I lived by myself, which I loved, aside from the wolf spiders that were common in this area. I came and went as I wished. I worked three jobs. Around this time, I had heard Oprah Winfrey say, "Find a job that you love, and you will never work."

"What did I love?" Hmmm.... Well, I loved to do my makeup. I had always loved this. So simple, and that is what I did. I went back to school to get a diploma in special-effects makeup artistry for film and television, while also continuing to audition for TV spots and ads. School and work kept me downtown again and meeting-up with friends afterwards was commonplace. After another disaster left me hanging my head for long enough, I began stringing together one month of sobriety at a time along the way. With glimmers of the program in my mind yet not wholly applying its suggestions, I managed to reach 2 years of continuous abstinence.

It was these episodes of restraint that fooled me into believing that I could beat alcohol's hold over me if left to my own ways and means.

I then decided to celebrate my achievement at my best friend's wedding by indulging in alcohol once again—I figured I had earned it.

Late one night a few months later, my landlord knocked on the door and let me know that they were being transferred back to England. The house would be listed for sale with unknown status of whether the purchasers would keep a tenant.

Once the deal was completed and the new owners moved in upstairs, it was clear that I could stay and that we would also become fast friends. Their biker ways were reminiscent of the duplex I grew-up in as a child—

it seemed comfortable and familiar. The loud Harley's were my childhood wake-up call from the *ape hangers*[67] and the stomping on the gas to the unmistakable roar from the exhaust pipes as they rolled down the oil-stained street.

The over-consumption progressed to the next level with us living under one roof.

I had grown-up well—loved and cared for—two kids, two parents. Board games. Bedtime stories.

But typically, you cannot pick your neighbours, and ours at that time were a multi-generational family of bikers, who went-out the upstairs window and sat on the roof to smoke weed (illegal at the time). In a flowing dress and biker boots, on more than one occasion I witnessed the woman of the house beating the dog on the front lawn and, nowadays when I go around there, I can still hear echoes of her bellowing down the lane to her children to come-in for dinner.

Their large fish tank in the inside of an emptied TV could mesmerize me for hours. This was not a life that I had experienced, and it was a far distance from the hard-working blue- and pink-collars my parents had donned. The heart-shaped bed in the downstairs bedroom adorned with red lacey shams and all the childhood stuffies and cushions one could dream of (courtesy of the woman-of-the-house's sister whose long-stemmed roses sat in a crystal vase on the nightstand with a card that read "Rock me Amadeus!").

[67] The handles of a motorcycle, "ape hangers encourage a more upright posture instead of creating the need to hunch over. On long rides, apehangers that fit your body type also decrease strain on the wrists, elbows, and shoulders." Black Gold Harley-Davidson. (2020, September 2). "Handlebar types" (Bullet 6). In *Should you put apes on your Harley®?* Accessed 2024-06-30, https://blackgoldhd.com/news-article/31322/ape-hangers-for-harley

Childhood—and all that came along with it in the 80s—all still alive *in my mind* today.

Though this was not the life that I had experienced when I was young, I was back in the comfort of "these sorts of people" upstairs, and their over-indulgence took us to the backyard, the front yard, and eventually around town. It was perfect.

And here I was, delving into a new darkness while arriving at the next level.

Fire

My boyfriend rented the penthouse of an older concrete high-rise with full-frontal mountain view. The days were full, the drinking was daily and, for the odd days we weren't drinking, those tricked me into believing I did not have a problem. The roommates went to bed as did my boyfriend, while I proceeded to set the scene for a bubble bath, music, and candles to support my magnetism towards all things fire-sign. It hadn't occurred to me that drinking alone like this was anything other than me just unwinding and creating some time for myself at day's end.

I reached the bathroom donned in my boyfriend's oversized grey bathrobe, disrobed, and slipped into the bath with my wine glass. Once out and robed again, the corner of the terry polyester blend whisked by the lit candle on the table and within moments my body was engulfed in flames from ankle to neck. I ran a-blaze through the apartment into the bedroom and he awoke screaming. Jumping towards me and tumbling me to the ground, he snuffed-out the flames with his body weight. We laid sobbing in a full embrace on the floor, a life-sized body-burn etched into the carpet below. Miraculously, we both escaped unscathed. Another memory charred into my mind of what was.

Time travelled onward and he went on to cheat on me with a stripper named Delilah. I was distraught, but my close friends cradled me through as did Toni Braxton's song "Unbreak My Heart." Around this time, the shootings and crime began to develop a presence in our city. I was in the nightclub when the first major gangland violence of this era ignited. Without seeing the assailant, I saw the weapon and grabbed my best friend's wrist with a tight grip and steered her quickly outside. We sprinted without her knowing why, and without speaking a word. Again, my training proved helpful. We continued non-stop at full speed for blocks and, when I couldn't run anymore, I vomited all over the sidewalk. I remember it well and could take you to that corner today.

A young man was shot and killed that night in the club.

It was around this time that we also lost our first friend by other means. Vibrant and in his early 20s, after a night out together with us he had passed-out at home and asphyxiated on his own vomit. It was heart-wrenching.

The funeral was well-attended. Our colourful friends celebrated his life and what it had been as we mourned what might still have been. His family gripped by the loss.

Mortality had kicked in—the threat of death—while at the same time, it had not. Our crew partied hard with hospital visits gaining in occurrence. After most parties, we went to my best friend's house where a knock at the door revealed through the peephole a friend had arrived back safely from the hospital. Bracelet still on and face still Jiffy-marked from the party the night before,[68] he ripped the electrodes from his chest and flung them around the room—an active frisbee game ensued in which all participated.

I was working at the coat-check of a local nightclub, my drink at the side of the cash register. The same club in which I had unzipped my 1-piece catsuit down-and-around my ankles and, after passing out, bra-less, I had hit my head on the toilet on the way down to the stall floor. The same club from which later I was wheeled-out of by paramedics. On our way through the club, the combination of the music's bass beating and the blue light strobing woke my body, I *came-to* blanketed and restrained on a

[68] Jiffy is a brand of *permanent* felt marking pens. His face had been Jiffy-marked with a black eye and Spanish curled mustache and beard.

stretcher. The same club in which I had partied with my friend a week previously, his whole life in front of him, now dead. Far from the glamour, laughter, or sequined ads.

It has always interested me that governments (cha-ching[69]) fail to expose the negative aspects and damage this legalized substance causes, while liquor reps,[70] developers, and alcohol companies (also) rejoice in their strategically-glorified advertisements. From early-on, these ads hook our children into the adult, fun-loving, and carefree side of consumption rather than the ruin, wreckage, and carnage that alcohol can play in our lives and societies. In contrast to the laughter and lights, I have often felt that real-life images should be included in alcohol advertisements as a warning—the flipside of the possibilities—with real people, the lives lost, the detriment.

It is important to note that Health Canada[71] recently classified alcohol as a Group 1 carcinogen and officially specified that any more than two standard-size drinks per week increases the risk of seven types of cancer.[72] Diabetes, heart disease, and stroke are also listed as risks associated with alcohol usage.

Aside from the brown paper-bag man in my mind—*I* was him—I was just encased in a different package. Likewise, from an early age mobile

[69] Cha-ching or ka-ching: Someone is making a lot of money.

[70] Short for "representatives."

[71] Canadian Cancer Society. (n.d.). *Alcohol policy: Canada should have policies that increase awareness about the risk of alcohol-related cancer and reduce alcohol consumption.* Accessed 2024-12-02, https://cancer.ca/en/get-involved/advocacy/what-we-are-doing/alcohol-policy

[72] Canadian Cancer Society. (n.d.). *Some sobering facts about alcohol and cancer risk.* Accessed 2024-12-02, https://cancer.ca/en/cancer-information/reduce-your-risk/limit-alcohol/some-sobering-facts-about-alcohol-and-cancer-risk

device companies manipulate young people while pulling them away from having *real* connections, being their authentic selves, and reaching their full potential. What are we, the people, doing to address this?

Next came a major car accident in which I totalled my truck and, not long after, another hospitalization due to over-consumption. Neither of these provided the wake-up calls to seal my defeat from alcohol. Though many times I had received much laughter for having been a "rock star," any remaining glimmer of the star had been extinguished inside. A sloppy, slurring, falling, sweater-less human was more accurate than any sparkle of a star. How could this be me? How could I change the way I consumed when I felt so driven for more. How? There had to be another way. My boyfriend at the time pulled a dark-blue book volume off his shelf that I had never seen. He said I should read it. Reading the embossed title[73] on the book's cover, I scoffed, laughed out loud, and exclaimed, "This does *not* apply to me!" Twenty-one years old—it does not apply to *me*!

Not long after, I found myself in a counselling session. My counsellor suggested I come to a meeting where there are lawyers, a doctor, business people, a super model—all who had previously lived similar detrimental lifestyles—I thought this not possible.

I went and found myself sitting, throat-choked, and unable to speak let alone have the ability to utter the word "alcoholic." So I didn't. I just sat, I listened, and I tried to find all the ways in which the word did not apply to me. From there he had me meet with a group at the Carnegie Community Centre. Often referred to as "the living room of the

[73] Alcoholics Anonymous (soft cover). Accessed 2024-12-02, https://onlineliterature.aa.org/Big-Book-Soft-Cover-4th-Edition

Downtown Eastside,"[74] the heritage building is located in the middle of what has been called the worst drug and alcohol problems in all of North America—possibly in the world. Homeless humans flailing in degradation, this is an area covered in graffiti, open drug use, tent-living, garbage everywhere, and violence; a tragedy to witness that made my life seem *normal* in comparison.

I parked and exited my mint-condition 2-door Honda Accord, dressed to the hilt (donning my silver faux-fur jacket and heels from Japan, of course), and made my way up the sidewalk. Dodging the dirty souls and loaded shopping carts littered along the sidewalks, I managed to escape their yelling, cursing, and antics, and scaled the library stairs. I would show the people at this meeting that none of this applied to me, I was even more determined to prove it to myself.

While not speaking, I listened and absorbed as much as I could. A 12-step book study group was introduced to me. As these times were foggy at best for me, I'm fairly certain I left those meetings and went home to my suite to have another drink. Those Carnegie Centre folks could shove it—"Alcohol was my master."[75]

Eventually the program had convinced my mind of better options and, at last, I collected my 1-month sobriety chip.[76] It was during this time that I discovered yoga—hot yoga. I found peace, release, and meditative growth within this practice. It freed me in ways I had not yet experienced.

74 City of Vancouver. (n.d.). *Carnegie Community Centre*. Accessed 2024-06-30, https://vancouver.ca/parks-recreation-culture/carnegie-community-centre.aspx

75 Alcoholics Anonymous World Services. (2001). *Alcoholics Anonymous: The story of how many thousands of men and women have recovered from alcoholism* (rev ed.; p. 8). New York, NY: Author. (Also referred to as *The Big Book*; available online at https://www.aa.org/the-big-book)

76 Small medallions earned with each month of consecutive sobriety achieved.

There was a warmth and self-development combined with a connection to source and a community of like-minded and -hearted individuals I had not yet known. Coming together in a battle between my mind and all that told me to give into the heat, to walk out the door, to allow the voices in my head to remain yet not prevail. Going against the discomfort of it all was a beautiful beginning.

After working on movie sets as a makeup artist, it was apparent that I had become somewhat resentful. I wanted to be back in the chair having my makeup done rather than doing others' makeup. So perhaps I had gotten it wrong making a career of something I loved to do, and my approach had been backwards.

At this point I shifted to a theatrical makeup and dance supply shop as one of my various day jobs. I decided to change course and return to work in real estate administration, which I had done on-and-off since I was 17 years old. I worked both jobs in tandem for a time.

During this period, I was convinced that I must have had a karmic debt to pay for the occurrences kept coming. A dark sun-glassed ballcap-wearing figure came behind the make-up store counter, reefed on my arm, and pulled me into his chest. His arm crossed the front of my body,[77] knife-blade at my throat, the tip jabbed into my jawbone. "Give me all the money!" he growled as my co-worker courageously grabbed the pepper spray from behind the counter and held it towards him. He intensified his grip. "Give me all the f***in' money or I will *hurt* her!"—and she did as he demanded. After several moments of being in his grip, he hurled me to the ground, my palms burned on the carpet as I skidded on its surface.

[77] At the time, this person carried-out a string of burglaries. He was a seasoned arsonist who, on this occasion, switched his choice of weapon.

In a flash I was up and escaping, running again, out the building's back door, into the alley, into the rain, a welcomed freedom on my face. Free again—once again.

But this trauma wasn't over. Next came the finger- and palm-printing to eliminate ours from those left on the glass showcases, police line-ups to attempt to identify the perpetrator, and victim-impact statements. Another experience to shape me, to teach me, to leave me questioning: Why? Me.

As I did (and as I still do), I kept going. A product of a family system, which did just that—kept going, kept striving, kept sacrificing—regardless. No excuses. The drive to continue, to seek forward, to heal—to not allow circumstances to define me and to shape what was to come. Determination, grit, in any and all circumstances.

One of the first examples I recall was at age 12, when my parents had saved enough for a down-payment on their first home in British Columbia—a mint-green vinyl-sided log cabin on one-third of an acre well-below the current market value. Built in 1911, the home had previously been owned by a pioneering family in the area. Backing onto a mountainous greenbelt, the yard was a haven with its terraces, old stone bird baths, and overgrown surroundings. This was where I found my first dragonfly who had crossed over, therefore allowing me to hold it to closely inspect its detailed features. A distinct lesson in survival through the (prehistoric) ages. Even back then I revelled in the mysteries of what it takes for a species to survive.

Seeing this as an opportunity to get into the market that was otherwise out of their reach, my parents bought the two-bedroom house, though it should have been condemned. They sacrificed having a bedroom in order for my brother and I to both have one for ourselves.

They slept on a pull-out sofa-bed in the living room for close to 3 years. My mom worked 12-hour shifts at the hospital and sometimes slept during the day as shift workers do. Sacrifice.

The bedroom that became mine had previously been a small library with glossy wood panelling and books shelved floor-to-ceiling on every wall. An entire room of classic antique volumes of literature—a delight to my father, which may have sealed the deal for us to take up camp there. Yet the musty odour would soon reveal that the dampness of the home had seeped-in to destroy the idea of salvaging most of the books, many of which had been lost to an over-growth of mold so thick that mushrooms grew between their pages.

A skeleton key was our access into the front door. The walls of the house were lined with old newspapers. The tarnished brass doorknob that led to the basement, upon opening, billowed a musty stench of drainage issues and dank water-pooling complete with a floating log. This is when I first learned the term "sump pump." It was also my first introduction to the possibility of rats taking-up residence in one's home—worlds away from the Pinterest boards of style ideas boasted by many now. Real, raw, part of my parent's story, and mine.

They tripled the home's value when they sold it less than 3 years later. Remarkable.

I always worked, I owned things, I functioned. I had managed to save enough to purchase my first condo, which was one block from the beach in an affluent West Vancouver neighbourhood largely occupied by retirees. I was beyond giddy at my accomplishment, the beautiful surroundings and ocean at foot. Somehow within the turmoil of it all, I had done it.

I met a man and was caught immediately by his charm and dark Eastern European features. We were off, and wildly in love. Yet high levels of consumption were a major factor in our existence, and this set forward several more years of drinking before I was levelled into making another true attempt at sobriety. I really felt I had found my match. The broken-bottle fights in the middle of a rain-drenched street would prove it, and this is all I will share about this incident.

Though I already stood-out from the crowd in this quiet community, soon after entering into our common-law arrangement my partner showed-up drunk and belligerent demanding to be let in via the entry-phone. I refused, so he took the liberty of kicking-in the glass panel beside the door, arriving bloodied and pounding on my suite door. These were my first indications of my "being stuck."

With all the cultural stereotyping he carried into our relationship, we battled to define our roles. The complicated dance between us was further fuelled by alcohol. He attempted to stifle my power and keep me boxed into filling what he saw as the woman's place. Through his own insecurities, he rendered me small and himself grand. He did his best to crush me and, at times, succeeded. In his defence (really?—I can't believe I'm saying this), he had learned this behaviour by example from his father, who adopted it from his father, and so on. Having said this, I am a firm believer that individuals need to be accountable and take responsibility for their lives, their traumas, their patterns whether these originate in their upbringings or adulthood.

My clouded vision tricked me into rationalizing that, if my parents could do it and be successful, then why couldn't we? Seven months from the time we met, we were married. I spent my wedding night scouring for my wedding rings in the laneway of the condo I owned, which he had placed on my finger earlier that day. Another symbol, a symbol of my arrival with a man, another dream upon which I had been raised and my first conscious thoughts of my reality being utterly misaligned with the bliss that is said to accompany this event.

I have sometimes wondered if anyone else in the world has spent their wedding night searching through crevices for their rings that were thrown out the window of a moving vehicle by their new husband? I do not need to know the answer really. It is irrelevant. But I have wondered. The following day he revealed that he had only motioned to throw the rings away, which only made my efforts to find them that much more futile.

While on a guided tour on our honeymoon in Tulum, Mexico, I began to exhibit signs of heatstroke. Becoming increasingly dizzy, with a newly formed embryo growing inside me, I shared how I was feeling with my then husband. His response was to tell me to suck it up and that I was "embarrassing him." I leaned against a tree, trying to hold back the looming vomit.

Later that evening he set forth on another disgusting bender courtesy of free-flowing bottles on our hotel room wall. (This did not include me, as I had entered into a newfound need to be responsible. Although this was an entirely difficult and particularly foreign place for me to exist, my cells craved to join-in.) Through years of counselling, I would learn later that abusive men can choose pregnancy as a time to further undermine their partners. Another potentiality-beautiful time in my life that was challenged at the hand of a man.

I was locked-out of our suite, my husband shouting profanities at me in a drunken fury. Sitting on the terracotta stairs, threatened and sobbing, custodians and hotel guests passing-by were asking me if I needed help. I figured I needed an entirely new life, and I was undoubtably right. After hours of listening to his drunken belittling and badgering, I resorted to obtaining another room. I contemplated leaving for home with his passport in tow but was too petrified to follow through.

Even now I can feel the power of the struggle from that time—the doom, the unknowing, the knowing. I knew that when I returned home, I would have to take drastic measures to begin freeing myself and my unborn child from a life such as this. But how?

I still felt so young at 27. The years between high school and then had blurred together in a clump of post secondary education, working, and over-consumption with a workhard/playhard mentality. My dreams of attending law school long since past, I had another set of circumstances fuelling everything. Pregnancy was a 9-month push to remain sober. The first term proved challenging beyond belief and, added to the abusive treatment while amidst my heightened emotional status, he continued increasing his usage. The unfairness of it all engulfed me.

I began studying for my real-estate licence while trying to fend-off the draining battles with my husband and feeling the loss of self even more all the while. In time, the cravings lightened, and the remainder of my pregnancy improved. I carried past full-term and a day before I was to be induced, I went into labour.

After 17 hours of back labour,[78] it was discovered that the umbilical cord had wrapped around our infant's neck and emergency procedures advanced quickly. I was given a total of 3 epidurals and went into shock on the table. Shaking violently, surgery staff instructed me to grasp both IV poles and "Hold On!" My teeth chattered uncontrollably. I delivered a healthy robust boy via emergency C-section. The first moments of his life were chillingly silent. I thank God for the gift that his breath was, and still is.

Cramming while working my day job, the day finally arrived when I was to write my exam our province's largest university. That morning, my husband met me in our small galley kitchen. I still remember the look in his eyes as he said, "I hope you f***ing fail, so everyone can see how f***ing stupid you really are." This is what I was up against. Unfortunately, in a variety of forms that is what many women are up against. This is what I had to leave the house with; this is what I took with me into that massive theatre-style exam hall. This.

This is what left me in the parkade after the exam combing through textbooks trying to calculate whether I had passed with the amount needed. This is what left me waiting, praying, holding-on to my way out. My out from him. The first steps away, away with my baby, the one he threatened to not come to the birth of, however later he boasted being the first one to hold our infant son. Some of the ways people move through their lives is staggering.

[78] Some "…women feel intense pain in their lower backs [during childbirth]. This is called back labor and is likely a result of where the baby is positioned inside the body….[Though] not a dangerous condition…[it] can make an already painful experience even more uncomfortable." Hamilton, V. (2022, April 7). What is back labor? *WebMD*. Accessed 2024-06-30, https://www.webmd.com/baby/what-is-back-labor

I failed that exam by three marks. It was crushing. What this meant was that I had to wait 90 days before rewriting. What this also meant to me at the time was that maybe he was right. Maybe I was those things he said. Maybe everyone else saw that too. Or maybe it was just another knockdown that I had to rise above, to wait out, to continue through. Maybe.

With our newborn in the bassinet beside me, I studied, and then I studied more. I was patient. I breast-fed. I waited.

I rewrote the exam at the 90-day mark and earned my license. I walked out the door with my 6-month-old baby boy after another big blow-out between us. This is where the cycle of his family's generations of males verbally- and emotionally-abusing their female partners was ending, at least for me. (Please understand, I dearly love his family, and have love for him now too, which I touch on later.) I would not take part in furthering that manner of male/female relations, and my son was not going to be brought-up in that kind of an environment. I knew better, much better—even at the (still) young age of 28. Although my family of origin had their struggles, it was not like this. A lifetime of this would be entirely depleting. No matter the hardships I would need to endure along the way, I felt called to leave for myself and for my son—a voice deep within me said "If anyone can put an end to this, it is *you*." *I* was the one who had to end this cycle.

It was difficult to say the least.

He had once said that his father had taught him that you never lay a finger on a woman. What I later learned was that his verbal undermining drew wounds that left deeply ingrained scars that couldn't be seen by others yet took-up immense space within. It felt as though there was a hole in my soul because, even when he wasn't present, my mind took the liberty of taking-over where he had left off. His frequent harassment had seeped-in to convince me I would be little without him.

The next months would see me entirely cut-off financially by my husband, living in my parent's basement, and getting myself into $50,000 of credit-card debt while I began my real estate career. I signed-on with a male-dominated office in which extra-marital affairs were common-place and the image to uphold was staggering. I showed-up looking the part and kept a firm distance from the rest, when one day early-on the owner told me, "You look really good, but you are not doing enough business."

The years to follow shortly thereafter would see the market crash of 2007/2008, which left me struggling again. It is during this time that I found sobriety, which finally stuck after the 10-year in-and-out battle to do so.

Again, "Difficult, but not impossible"—one of my "live-by" statements.

Battle in, Battle Out

From the time of the market crash, I continued to crawl my way out from under alcohol and my tendency towards demise. A young and vibrant highly-functional woman, but add alcohol into the mix and the poisonous depressant hijacked her system in ways she had not known possible.

As previously mentioned, I was far from the designer advertisements for alcohol—the marketing campaign of flashy glamour with tanned and toned bodies partaking in an oiled-up game of beach volleyball, ice chest in-tow. Or the holiday cocktail party with sparkling dresses and the glistening glass embodied by the smiles and laughter of its consumers. Not I. That was not what happened for me once this liquid was consumed. The combination of the craving for more and the obsession with how (this time) I could make it look like the ads and their illustrations—that did not happen for me.

Drinking with my dad made for times of bonding while filling a void—my tea-totalling mother did not partake. The alcoholism from her father had skipped her, so she was not predisposed. The draw towards alcohol on both sides of my parents' families resulted in a flawed recipe, which left my DNA intolerant of any blend, distilled or fermented, grape or grain, neat or mixed, which touched my lips.

My internal system would try any and all ways to make it work. To just be able to drink like others, to drink less, to drink something different. Being able to swear-off for weeks and months, my binge-drinking tendencies had tricked me into not pairing "alcoholic" with who I had become. Yet the moment I consumed the substance again, I was back to how I had been previously, and worsening with each episode.

To Nourish Thy Infant

I had thought that once the baby was born, I would be able to drink freely. I was graced with a firm flow of milk from my bosom for which I was grateful as I know there are many who are not as fortunate. Based on the research findings, I had the firm resolution that the most wholesome start (breastfeeding) would keep my infant and I bonded for some time to come while increasing his immunity in life. Though pumping milk didn't seem to be a friend of mine, I would attempt it once again at a friend's wedding shortly before my husband and I separated. Another disaster of trying to drink with the crowd, highly intoxicated my breasts were painfully engorged and drew blood into the pumped milk. This had to stop. The pull to be *normal*, to take or leave the drink, to mother, to escape my relationship, all at once, stringing together some time of abstinence. I attempted sobriety again.

With baby stroller in hand, arriving at the bottom of the Women's Centre's stairs that towering steeply, it seemed as if I were to ascend the Great Wall. After minutes of being stuck there, another member passed and offered help to climb together, bringing stroller and baby upstairs. Inside was a calm quiet environment full of the feeling of love, hot tea, and bright expressions. I would remain quiet for quite some time, passing when asked to share.

Months later when attempting to utter the word "alcoholic," I at long last verbalized this in Porky Pig fashion. From that point, the disease of alcoholism and the reality of my illness became more apparent. I had crossed the threshold. Once I began to see how my life flourished when the bottle was consistently removed from my presence, I was willing to make a solid attempt at staying sober. Beginning again was not easy—a complete change in friends, some family, places, and habits. Everything had to be changed and at times it took every ounce of strength to transform specific pieces of my life.

At first, I attempted to keep my group of friends intact, clinging to what was. This proved futile as I quickly discovered that the two could not co-exist. I remember crying while standing in a pub washroom stall when a girlfriend of mine came in and joined me. (Do not go to a pub if you have recently stopped consuming alcohol.) The cells of me wretched at the unfathomable feeling which made me want to jump from my own body. With all the pain inside me coming forward, I said to her, "I would rather have cancer, than have this [alcoholism]!" It was strong. It gripped my everything. My cells longed for liquor—in any form—to once again come and soothe the anxiety and turmoil that lived within me.

Years later with my dad's diagnosis, I discovered the devastation cancer causes and the fact that it affects so many—I was embarrassed to have uttered those words.

The grip alcoholism had on me was astonishingly powerful and yet, at the time, I did not understand what "I had" or that there was a remedy for it. A complete spiritual shift was required to free me from the pull, though in the state I was in I could not see how that could be attained. Now looking back, I realize I just needed to stay willing to have a power greater than myself to help restore my sanity.[79] I managed to show-up at meetings amidst the heart palpitations that filled my chest. As my son grew, I nourished him from my body, and I continued to be nourished from the teachings that I was slowly absorbing.

[79] Step 2 in AA.

Though the Carnegie Centre had come and gone for me, I later realized the efforts of that counsellor to show me the potential of where I could have ended-up if left untreated. I stayed surrounded in the centre of women who had walked before me and held my spirit and best intentions at the forefront. While I was being shown the way, time endured, and my boy found a place to play in a neighbouring room with a frequent pal whose mom also attended the meetings. I managed 3 years of continuous sobriety doing the program as suggested, set out in parts with some alterations of my own, which in hindsight proved to be unsuccessful.

On a sunny day, April 12, 2008, one of the first times my son stayed overnight with his dad, I went out with a handsome Black Irish man I had met some time prior at an open house. I parked my Mercedes at the marina and walked down the wooden dock. He and another couple waved to me from their boat in the harbour, their jovial smiles beckoning me in the sunlight. We exchanged introductions and they quickly pulled-out a bottle of chilled champagne. There it was. How could I not have considered this possibility ahead of time? I quickly told them, "I don't drink." "What do you mean you don't drink?" said my tall dark friend. "No, you don't understand," I said in a low tone. "When I drink, I go crazy." "Ahhh...," the laughter escaped from their mouths as if to say, "Awesome, bring it on!" But they left it alone and poured their three glasses as we departed.

We travelled to Bowen Island where we docked and climbed-up the steep stairs to a gorgeous home built on a towering rock. There were so many stairs to reach the home's entrance—100 minimum—I recall them with distinct clarity. Inside, the ruby-red ornate furnishings and Persian rugs saturated my senses. I would not drink that day. I would continue as I had. I was different genetically than them and I needed to hold onto this fact tightly. I went to the beautifully decorated powder room with more ruby-red wall coverings and lavish finishings inside. I sat down, and the thought crossed my mind that it would be alright to have just one glass of wine.

I went back out to the living room and made an announcement that it would be okay to have a glass of wine. They gladly poured the robust red into a crystal glass for me. The first sip, I recall, was followed by the next 10 hours of complete blackout. From the Bowen Island home, how I descended down all those stairs, into the boat, and miles down the inlet to the shores of downtown Vancouver was entirely absent. Nothing.

My next memories of that evening where patchy recalls of being at the bar of a Coal Harbour restaurant and another bar late into the night, where I shot Tequila, drank red wine, ate raw oysters, and smoked cigars outside. I had lost my cardigan, which meant that now my long-fitted skirt and top did not meet at my mid-drift. I was put into a cab, started vomiting profusely, the driver screaming at me, which led me to vomiting in my Louis Vuitton purse instead of on the taxi's floor. I hit the driver, and he threatened to drop me off ahead of the bridge I needed to cross. Thankfully, he went the distance and dropped me at a gas station on the other side. Shoeless now, lost wallet, lost dignity, I used the station's landline to call my sponsor (lost phone, but I survived, even in this state). A dear friend, Thad, picked me up and drove me home. He had years of witnessing this kind of depravity, which was outside of how I presented myself when away from alcohol's flow. We arrived at the apartment that I had just moved into, the mattress still leaned-up against the wall with boxes stacked eye-high. Putting the bed down onto the floor, I crawled on, sheetless. He left me to sleep it off and awaken to my own demise.

The next morning, I awoke stunned. Searching for my cell phone in my purse, I was greeted with the putrid remains of what I had become: the stench of partially digested seafood, Mexican hard bar, and Merlot. A one-night relapse that left me levelled and desperate for a lasting change to be made—this time had to be my last. One night.

I peeled the tape from my sealed filing cabinet and, hands shaking, searched inside for the one phone number I needed. My cell phone gone, I called from the landline. Central office, where a woman cheerily answered and helped direct me to a meeting to begin the journey again. Today had to be the first day of my forevermore.

Complete surrender would be what was required for me to give myself wholeheartedly to this program now. During these days I came to grow closer to a "higher power"[80] from which I felt distanced. It would take time. I began doing yoga again and attended meetings with a new-found vigour, while this time strictly doing what was suggested while also removing any residual thoughts that I could run certain aspects of this program my own way. I had tried this time, and time again, and had failed miserably; left without a defence against that first drink, that one glass of red, that sip, that thought. In these moments, I knew—it was ingrained in my brain—that momentary thought flew across the top of my head with lightening speed to the reality of what that was for me. *Now* I knew.

[80] Alcoholics Anonymous World Services. (2001). *Alcoholics Anonymous: The story of how many thousands of men and women have recovered from alcoholism* (rev ed.; Step 2). New York, NY: Author.

Beginning Again

The first months were blurred with flashbacks of that night, and the shame and guilt that walked with me as I began to heal. The eyes of the Black Irish man haunting me as we met the following morning, while I first retrieved my vehicle and then went to work. I always made it to work. Running into him in the hall, our eyes met, his voice lowered and he quivered, "Next time someone says they go crazy when they drink, I will believe them." Later that day a woman to whom he had introduced me to list her multimillion-dollar home that week called to let me know she would no longer be needing my services. None of this could matter anymore. In the absence of sobriety, I would have nothing.

I continued to show-up at meetings and "fill a chair."[81] I followed the clearly outlined suggestions, including getting into service, which prior to that I didn't understand held much weight. But I did it anyway. First working at the counter of a local breakfast meeting taking orders and cash. This pushed me to speak, which I still had immense difficulty doing when sober. I next accepted a position to chair a large weekend meeting that drew upwards of 200 people. This also held me accountable. It was a colourful lively group to stand in front of at the podium. I chose to face my fears head-on. I had forced myself to read the cards provided—to emerge from a shell that protected me like finely-crafted heavy-duty armour. Heart palpitations aside, somehow, I slowly arrived.

This time morphed into gaining more sober time, knowing more completely, and feeling able to begin working with other women who felt it difficult to *find* themselves. I understood. I had been there, and I too

[81] "Fill a chair" is a phrase used to describe those who attend AA meetings.

had struggled to stay. I sometimes shared with them how to break a day into units—each second ran into a minute, minutes became an hour, hours led into a day and, eventually, days progressed into weeks, weeks into months, and so on. I felt their pain while healing my own. I did the work. It was gradual. I applied the 12 steps and, one moment at a time, I managed to stay sober.

My first husband and I had begun healing our relationship, and I can assuredly say that he also worked to gradually better himself. The turmoil from our union and separation had caused him to shift to looking within himself as well. We did share love back then, and our child was created in the union of love. Prior to our separation, he spent time away working while I stayed home with our child. The song "Here Without You"[82] by 3 Doors Down was our song when times kept us apart. We did hold a bond together. It was not all bad—there were positive aspects.

Time and circumstances did not allow us to be healthy together. I do not dismiss what happened between us, but today I have a firm forgiveness towards both him and I for what we endured. We did what we could given the tools each of us had, and lacked. From our union, the miracle of a son graced our planet, and he has grown into a fine young man.

> We want to be grateful for the lessons we have. Don't run from lessons; they are…packages of treasure that have been given to us. As we learn from them, our lives change for the better.[83]

82 3 Doors Down. (2003). Here without you [Song]. On *Away from the sun* [Album] (Songwriters: Brad Arnold, Todd Harell, Chris Henderson, Matt Roberts; Producer: Rick Parashar). Labels: Republic, Universal.

83 Hay, L. (2018). April 13: I am willing to learn what life is trying to teach me. In *Trust life: Love yourself every day with wisdom* [A daily devotional]. Carlsbad, CA: Hay House.

We have come so far. To this day my first husband and I openly express love towards one another, and look to the past as a necessary, albeit excruciating, time in our lives. I also have a deep bond with his family, who play an active role in all my sons' lives for which I am eternally grateful.

Social NeedyAh

Going back to where this manuscript began, let's take some time to look at the words "social" and "media." The *Oxford Learner's Dictionaries* describes the word "social" as "connected with society…connected with activities in which people meet each other for pleasure."[84] When one is social, they go out and spend time with others or have others over to share their space. Even talking to someone while walking (or otherwise) is being social. Media is defined as a "means of [mass] communication."[85] Social media is the digital technology through which people can connect and share ideas, information, images, etc. which, overall, sounds positive yet there is mounting evidence to the contrary.

Now that we have defined social media, let's take a look at it in terms of how we feel about our lives, how it sits with us, and how we are evolving with it.

I often think of a boardroom in which a meeting took place when the founders of a company in its early stages were looking for a catch phrase for what they were developing. A small group of individuals coined *social media*, which has/is gravely affected/affecting mental health in record-breaking ways with enormous repercussions, such as increased suicide, eating disorders, depression, low self-esteem, and anxiety.[86] These illnesses (and more) are at an all-time high. Also at record levels are online fraud, sexualization, predatory behaviour, online scams, hate speech, and

84 *Oxford Learner's Dictionary.* (n.d.). Social. Accessed 2026-06-30, https://www.oxfordlearnersdictionaries.com/definition/american_english/social_1

85 *Dictionary.com.* (n.d.). Media. Accessed 2026-06-30, https://www.dictionary.com/browse/media

86 nutritionhouse. (n.d.). *Is social media causing you stress?* Accessed 2024-06-30, https://nutritionhouse.com/blogs/better-mental-wellness/is-social-media-causing-you-stress?_pos=1&_sid=b82456891&_ss=r

bullying just to scratch the surface, and so many others that are not reported.

Take a closer look at what you see, and not just the positives, but the negatives as well. For the positives that you view, what are the negatives that influence you? For example, the ads that bombard you and the money that you would not have spent. There are hooks programmed into the software driven by algorithms. Data about our shopping behaviours and patterns is collected. These are powerful manipulation techniques that are used to target us with specific-interest ads when we are most vulnerable. Damaging effects go on *ad infinitum*: the negative self-image that comes from viewing others' *seemingly* perfect lives and the potential comparisons and feelings of competition that arise; the trip you didn't go on, the hair-type you'll never have; the waistline having multiple kids, genetics, or age seldom allow; the love between another couple that flashes in front of you after a massive blow-out in your own relationship. Please feel free to pause, continue with, and add your own observations.

Is this *truly* social? Do the feelings that arise from swiping through such images help to uplift you and add to your experience of life?

Let's examine more closely where we are focussing our attention. How does the pull of *the thing* draw us away from our present lives? The images we view, others' opinions and comments—how do they infiltrate and affect our thinking? Aside from the pocket hedgehog wearing flipflops under a beach umbrella, there are so many things we view that affect our thinking, the way we value ourselves and others in the world. I suggest that it is time we get back to living in the now, savouring the gifts, experiencing the interactions that simply come from being alive—away from a screen's influence. Remember, "every choice we make, every thought and feeling we have...."[87] How many times a day do you make a choice to pick-up *the thing* and engage elsewhere, view more, feel less than, feel more than, all while squandering your time *away* from yourself? All that energy from all those people wasted away into an externalized web in an unconscious world.

> The Attention Extraction Model[88] is not how we want to treat human beings....The fabric of a healthy society depends on us getting off this corrosive business model.[89]

Choice.

A high percentage of what I follow includes inspirational quotes, betterment sites, environmental groups that examine and attempt to make change amidst the downward decline of our planet's ecosystems. Yet even focussing on these positives, there is so much negative that manages to creep-in. I allow myself to look at the first five posts from my friends. However, these days usually the first five posts contain two or three ads or *hooks*,[90] so now I'm down to two or three friend's posts. Didn't make that top-5 cut? I'm not sorry as, at this time in my life, this is what works for me. I am consciously decreasing "Social NeedyAh" from my life.

As I stated early on, I do appreciate being able to view the milestones and accomplishments that others in my inner and outer circles experience. I can honestly say that I would not know of these events in their lives without social media avenues. Yet as time moves forward, I feel it has a greater downward pull as we continue to evolve under it. With little

87 Myss, C. (1996). *Anatomy of the spirit* (p. 220). New York, NY: Harmony Books.

88 Also known as (aka) the Attention Extraction Economy.

89 Tristan Harris interview in Orlowski, J. (2020). *The social dilemma* [Documentary film] (Writers: Davis Coombe, Vickie Curtis, Jeff Orlowski; Producer: Larissa Rhodes). Exposure Labs, Argent Pictures, The Space Program; Netflix.

90 "Hooks" are suggestions "recommended for you" (personally) that are based on algorithms.

investigation into the time between signing the mobile contract and pulling away from socializing in-person (without devices) and with no rules surrounding their usage, I believe we are heading into social catastrophe of epidemic proportions.

We have allowed this gadget and its apps to completely re-shape human existence. Are we really so weak that we will simply let ourselves float away into the Heads-Down Generation (H.D.G.) without serious thought and consideration about this?

The last time I checked, we have spines. *Homo erectus,* designed to extend one's head in an upright position. We are not jellyfish, floating mindlessly in an ocean of (often mis-)information, or some malicious troll spouting their two (thousand) bits our way for us to absorb and/or counter. I mean nothing against jellyfish. They serve their purpose with their delicately moving glow-filled stinging array of goodness. But we are not them.

We have become pawns in the insidious marketing of the corporate digital world—all with little awareness of this fact. Are we afraid of doing things differently than others? Why do we feel we have to bow down to this way of being in the world? Do we *truly* want to live this way? My intuition says, "We do not." There *is* another way.

We are designed to make eye contact with humans and to engage and communicate with body language, spoken words, affection, compassion, empathy, among other forms of expression. *Homo erectus.*

I have already discussed some of the ways in which I am different than others who are able to safely consume alcohol. Although I suspect there are many who may not realize the extent in which it, too, negatively impacts their well-being, but this aside. I have also brought forward some of the life experiences that have shaped who I am today. From the vast number of reports, talking with others, and my internal intuition and intellect (which I now trust and value immensely), I truly feel that we are undercutting our own potentials by having allowed *the thing* into our lives with such pace and strength. Many alcoholics are familiar with the loose term that at times is used to describe us. It is said that we have "the disease of more."[91] It is my opinion that this *device addiction* that has claimed so many largely falls into this category as well.

While writing this publication, a friend of mine whom I consider to be a person closely tied to her device announced that, at the end of her current contract, she would be purchasing a simple flip-phone—one of the old ones with only talk and text capability. "Wow," I thought, "of all people!" I said to her, "I thought you were a serious FB'er." (To contrast, I joined FB very late in the game, having avoided it "like the plague" until it was *suggested* I needed it for my multi-level marketing [MLM] business.) She seemed somewhat offended that I thought this. I suppose she hadn't recalled scrolling-through FB while we were at the (Sir) Elton John concert, so she wouldn't feel that she qualified. (Sorry love.)

For those of you who do go out and socialize, how have face-to-face exchanges been reshaped for you? Do you, or would you be willing to, adapt a deviceless rule when dining out? There, I said it. Yes, rule.

Another thing I've seen is people being so rebellious in their ways that they feel there need not be rules when it comes to so many areas. This insurgence is so prevalent online. It is also seen in parks, on streets, in public spaces and stores. Why is this I wonder? What is it about *the thing* that makes it a free-for-all? It really doesn't matter if you wish to have some

91 A phrase I've heard used in AA.

time to flip through clothing racks and get into your zone, because I am about to land into your sound- and sight-space. In fact, I will even bring along my sister into the store and Facetime *loudly*. One's image on their clothes-finding spree may even show-up on their call, but what do they care? No rules. Sure—and loud volume please—this is my favourite. Sure, bring it on. Let 'er rip. No rules. Have at 'er. How about in a different language—or a business call? Great. The world is your office. "Sorry, I couldn't care." Mine. No rules. You don't wish to hear about it. Boardroom—remember? An idea. Social. Internet. Face call. Photo-sharing site. A place to connect. Idea sharing. Remember?

Now ads (lots of them), sexualization, bigotry, hate, so many detriments—the sky's the limit for where, when, how—all the time.

In schools, difficulty concentrating, young people killing themselves (pause on that one), negative body image, teen pedestrian struck and killed while walking against light through intersection, distracted driver kills family of four.... Whoa. Boardroom. Whoa. Is it just me? Really? I am the same, yet I am different. Is it just me?

Say you are on three social media sites for example. How would it feel to scale back and go to one? Within your brain, is there a scurrying or darting back-and-forth as to which one that might be? Does having to make a choice make you anxious? Isn't that telling in its own right? Ask yourself: When you pick it up, what is it that you are seeking? Become aware of this. Think about how you could use the extra time.

I love people and, though it has taken some time, I have learned to love myself wholly, which continues to expand. How do we gain balance while optimizing this precious gift of life in this short time that we have?

How can I best show those around me how much I value them, whether they be the ones in my close circle, or anyone and everyone including those I pass on the streets and the homeless person I make eye contact with to show them that I see them? They are alive—and they have value.

How can I land and set parameters as to how much space I allow for the ping and the ding of *the thing*? "Oh—I have my notifications turned off." Sure. Yes. All sorts of excuses can be made. What are yours?

What if gyms, schools, churches, stores, public transit, etc., all had a device-free zone policy? Would we see people dropping their goods to leave the store to take that call they have been waiting for and then come back inside moments later when it was completed? Can we excuse ourselves and leave the room to make a call in private, or stand over to the side of the walkway rather than conduct the call for all to hear? How would things change?

I struggle with leniency in other areas as well. If a municipality wants to do something like ban single-use plastic bags, why wait to have the ban go into effect in 5 years? Let people know that in 90 days there will no longer be plastic bags—period. What would we do? We either walk out of the store with our items and receipt in our hands or we bring our own bags. Humans are adaptable creatures. It won't take long for us to remember. Remember, *Homo erectus,* not jellyfish. One life. But I digress.

Many of us have been sucked downward into the head-burying vortex of modern-time *smart*phones. It does not *have* to be this way. But the skilled craftspeople who are hired to design these devices to permeate our brains would have us think this is the *only* way.

> We curate our lives around this perceived sense of perfection, because we get rewarded in these short-term signals—hearts, likes, thumbs up—and we conflate that with value and we conflate it with truth. And instead, what it is is fake, brittle popularity that's short-term and leaves you even more, admit it, vacant and empty before you did it....Think about that, compounded by 2 billion people.[92]

Another way lies *within*.

Some time ago, I did a strengths-finding workshop[93] and found that my Number 1 strength was connectedness followed by positivity and that I am also a maximizer. Connectedness. Right. I believe that it is an inherent trait for all of us humans to be connected with others. From the moment we take our first breaths, we long to be held, to have our eyes meet with others' eyes, to be spoken to, to have attention and affection.

These are not traits that we grow out of—they stay with us.

We also require independent time as we grow, though essentially we need balance in order to thrive. But we are replacing our innate needs with outer stimuli that have been disguised as a substitute for in-person connection with ourselves and others. *The thing* is leaving us feeling further depleted with less time and more pull away from true relationships and real interactions, and I am alarmed that we are not giving this the enough attention or addressing it fast enough with the fervour and momentum required.

[92] Chamath Palihapitiya, founder and CEO of Social Capital, Facebook VP for User Growth (2007-2011). Wang, A. B. (2017, December 12). Former Facebook VP says social media is destroying society with 'dopamine-driven feedback loops.' *The Washington Post*. Accessed 2024-07-15, https://www.washingtonpost.com/news/the-switch/wp/2017/12/12/former-facebook-vp-says-social-media-is-destroying-society-with-dopamine-driven-feedback-loops

[93] If you're interested, this workshop facilitated by Eddie Villa was fascinating. See https://unleash-your-strengths.mn.co and https://riselovelive.com/guest-post-dont-ever-dim-your-light-not-for-anyone-even-yourself

Though a few elementary and independent schools in our area already have a no-device policy in place, in high schools, there is no such mandate. Teachers have to turn a blind eye to students with their heads down, looking under their desks during class. And then once the bell rings, they flood the hallways device in-hand to have a head-down culmination with other head-downward individuals to feast on profanity-laced sexualized-image screen viewing or some other mockery of life itself.[94,95,96] Sure, not always, some fluffy animals wearing hats make the cut here and there, but more often it is otherwise.

This is problematic, so we will put a stop to this now. Nope—jellyfish unite—another no-rules free-for-all. How does all of this affect young people's learning potential and how they relate with others? But they *need* their devices for study purposes. Right. Yet, clearly, this is not what is happening.

So when do we re-assess?

There was a full-week focus on the radio station (*CityNews* 1130) about the never-before behavioural issues becoming rampant in schools. Unprecedented extreme behaviours bombard classrooms that have been

94 I have witnessed such viewings numerous times in my personal life and while working in schools.

95 Abdoli, M., Khoshgoftar, M., Jadidi, H., Daniali, S. S., Shahrbanoo, S., & Kelishadi, R. (2024, February 29). Screen time and child behavioral disorders during COVID-19 pandemic: A systematic review. *International Journal of Preventative Medicine, 15*(9), PMCID: PMC10982732; PMID: 38563038. doi:10.4103/ijpvm.ijpvm_78_23

96 Wiguana, T., Minayati, K., Kaligis, F., Teh, S. D., Sourander, A., Dirjayanto, V. J., Krishnandita, M., Meriem, N., & Gilbert, S. (2024, January 15). The influence of screen time on behaviour and emotional problems among adolescents: A comparison study of the pre-, peak, and post-peak periods of COVID-19. *Heliyon, 10*(1). e23325

linked to increased levels of device usage and screen time along with the desocialization after-effects of the COVID-19 lockdown.[97,98]

And what about the parents who do not give focused time, attention, and nurturing to their children as the result of their own device addictions? Whether alcohol, drugs, or any other addiction, if a child isn't emotionally supported so they feel seen, heard, and otherwise tended to, they have a far greater chance of not growing into healthy well-balanced individuals.[99] As with other addictions, modelling ODC behaviour is likely to be passed down through generations. We have yet to fully comprehend the ramifications of *the thing* and the impact it is having on human*kind*.

My oldest son recently obtained another job—his third job at age 17. The employer reported that he "is a breath of fresh air": personable, teachable, and able to build and withhold relationships with both staff and customers. Another employer from a major sports-brand store stated it was extremely difficult to hire young people these days; so few of them are able to hold eye contact for more than a second or two, and they all seem to carry a feeling of being distracted or wanting to be somewhere else (enter *the thing*).

Acute mental health crises are at an all-time high and are currently plaguing our society, and there is little finger-pointing towards *the thing*

97 Abdoli, M., Khoshgoftar, M., Jadidi, H., Daniali, S. S., Shahrbanoo, S., & Kelishadi, R. (2024, February 29). Screen time and child behavioral disorders during COVID-19 pandemic: A systematic review. *International Journal of Preventative Medicine, 15*(9), PMCID: PMC10982732; PMID: 38563038. doi:10.4103/ijpvm.ijpvm_78_23

98 Wiguana, T., Minayati, K., Kaligis, F., Teh, S. D., Sourander, A., Dirjayanto, V. J., Krishnandita, M., Meriem, N., & Gilbert, S. (2024, January 15). The influence of screen time on behaviour and emotional problems among adolescents: A comparison study of the pre-, peak, and post-peak periods of COVID-19. *Heliyon, 10*(1). e23325

99 Lee, M. (Producer). (2023, November 7). Around one-third of people globally may be at risk of smartphone addiction: Canadian-led study. *CTV News.* Accessed 2024-10-04, https://news.ucsb.edu/2023/020867/screen-time-concerns

and the possible repercussions it has on our lives. I've seen smatterings of conversations towards how social media is playing a part in the increase of teen suicides[100,101,102,103] and some research about how personal relationships are being affected. As previously mentioned, the conversation has extended to dogs and how they are being negatively affected by our devices taking precedence over them.

Overall, the negative impact extensive device usage is having on our society has not been given the attention it requires.

What about the implication of raising a whole generation of people who do not, or cannot, give eye contact to another human being for more than 3 seconds as this feels too uncomfortable and foreign to them? Hmmm....This is a startling question and observation about an issue that has reached epidemic proportions that has not been recognized to the magnitude that is required.

Overall, the negative impact extensive device usage is having on our society has not been given the attention it requires.

We live on a planet with other beings. Does that not in-and-of-itself blow your mind enough to make you want to wake-up and begin to truly

[100] Abi-Jaoude, E., Naylor, K. T., & Pignatiello, A. (2020, February 10). Smartphones, social media use and youth mental health. *Canadian Medical Association Journal, 192*(6), E136-E141. doi:10.1503/cmaj.190434

[101] Wiguana, T., Minayati, K., Kaligis, F., Teh, S. D., Sourander, A., Dirjayanto, V. J., Krishnandita, M., Meriem, N., & Gilbert, S. (2024, January 15). The influence of screen time on behaviour and emotional problems among adolescents: A comparison study of the pre-, peak, and post-peak periods of COVID-19. *Heliyon, 10*(1). e23325

[102] *The Economist.* (n.d.). Suicide rates for girls are rising. Are smartphones to blame? Accessed 2024-06-14, https://www.economist.com/graphic-detail/2023/05/03/suicide-rates-for-girls-are-rising-are-smartphones-to-blame

[103] Flora, C. (2018, February 1). Are smartphones really destroying the lives of teenagers? *Scientific American.* Accessed 2024-11-05, http://scientificamerican.com/article/are-smartphones-really-destroying-the-lives-of-teenagers

interact and connect with those who have been given this journey as well? These are *our* lives. Would you rather choose to continue to bury your head downward in a pool of often-times false representations and unrealistic glamorized fantasies?

Here's the good news: Our power, that is our human strengths and the gift of life, allow for choice—the choice to continue to be buried or to rise above and choose differently. Full stop.

On a recent radio news program, I heard several reports about a horrific stabbing in our city. Several onlookers recorded the footage and posted it on social media. Beyond sickening, truly. I cannot fathom, not only the tragic loss of this individual, but their family then having to endure this as well. Further to this, another man took photos of himself with the deceased body and posted them to social media boasting and making a mockery of his actions by saying that he is part of the problem the world is facing. The media platform's spokesperson said they were working towards ensuring this post was removed completely and would not be posted further.

Really? That is *all* we've got to rectify situations such as this?

This is only one instance of so many others that ought to not reach people via social media. So many forms of illness, sexualization, misogyny, depletion of one's character and views, racism, violence, so much negative behaviour exhibited in our daily lives—and glorified—it is horrific.

We will wonder how we arrived here. We will wonder.

What about implementing a full-fledged *pre*-posting process on social media sites? The public would not be able to see such posts instantly—they we would only be able to see them *if and after* they had passed though a pre-screening process. Penalties could be issued to media sites for non-compliance with the potential for complete shutdown.

I am not saying that it would be an easy transition. For the younger generations, it will require:

- First, positive modelling and (likely) assistance from their adult counterparts.
- Second, taking a clear inventory of how many social media sites you frequent, and seeing which ones you are ready to purge from your life. You may choose to jot down the things you have been putting-off or procrastinating about that can fill the new-found space you have created.
- Third, making the decision to allot a certain amount of time to answer emails on your home computer while also taking time to unsubscribe from unwanted bulk emails or ads that have also taken hold of your life.

And how many email addresses do you have? Perhaps now is the time to also decrease them in order to lessen the amount of time required to look at *all the things* available on a device. Notifying important contacts of this change prior to shutdown is important. Then brush your hands of it all and move into the re-connection with real life, with people, with causes that require your immediate attention, and living life in the H.U.G. will begin again for you. You are the only individual you have power over.

Others around you may feel uncomfortable with you having decided to land on the planet again, fully present, undistracted, eyes up. That is alright. It is like a person who begins a journey of sobriety, who find themselves making different choices than going to the bar or a boozy lunch will oftentimes find themselves in need of a complete association overhaul. Another example could be a person who goes on a weight-loss journey and finds when, on the other side, there are those in their lives who find it difficult to accept. The friends want to continue to go out together for cheesecake with extra whip like the old times. Of course, there is the other side of the equation in which the person making the change cannot be in those habitual situations again because of the pull of peer pressure and the desire for their nemesis.

Perhaps not as extreme as the issue we are discussing around device usage or, then again, maybe just as extreme. This depends on the habits of those with whom you surround yourself and how much time they devote to their devices.

Remember, we all have a story. Each and every day that story expands. Sometimes it is full of amazing achievements and feel-good moments. Other times it is tumultuous, full of upheaval and everything in between. We all have a story. How many of us share our stories: where we came from, the trials we've experienced, and the gut punches we've received along the way. Did they level you? Did you share this or keep it locked inside? Were you able to dig deep and find strength regardless of what was placed in your path? As these situations arose, did you share with your close friends, or did you post only your rosy pieces on a reel?[104] Or perhaps you were the one with your leg in-traction in those hospital pics you posted? Respondents posted "wishes for a speedy recovery," "sending healing," or "get well soon." How about a call to a family member or someone close to you instead, so you have the opportunity to receive *real* comfort and support?

Which brings up the question: What is it that we are *truly* seeking when we create such posts? What is it that we feel we need or want? And

[104] "Reels" are short video clips that your social media friends post for your viewing.

why? Is there a void that needs to be filled? If you require coddles from every direction, then perhaps it's time to dig deeper.

In contrast, more recently I have witnessed an increase in videos and photos being posted of people upset, crying, or visibly shaken, which contrasts the perfection of how lives have typically been portrayed. What is the goal here? Wouldn't it be better to share our vulnerable times with those in our inner circle—those who are there for us in times of need to help us through on a more personal and deeper level?

From the elevator to the bus stop, "Life is like a box of chocolates."[105] We can all return to the moments of niceties or conversations that previously occurred. When saying, "Good morning" to someone or asking how they are post-workout, I am often pleased to see how their demeanour changes when I simply acknowledge their presence. It seems like a lost art has been resurrected if only for a moment. Though it doesn't always land this way, that too is alright. All good, either way. I am there, present. This is what is important.

Each and every day our stories continue, they evolve. So, who are you anyway? Have you spent time revealing this? The extra time away from *the thing* could help you to rediscover yourself while also discovering, even rediscovering, others. There are experiences to share, similarities and differences. Some of them make us feel closer having known these places and feelings ourselves. Other parts intrigue us; we wish to know more as we have never experienced this before. Shock and disbelief that someone could have encountered something that is far from what you have had to face. Compassion, empathy, introspection in sharing, listening, and

[105] Zemeckis, R. (Director); Finerman, W., Tisch, S., & Starkey, S. (Producers). (1994). *Forrest Gump* [Film]. The Tisch Company; Paramount Pictures.

talking on the experience. It feels so good to share and confide in each other.

But when we paste our lives on online forums, there is the potential of leaving ourselves open to those who prey on others' opinions, experiences, and images. By lessening our exposure through these avenues and going back to face-to-face interactions, we have a choice (for the most part) with whom we interact. Seems simple right?

Heads up humans!

> Here's the good news:
> Our power, that is our human strengths and the gift of life, allow for choice—the choice to continue to be buried or to rise-up and choose differently.

Flashback 2007

Seven months prior to the stench of oysters bathed in tequila wafting through my nose on command, a woman in a neighbouring province whom I had not met and would never meet was giving birth to her second son. I did not know her or any of the struggles her life held. I did not know that I would come to raise this son alongside my own.

Eight months after the boy's birth, the province's ministry responsible for children and families took her son away from her. The circumstances were dire for both her and the child and, although I will not disclose what these were, I will say that she too was trying to find a way out. Affected by a different beast than I had known, she too had wanted a way out from her addiction. She too.

I had not yet met the father of the infant being birthed. At this time, I also did not know that I still had 1 day of drinking to do before I completely surrendered to abstinence.

My firstborn and I were continuing to make a life together. When my son was 4½ years old, I sat in a meeting admiring a broad-shouldered man encased in a black-felt coat with mock-neck collar, which spoke as if to say, "I have arrived." (Later I learned that he hadn't arrived yet, and wasn't about to anytime soon.) That same coat spoke at the podium, to which I listened intently in my first year of sobriety. He shared his story which included his attempts to re-gain custody of his son who was in the care and custody of the ministry. The rules in that province allowed a child to be in foster care for 500 days before being adopted-permanently. He had been advised to get through the Step 9 in our program prior to becoming further involved in this attempt; and he was struggling immensely with this process.

Enter me, an open heart with a willingness to help this man with his struggle. Enter me. If he does not have the gumption to take this on, "Well, I sure do!" I thought. I will save his son (and him!). With the momentum I had to offer, we began at once with my detailed ability to do *all* things.

In our recovery program, it is strongly cautioned against beginning any personal relationship in one's first year of sobriety. Yet just like my heeding of other issues in the past, I felt I would prove the exception to this rule. Our speed at tackling this new venture allowed little time to really dig into who this father was as a person. His workaholic tendencies were obvious, but I had not had conversations with him about his habits and patterns. Nor was I aware that he had already been in treatment facilities 11 times. Read that again—11 times.[106] No knowledge. The child—in need. Save him.

We began to travel to Alberta to visit his son who had already been in three foster homes since his apprehension from his birth mother at 8 months old. At this point, he was 18 months and in the care of a good family with the best of intentions, who were unable to conceive a child and would adopt him upon completion of the 500-day term. During visits inside the ministry facility, we were being watched behind 2-way mirrored glass. Plane rides and road trips through intense lightning storms and pitch-black nights with glowing deer-eyes and steep mountain passes, his father deeply asleep in the passenger seat and me, alone again. Visits. Visits to take the boy away from the adoptive mother who now held him,

[106] I learned of his repeated rehabilitation attempts several years later.

the prospect of life growing-up on a farm with vast land, siblings, other adopted children, a loving couple, and many animals. (To this day, this still stings if I allow it to.)

I thought I knew best—that if given the opportunity, it is always better for a child to be with their biological parent. Upon reflection, I realized this impression had originated in my upbringing. In the years to come, I would learn that this is not necessarily the case. I really had not known this man well-enough to have supported him through this process.

Ready for Take-off

There was much contact with the ministry case-worker, Conrad, who was thrilled that the biological father had suddenly taken such an active interest in re-gaining custody of his son. The wheels were in motion. As the 500-day deadline approached, he was granted custody of his son after the final court application, which required posting several newspaper ads in the attempt to locate the child's birth mother. There was no response. The custody preparations were finalized, and flight arrangements were in place for the father to pick-up his son. It was happening, and my role had been pivotal in the process.

Days before the flight, his father (now my partner) disappeared. A pocket call (damn *smart*phones…) came-in early-on in his disappearance. I heard the back-and-forth exchange of two male voices and laughter. One encouraged the other to enjoy himself, then the phone went dead. I did not hear from him for several more days. I searched the city and suburbs for a sign of his vehicle near places he might go. Nothing. (This was my first experience of several painful disappearances to come.) Still, I took it upon my newly sober self to maintain conversations with the ministry and respond to important emails that came-in to finalize plans in the short days ahead.

Looking back, I behaved insanely. This was the first indication of the state of this man and his inability to be in a healthy place to take this on. Somehow I wasn't able to see it that way. There had been so much work done already, and I was sure this would just be a momentary blip on the father's road to recovery. Insanity.

Several days later he called, gave me a story, and came home to detox in my newly-built condo in which he had previously taken-up residence.

Though I am an alcoholic and we are said to detox from this substance, this was an entirely different animal. It was then that I learned his drug of choice was crack cocaine. I viewed the convulsions, moaning, twitches, sweats, and scratching that can accompany its release from the body. He recuperated with my support and promptly returned to work not wanting to get into much discussion surrounding what had happened, stating "It is in the past now, and we don't want to live in the past."

His young son arrived with him to the airport days later. The paternal grandmother was there in tears with sobs of "He did it! He got his son! He did it!" (His mother would be another source of toxic detriment I would come to know all too well.) *He* did it—I swallowed.

The next months were fully immersed in getting to know this fair-haired boy while integrating him into life with my son. I would take long walks with the two boys, shoulder-to-shoulder in a double-wide stroller I had purchased second hand. With a rain cover for two, which I felt would be a great way to get them accustomed to each other, we took long walks in nature and down rain-drenched streets. I even picked-up a rain hat from the local military supply (definitely out of my realm of fashion) as who had extra hands to hold an umbrella?

My common-law partner was rarely present as he had thrown himself back into work with a new-found vigour towards recovery. I took to my attempts at rehabilitating this child as the tantrums and outbursts were frequent from this mostly non-verbal being. I started working at a real-estate firm in the community into which we had recently moved—a house with a yard and a 25-foot vegetable garden to tend. The springtime met with apple blossoms filling my eyes as I stared through the bathroom window while showering. My expanding pregnant belly was again growing life inside, which was expected shortly after kindergarten began for my firstborn. This would firm the foundation and amalgamate our family's blend.

Summertime came and the mature apple tree in the backyard yielded too many apples to make use of. The corn grew high, and our children played outdoors and made much use of the tree swing. One of the attributes that my partner had was his skill of cooking. We feasted on barbecue and garden-ripe vegetables. The neighbourhood was beautiful with many childhood playmates and friendly neighbours to talk to in the streets while the kids drew sidewalk chalk racecourses to ride their bikes through. The streets were wide and quiet, and the small-town feel had me waving to acquaintances at the 4-way stop. It was a beautiful surrounding.

My pregnancy went well. I carried very large with an ultrasound being needed to try to estimate the size of the child whose gender we did not want to know—9 lbs was the estimate. My second son (our third) was born shortly after school began. On his due date, I worked a 7-hour parent-participation shift with my heavily swollen feet holding me up. He weighed-in at 9 lbs 9 oz and was a beautiful bright-eyed being "ready to move mountains," my brother exclaimed.

Time passed and my father was diagnosed with colorectal cancer. With his determination and strong mental and physical state, I had no reservations: He would beat it. Treatment commenced and he had solid progress. During the day a couple times per week, my son and I drove an hour each way to visit him. The prognosis looked good.

Now 3 years sober, I had gained headspace and began to be accountable. I still remember the chill of my father's skin post-op, yet my eternal optimism held onto the ideal that this too would be another stepping-stone in his recovery. The doctors said they "thought they had gotten it all." He regained consciousness and began to heal somewhat, but the recovery did not progress as we had hoped. His body was not gaining back the strength or tone that was expected. He was tested again and given cancer-free status. My mother, brother, and I were elated.

After continuing to deteriorate and being confined to a wheelchair with little strength from the neck down, 3 weeks later an MRI revealed the cancer had spread to his lungs, and he now had seven new areas of cancer in his brain. It was crushing.

Two years old now, my youngest and I would travel the distance to spend time with my dad who would cheerfully suggest "Why don't we go have a lie down together." He always had a beautiful way of making others feel like it was a good thing to rest, and sometimes we needed that more than other times. The days passed and my visits became more frequent as I was able to stop by after I dropped the kids off at school (preschool now for the second child). I am eternally grateful for this time and the sobriety I'd had at this point as it allowed me to be present, accountable, and reliable in ways I hadn't been in previous years.

I received a call from my mom saying that they had decided not to do any further treatment. "How could this be?" I thought. What did this mean? I drove through the tunnel, across two bridges, through yet another tunnel with tears streaming-down my concerned cheeks. Crying, I entered our family's home to sit beside my dad. "What is it—What's happened?" he said. "What's happened?—What's happened?!" I replied. "What's happened is that you have decided not to do any further treatment!" I sobbed. "[Love], I've had a good life, I've had a long life," he said. "It's okay. It's okay." But it wasn't to me. It wasn't okay, and I could not fathom life without the one man who had been my greatest inspiration, who taught me not to take s*** from anyone.

My dad fascinated me, and he was brilliant. He was a body builder, a creative force, my biggest advocate, and my greatest teacher. He taught me to strive, to never give-up, regardless of what life threw you, to fall and then get back-up. He taught me to sprint and coached me not to stop until far past the finish line, literally and figuratively speaking. On that soccer field, between those net-less goal posts, to push through, to dig into that internal God-given strength from within.

Dad taught me, and so did my mother. They were present. They might have had their heads down in a newspaper, but that was world's apart from the mindless vibe of *the thing*. Newspapers contain content (at least that would be the hope) and can be easily put down—there isn't an addictive pull like there is with devices, which cause people to attend to them everywhere.

A nurse for 35 years prior, my mother cared for my dad, which enabled him to remain at home and not require hospitalization. This is what he wanted. She was "a saint" as others in her profession had called her—full of care, and so giving. As I mentioned, they were married for 43 years, and they were a beautiful example of union, despite their differences. From different upbringings, circumstances, and knowledge bases, married by elopement after having known each other for 7 months. He was 9 years her senior. Their struggles were real, their sacrifices plentiful. The yin of light-skinned fair-haired farm girl donned with nursing-cap and the black-browed dark-eyed yang complete with organized religious affliction and apartheid damage.[107] Both experienced generational traumas served on a platter of guilt and shame. But they made it work. Having grown-up with their example, I have often

[107] From Chinese philosophy; for the meaning of yin and yang please see https://www.britannica.com/topic/yinyang

pondered how I ended-up in such dysfunctional relationships. Yet, I honour that we all walk (and sometimes trudge) along our own paths and mine was learned (often painfully) through being given the tools I needed. "Onwards and upwards" I say freely, eyes cast ahead.

My dear dad passed away in hospice, which he had arrived at 3 days prior, surrounded by family at 4:32 a.m. Through my grief I smiled within as I thought "Of course: 4 3 2 1—blast-off!" Brilliant—This was his way.

The Service

The crisp November air brought with it my father's service. It was peaceful and beautiful—a touching tribute. My mom and aunts worked tirelessly on the photos, personal items, music. Our three young boys wore navy-blue suits and transmitted playful light to the guests. My mom, my brother, and I spoke and shared from our hearts. This was the poem I wrote and recited. It amazed me how on paper the shape of the reading looked like a rocket-ship—a tribute to launching him up to the heavens.

All
Eternity

Come Soar with me
Sprout wings and fly
Into an eternal & limitless sky
Where dreams grow wild
Futures unfold
Take with me heart & memories Gold.
Of Peaceful state where time stands still,
No lines to wait ~ no one gets ill.
Where no more days sit idle by,
We talk, we laugh, no tears to cry.
No one grows old and no one sick,
The hands of clocks no longer tick.
Come hold my hand away we'll go,
Of parting ways we'll never know.
Yours forever I will be, your daughter all Eternity.

It was Christmas again, and I shouldered the loss of my dear dad throughout. (For the parents of young kids, you know all that Christmas-time brings.) I ached and had wanted to go and be present while his cremation took place, so he did not have to be alone. I was beside myself with grief, disbelief, and the processing of my feelings while keeping the ship at home afloat. I never truly had the space to grieve. We had two birthdays in our house in January, and then my husband relapsed—again.

This time it was different, and yet it was the same. Reeling from the loss of my father, the holidays just past, my emotions were ragged. I began driving around looking for my husband once again and, ironically, I received a pocket-dial from him, only this time it was different. This time, I heard a woman's voice accompanying his while picking-up from their dealer.

I took the kids to school, and I drove looking for him again. Looking for his vehicle, looking for him—again. There was so much I did not understand. Didn't he fathom all that was going-on, all that was at stake? What about the kids? Why couldn't he see, why couldn't he stop? He had said he could only aspire to being half the man my father was. So why...how...this...again? I thought we had moved past this. And what about me? Couldn't he see all that I had done and continued to do?

Six days passed and I received the call I had been waiting and praying for. He was on the other end. Relieved and elated, rather than call the authorities I had used the amount of time he was missing on his previous relapse as a possible time-gauge for when he would again come back.

On the other end of the phone, he told me he had crashed his vehicle and these "amazing angels, Mary and John" had been first to the scene to rescue him. They brought him back to their home and had tended to him since. I was overjoyed and thankful that these people, whom I had pictured as an older loving hospitable couple, had taken him under their wings until I could step-in. He arranged for me to come and pick him up later that day at the address he had provided.

I arrived. The curtains closed tightly; I waited. It took a lengthy time while for him to surface and, when he did, he stumbled down the front stairs. I was shocked at his appearance. His loose dirty cargo shorts noticeably hanging-off him, no underwear underneath, with beard stubble and dark rings around his eyes. Coming closer, the sweet stench of him getting into the vehicle, putting the seat back with tremors visibly running through his legs, twitching spasms jutting through his glossy slack skin.

Pulling away from the house, police lights in the rear-view mirror caught my attention. I pulled towards the side of the road. Two officers approached my window, the female came forward and asked me the relationship to the man who was now in my vehicle. After I told them, they then asked him what his drug of choice was; he answered. They then informed me that the premises I had just retrieved him from were highly dangerous. The house was routinely known as a place of criminal activity; two homicides had been committed there this month alone. I had been put at far greater risk this time. How did I get here? How was this my life now? Oh, yes. Save him. Save them. Right.

This time I clearly stated that there would be no further detoxing in our home, that he would have to go to a facility.[108] He obliged, begrudgingly. I later came to find that the supposed sweet couple who had saved him were actually a pimp and his prostitute girlfriend. The wool covering my eyes was becoming thinner in its veil. He surfaced from detox

[108] This is when I learned of his extensive history in rehab treatment centres.

once again with a new-found resolve to be reformed further, a firm commitment to getting back on track and closer to spirituality and, again, not wishing to discuss what was now in the past.

He resumed his workaholism, and I resumed doing what it was I did to keep everything else together. Now 5 years sober, it was said that this is about the time it takes to start becoming clear in one's mind and spirit, although it is expressed more crassly by people in our program.

I unmistakeably stated to him that he "may have another relapse in him, but I did not have another of his relapses in me." If the history of math repeated itself, I had approximately 3 years until I saw this again.

Writing this now, I truly wonder why I stuck around for more. Keeping the kids and the home together, isn't that what women so often do despite dire circumstances that should inevitably dissolve any union? Something inside of me seemed to hold-on to "perhaps this time will be different." Yet gradually, I grew closer to the understanding that I could not change him. He had to be the one to change himself, or not. I had to begin to let go.

The next time would be the final straw for me. He had to be the one to recognize the nature of his illness and the ruthless application of principles required to keep him sober and stay that way. Like the oyster stench from my purse after the 10-hour blackout that made me stay sober at long last. Only time would tell.

Onward

So, shall we step back and re-examine the issue at hand? The plague of the desire to stare blankly, to float away, to blindly lose contact. The pull away from engaging in being authentic and truly knowing oneself and each other. The feeling, the experiencing, the savouring. After all, this book is about our loss of connection and how many of us are unable to identify the havoc that creates in our lives. *The thing* has been ingeniously presented. It has evolved bit-by-bit to take-over, to build upon itself, to creep into the palm of our hands leaving red stars across our vision and enticing us to pay attention to its demands. Dinging, pinging, and ringing its way through our senses. Casting your gaze downward, leaving you feeling shallow and hollow, yet not able to consciously recognize why.

Perhaps you are at the age of when you haven't yet experienced a time without *the thing*. Life without it might seem unfathomable. I can sympathize. A beautiful soul once said, "Wise men know not what they don't know." She had said this to me when I most needed to hear the message and yet, at the time, I battled with understanding what this meant. Weeks later I began to unravel it's meaning:

> "A wise man [or woman] knows that he [or she] knows nothing" means that you have to have the wisdom to understand that you can't learn everything. Even when you think you know a lot, you should still be wise and humble enough to admit that there is always more to learn in the world.[109]

[109] grammarhow. (n.d.). *'A wise man knows that he knows nothing'—True meaning revealed.* Accessed 2024-07-29, https://grammarhow.com/a-wise-man-knows-that-he-knows-nothing

There is so much we have yet to learn, and being shrouded in our addiction(s) clouds the connection to our *true* being. We need to consciously and continuously work on being better people. When our intentions are *truly* good and we make changes for the better, the universe sends us the help we need to continue on our paths.

Living a sober life and making the conscious choice to detach myself from distractions has opened-up my ability to express my thoughts and feelings while reigniting my creativity. My intuition allows inspiration to stream through me in words which, ultimately, led to the writing of this manuscript. For instance, the title of this book was *sent* to me, and I was guided surrounding the next steps. The momentum gained as I progressed through each step. Too much for you? Too woo-woo? That's okay. I don't expect everyone to be on the same plane as far as reliance on guidance goes. Then again, others are further ahead in this area than I. We all journey at our own pace, and we all have varied capacities for following internal guidance. The more space we create within allows for more insight to flow through.

Choosing our teachers is vitally important. Perhaps you have a multitude of YouTubers you rely on, or those who make clips on TikTok. Are you choosing your teachers with your (and others) highest good in mind? Take great care in choosing your teachers.

> "My thoughts are my teachers.
> Are they teaching me to love and appreciate myself and others, or are they teaching me to practice isolation?
> Today I will choose my teachers with greater care."[110]

[110] Al-Anon Family Group. (1992). Today's reminder. In *Courage to change: One day at a time in Al-Anon II* (p. 33). New York, NY: Author.

As you have read, a good deal of my adult life progressed in a less-than-conscious state. Now I am here sharing my story and encouraging you to also dig deeper into conscious awareness. Limit reliance on mood- and mind-altering stimuli or device-dwelling. Arrive. You have the power. You *can* get out from under *the thing*. You can choose differently. And while you are distancing yourself from the pull of the screen, not only will you be setting an example for those who surround you, you will be living more wholly everyone else aside.

Yesterday I walked past a parked car with a mother and daughter in the vehicle. Both were sitting without lips moving. Both were staring into their devices, preoccupied, and neither paid attention to the other. This is a common sighting nowadays. Sure, I had no idea what their circumstances were in that moment, and it certainly wasn't my place to judge them. Perhaps one of them was forming a letter to the government to address concern for toxic pollutants entering our waterways, while the other was looking-up the phone number to order take-out from the restaurant by which they were parked. Sure, why not give them the benefit of the doubt? More likely though, one was checking Facebook (FB) while the other scrolled through IG. Another missed opportunity to converse, to watch passersby, or to simply be in the moment, just be together, to share, converse and be attentive to their surroundings. When my kids were young and longed for a car with movie screens in it, I would calmly reply, "There is a movie going on right outside your window, love."

The changing seasons fascinated me when I first became sober. Like I had suddenly awoken to the blooming of flowers, the floating clouds passing above, or when raindrops bounced against the sunroof in a melody like no other. I had awakened to the beauty of the ever-changing bounty I had not seen clearly since I was a child. Sober or not, unless we have booked a predetermined unplugged venture,[111] I suspect that many of us in the modern world rarely limit the use of *the thing* long enough to revel amidst the natural beauty in the world or true human exchange.

What I am referring to (and highly suggest) is a complete reboot—a re-vamping of how you cradle this baby in your everyday life and a look into your deep attachment to *the thing* and how you can arrive in your life—undistracted.

If you would like to land in the H.U.Generation, the power is already within you. As with the plastic bag abolition, it doesn't require 5 years to take effect, or 90 days for that matter. Chances are you already know that something has been *off* for awhile, and perhaps you have yet to pinpoint it. With all the turmoil in the world, it is difficult to sift through to any one thing as being *the* culprit. I am not suggesting that the *smart*phone is to blame, I am however saying it has had an immense impact on how we show-up in the world. One might say it's just another material object, however *the thing* can become all-consuming in comparison to others. When it is within our eyesight and earshot, it commandeers our attention. It becomes both a force that serves as a diversion from ourselves while also amplifying the chaos in our world.

I'm not saying *the thing* is all-bad, there are positives to it, like those celebratory photos or vacation pics, needed text messages, calls, or times of emergency. I believe the cell phone is useful, and I hope I've relayed this. But we have one life. Remember—one life. This is not a dress rehearsal. Sure, some may believe in reincarnation, some people believe in multiple lives. Yet how do we want to show-up in this life? Right here, right now, present, held-up. Do not continue to be fooled into following

[111] For example, an off-the-grid hiking excursion, a yoga retreat, etc., specifically with a "no-device usage" rule.

the H.D.G. herds around you. Next model, more apps, increased clarity, more gigs, 5G, 6G (its coming), and then some. Supply, *demand*. More—More.

I'll show you more—more time, increased head space, higher body image, closer relationships, fuller connections, more attention to deal with issues truly requiring your attention, more acceptance. The list increases *ad infinitum*. More.

Choice—you have it.

I have already shared that I am a solo parent of three sons with 5 years between each of them (i.e., a 10-year span altogether). They all play sports and have other extra-curricular activities. Each requires a different set of age-appropriate nurturing, involvement, and care. The upkeep of our home, laundry, pet care, cooking, driving, scheduling, and working are a few other areas that require my attention including the extra energy it takes to deal with my (soon-to-be-ex) husband. I have never hired a nanny and had limited help when my children were young as we didn't live in the same area as my mom.

I focus on my family, my sobriety, and God, first and foremost, and manage my brain and its flow and flux of ideas and processing at any given time. I do Kundalini yoga[112] twice a week and workout three times per week, which helps with balancing both body and mind. And somehow, I still manage to write letters of concern about causes and world issues from writing governments regarding dolphin slaughter missions, whaling, and shark-finning practices (Japan, Taiji Cove, Faroe Islands) to local coffee shops (that could use some adjustment in their over-use of unnecessary

[112] Several years ago, I happened upon Jai Dev Singh and his life-changing Kundalini teachings. His wife, Simrit, plays beautiful music which further enhances the practice. If this is of interest to you, please see https://teachings.jaidevsingh.com

plastic, etc.) and many others in-between. I also routinely contact my MP to address local issues that I feel require attention.

Sometimes just doing *nothing* is amazing, too, which can be difficult for so many.

How would you utilize your freed-up time and space?

Voices

At this point, life had returned to a more stable place. I was attending regular meetings for both Alcoholics Anonymous (AA) and another fellowship (Al-Anon[113]), which helped me immensely in dealing with the addict in my life. I had to let go of the resentment I held and get back to living in as stable a place as I could create. It was around this time that I felt an increasing pull towards God and a faith that was strengthened more than I had experienced before. Our kids were growing as was our St. Bernard/Bernese Mountain dog. My business was thriving, and the market conditions had improved. I began getting back to other things that had previously brought me joy in life.

I enrolled in flamenco dancing, which had always been of interest to me. It was a form of dance that came from my roots. We danced twice a week, and I found release and great freedom with the women and the music, which replenished my soul. My dad had encouraged this form of expression as something he felt suited me—he was right. We rehearsed and performed shows—and the *little voice* inside continued to nag at me.

I had never been able to shake the fact that I had not had a daughter. Growing-up I had chosen her name. It felt like I could see her, and as an adult I still envisioned her arrival. My oldest son had wanted a sister since the first of his brothers arrived. Given all that had occurred and was still going on, it seemed ludicrous to think of taking-on more.

[113] Al-Anon is a support organization for families and friends of alcoholics or addicts; see https://al-anon.org

I was bombarded with Individual Education Plan[114] (IEP) meetings, speech pathologists, hearing tests, dental and orthodontist appointments for our middle son. His defiance, stealing, and outbursts were at times severe. He had been diagnosed with a condition referred to as static encephalopathy, severe Attention Deficit/Hyperactivity Disorder (ADHD), and Oppositional Defiance Disorder (ODD). All of it was beyond challenging. I had worked closely with a social worker to provide an *acceptable* story to inform him of his birth mother, as thus far he had been living as our son with no mention of her. It took much time and attention to formulate the best wording to express this to him. Less than 6 months after having provided him with this information, we were notified that his birth mother had passed away. Apparently clean and sober for 3 months, she had died of a severe asthmatic attack. This brought on another level of complexity.

Yet the voice inside my head was relentless—I was meant to have another baby. It became so loud at times that I would have to thrust the heel of my palm into my skull behind my left ear to make it go away. As I drove-around, my head calculated the year in which the (unborn) baby would go to school. How far would he be in age from the others? Busy mind, racing thoughts. I informed my husband that this voice kept nagging at me and I was not sure what it was about, but it had not let-up for years. With the age-gap growing, according to my calculations we had 6 months to conceive this child.

[114] "A plan or program developed to ensure that a child with an identified disability who is attending an elementary or secondary educational institution receives specialized instruction and related services." University of Washington: Access Computing. (n.d.). *What is an Individualized Education Plan?* (para 1). Accessed 2024-06-30, https://www.washington.edu/accesscomputing/what-individualized-education-plan

I suggested we roll the dice and see if it was God's will for us to have another baby. No guarantees of a daughter, but we were both willing to try, nonetheless. This sort of *rendezvous* was not commonplace for us. Aside from this, it also required scheduling and conviction. Yet 3 months later I was pregnant with child. We would not find out the gender until the day of its birth—the baby was due 1 day after my birthday.

I continued flamenco dancing and prepared for my upcoming dance exam. I practised on a sheet of plywood on the floor of our cold garage. The rhythm of the stomps of my heels moved through my legs with the vibration of being alive and this growing life inside me.

When I turned to the side, the examiner from Spain squealed with delight at seeing my now 5-month pregnant form. At 8 months, I continued to train, rehearse, and perform the stage shows with the rest of my group. The baby laid sideways[115] the entire time. I felt fully alive when I danced. The music and feelings were like the music that my father had played and adored. The percussion of the hands with the feet, the castanets, the women, the vibrant costumes, the community. Alive.

I was *sent* a name during the pregnancy—sent to me because I had created the space to allow such messages to come. Expanded clarity in the place of toxins that had numbed and dumbed my body and mind in years past. Names hit me on the right side of my head towards the back of my ear lobe. It was a name for a boy that I had never heard before. Hmmm…I wondered, "What did this name mean?" Upon arrival at home, I looked it up—a Spanish name with a meaning that would represent the voyages my parents had taken to Santiago de Compostela. Time and space. Time

[115] Transverse abdominal.

and space. We can expand the space within by not allowing devices, other dependencies, and external distractions to bombard us.

Our beautiful wide-eyed baby was born. "It's a boy!" the doctor said from behind the surgical curtain.[116] My eyes cast-up to the left, I smiled having felt this all along. The total now—four sons. We never referred to any of them as *step*-children. We integrated them all as our own. Although a daughter was not in my deck of cards, I didn't think about that for a moment.

Arriving back at home, the front door opened to remind us that our renovation had been going-on for some time and, as my husband was in the business, ours received last priority. The floor had been ripped-up in areas and the walls (which once were) made for an uneven stepping surface. Electrical boxes hung from cables in the ceiling. Nursery decorated just so? No. We were making do with what we had, and I had accepted that things were not often where I would like them to be. The main thing was that we had our newest amazing baby boy. His eyes shone with depth and the gifts of my father's ancestry along with his appearance and build. Interestingly with this addition, the first letters of our four boys' names spelled my dad's abbreviated middle name. Another delightful synchronicity.

Our bedroom, now downstairs as the renovation continued, the baby and I took-up shop on the upper-level's pull-out sofa-bed in the evenings, which permitted for late-night nursing and a lack of disturbance to my husband who awoke early in the morning to go to work. I appreciated all the boys being on the upper level with me.

[116] Though I wished to experience a natural birth, this was my third Caesarian. All attempts were made to flip the baby's position including, among other techniques, the doctors having me stand on my head.

With the continuing support of Al-Anon I grew in my understanding of detaching from what I had no control over, that is, my husband's usage, his emotions, and his behaviour. Increasingly I noticed that the boys were taking-on his attitudes and his treatment of me was at times less than favourable. In one instance, we had left a car show and, while I was trying to get into the vehicle, he hit me with his truck by moving it while I was standing there. Upon entering the vehicle, he said "What do you want me to do, call the wham-bulance?" Along with him, my boys laughed wildly in the back seat while I sat silent in the front, eyes forward. On another occasion, I held-up my finger to prove a point and he let me know that "If you hold-up your finger to me again, I will f****n' break it." We did not have blow-outs. I seldom raised my voice, which infuriated him further. But an underlying toxic seep flowed between us at a low vibrational level. There was an increase in things said and done to my oldest son that grew exceedingly disturbing. I paid close attention to protect him at all costs.

Life continued. I continued. The boys grew. My husband went to work. I cared for our kids amidst the rubble of our half-renovated home and the ruins of our dissolving family. My exit plan was slowly formulating in my mind and gaining momentum.

At one point, our garage developed a rat infestation. When it became bad enough, we hired a pest control company to come and set traps. The storage room off the garage needed to be cleared out. I was summoned to assist a friend of his (who, also, had detoxed years earlier in my newly-built condo) and an ex-con (who had recently been released from a treatment centre). The three of us moved totes with pools of rat urine and feces on them, several bags of stuffed animals, and a coat of mine from Japan (not *the* coat) that the rats had used for bedding. The lawn was littered with numerous traps we had tossed-out containing dead rats, their broken necks etched into my memory. It was hard for me to witness these dead rodents. Since childhood I have resonated with animals. Even killing mosquitoes and silverfish causes me great pain.

This was a far cry from my pageant days with rhinestone tiara and sequined sash as I gracefully crossed the stage, flower bouquet cradled in arm, waving. How did I get here? Oh right, save them. Save him.

Between couples-counselling for other issues I, too, began intensive counselling, trying to unravel who I had become and the how and why of it all. Sitting in a downtown Vancouver office tower, my female counsellor looked me square in the eye and said, "This is certainly not an easy road you have chosen for yourself." "Chosen?" I thought. "How could she say that? What else could I have done? How *could* I have chosen differently?" I thought.

But you see, I did have choice then, and I do now, as do you.

We all have choice—and we *can* choose differently.

In the months ahead, it gradually became clear to me that out of the approximate 8 billion people who grace this planet, I had chosen this man. "Eight billion people," said the voice in my head. Sure, okay, there are around 4 billion females, and how many of those remaining are adult male heterosexuals. Well, that figure is unknown. The point is, there are *many many* choices. "Eight billion people." We all have many choices. Being on my own also became an increasingly viable option.

Something inside me said there was a different level of serenity that I had not yet tapped into. I went back to hot yoga when my youngest son became old enough to go to the facility's neighbouring child-minder. I went deeper into AA's steps again. I wrote, I sang, I parented, and I continued to stay sober, putting one foot in front of the other each and every day.

I knew with clarity that my husband was not functioning well. Though I was largely outnumbered in testosterone levels within my home's walls, I did not loose hope, and my faith did not falter in my attempt to move forward. I was in awe of our children, their life stages, their difficulties with one another, their play, their sports, how they came to me for support. Though they did not know all of what their parents were going through, our ability to carry-on was truly remarkable.

I couldn't quite put my finger on it at the time but, in hindsight, my awareness had deepened, and a new-found grace was building within me.

We all have choice—and we can choose differently.

Leo, Fire Dragon, Life Path Number 1[117]

Leo, Fire Dragon, Life Path Number 1 are my symbols, which some may see as signs of power, strength, and resilience. Though for several years I did not put much thought into these gauges, I have come to learn that the exact time of our birth and the location of the Earth in relation to the sun, the moon, and the surrounding planets determines a large part of the traits we may possess. Further to this, ignoring others' inherent traits can be a foolish and unwise gamble where personal relationships are concerned. This has been my experience.

I consider myself to have firsthand experience with this as I chose to marry two men with the least two astrologically-compatible signs to mine. In hindsight, I recommend against this. However, if you have done this and have found a successful and joyous union, may your blessings and fulfillment within this relationship blissfully continue. I wish nothing but the best for my fellow humans.

I often recall the first line in the amazing book, *The Road Less Travelled,* by M. Scott Peck: "Life is difficult." I first read that publication when I was in my early 20s. It seems to me that, at the hand of *the thing,* many of the younger generations are losing site of this fact. It is often perceived that one can coast-along shielded from this simple fact. Life is difficult. Without having to put-in the time, patience, and resilience to stumble, grow and, therefore, evolve as a human. The *instant* message mentality has a trickle-down effect to other areas of our lives. And when the *real* world does not conform to instant gratification, it can leave us feeling even more restless about life itself. We have been trained and are

[117] These are my signs in Western astrology, the Chinese lunar calendar, and numerology.

instructing others that we are *always* available. Not receiving a response within moments can leave some spiralling into all the imaginable reasons why this could be.

What would happen if you were not so readily available? Within your search to get away from the most profound distraction our modern world has encountered, what if you decided to take your personal power back? Would those around you adapt? Would the teenager-in-need of you to bail him/her out in that moment have to find alternate ways to cope? Would your friend-in-crisis have to find a different outlet to make an unmanageable situation manageable, or perhaps dig within in order to get to the other side? How would we teach those around us to show-up for themselves while also showing-up more wholly for others in the process?

In order for humanity to heal, each of us must travel our *own* personal journey to heal ourselves. The ancestral patterns we inherit require effort in moving away from that which burdens our genetic makeup. Every human encounters hardships in their lifetimes. There are those who have experienced abuse, trauma, and/or victimization, which can make their healing journeys considerably more challenging and involved. My experience has been that the lessons I needed to learn have continued until I evolved from that particular lesson.

Regardless of our upbringings and experiences, we all possess distinct gifts and abilities meant to be shared with others. Regardless of astrological sign, numerology, or other symbology applied, one shows-up more wholly when distanced away from the rat-race of constant posting and scrolling into oblivion. Otherwise, we continue to flow toward empty shallows of soul-less communion.

My hope is that we can come together in true connection again—so that we can share our stories authentically and healing can take shape.

Further Education

Through the process of all I had learned in having a child with special needs, I decided I would assist him a step further. I reschooled in the area of special education, while also preparing for the next market-dip to help with the lack of a steady paycheque. I set my sights on gaining new knowledge while also preparing for the day when my husband would again jump ship.

An incident occurred between my sons and my husband on Christmas Day that year, which made me realize that we could no longer endure my husband's bouts. I knew that day. That day—I knew. I had done this before—newborn, studying, exams, work, and family life, but this time I carried an entirely different plate.

My boys were not those who walked down the street in calm procession but, rather, they swung from the phone polls, spun-off the curbs, jumped from the mediums. Multiply that by three with me pushing the baby stroller, grasping the dog leash, and constantly scanning for any one of them narrowly missing sudden death at any moment. I imagine you get the picture. Frequently others in the community would comment, "Wow, it looks like you have your hands full!" Yes, I did. At every turn. Please also remember, none of them had a device to occupy them.

I do not understand how any of them had not had a broken bone, stitches, or antibiotics in their lifetimes. A couple of visits to the emergency room for x-rays or to take-out a pen-flashlight's rubber-tip from up a nostril, and a trip to the firehall to have a metal washer taken-off a finger…. But I digress.

The rats had fully-vacated and the slow renovation continued with me spending the last of my savings on its completion. The downstairs suite was completed with original hardwood floors from a 1920s cruise ship, which I had fought my husband and the floor installer to keep. It also had a walk-through closet and beautiful Spanish-inspired bathroom with floor to ceiling shower, herringbone patterned floor tile, and full view of my magnificent apple tree. Yes, at this point I felt like it was mine. My dad's tree was planted in the rear corner of the backyard and growing stronger each year. The same tree at the foot of which I buried my son's hamster while he was at baseball game as he didn't want to see.

Back to college. Back to new people, online learning for the first time, in-class learning, cohorts, nursing practicums, assignments, and completing components. This was a world I had not yet known. I remember writing "BLOOD, FLOOD, FIRE" on a piece of paper in a column and drawing a red line under them. I explained to my sons that they were not to disturb me while I was in class sessions unless one of these three things were happening—that they needed to sort through whatever they were dealing with, independently, as I sat off to the side in our kitchen on our computer, headphones donned. Their dad typically asleep in the living room, if one of them presented himself at my side, I would hold-up the piece of paper and they would usually retreat. I did the 2-year program in 10 months, which kept me occupied, and my sons learned how to better cope in this new phase of my development. As time passed, I grew to appreciate the increased distance this had brought between me and my husband who, along with his mother, had a strong distaste for this most recent venture.

I made $50,000 that year in commissions aside from completing a full-time diploma program, raising the children, and being responsible for everyday domestic responsibilities. Yet they both had something to say about how *I* should be doing more and contributing further. I was accustomed to this. I had become accustomed to a lot of things.

You see, this is part of my point. Many of the younger generations feel a sense of entitlement. Without expanding their prospects, some hold on tightly to the pipe-dream that they will be a YouTuber and make it big. Maybe they will. Or maybe they will marry rich, their over-plumped lips and augmented parts attracting a suitor, who will meet each and every one of their needs, and life will be the freest of rides. Maybe. This wasn't my experience—and it is not in my nature. Though I did not *choose* an easy life, eventually I was able to acknowledge and own this. I was going to continue, to keep my faith, to be guided, and to tap into my strengths—to make it through this time as I had previously gone through so much else. Through all of this, my sons were such a blessing in moving forward. I have immense gratitude for them.

My sobriety had been unshaken through my treasured father's passing, my husband's relapses, the toxic spew coming at me from others, and my general daily challenges. I was conscious of putting my head down, immersing myself into what I needed in order to get to the other side. My dad used to refer to this as "putting your head down," meaning giving it your all and not letting anything outside penetrate your focus. Of course, this is contrary to that of our society which now largely falls into the H.D.G. Strength and determination flowed freely through my veins now, and this time was no different.

Tunnel-Vision

In my late teens, I had a boyfriend who was influential in my life and had many catchphrases which were highly memorable. He was a gift to me. When he talked about "tunnel-vision," he created a telescope with both hands, fingers touching his thumbs, one hand in front of the other, and raised them up to one eye. He would say, "You only allow the things that help you get to where you want to be in your tunnel. Everything else stays on the outside." This was just one of a number of the things he said that stuck with me all these years. He was also a beautiful example of an upbeat yet commanding personality who was raised with little—he was an unstoppable force who knew with clarity where he was heading. At the time, my focus was elsewhere. He didn't drink alcohol yet was the head bartender in the place in which I first worked as a busser at age 16. I stayed at that job for 4 years, eventually climbing the rungs and moving-up to server. We stayed together for several years, and he taught me many valuable lessons. I still had many years of drinking to do, and he had his tunnel tightly set. He went on to be a highly successful multi-millionaire in the US.

The 10 months felt like an eternity at times. With lectures and cohort meetings, headphones on at the computer, I was centred in my tunnel with God surrounding me. My partner's negativity was on the increase with his crunchy atmosphere towards me and the world in general. My oldest son would be going onto high school soon, and his confirmation from our church was during the same year that the second youngest would be receiving his first communion. Though I did not grow-up in an organized religion setting, I found faith, comfort, peace, and togetherness in our tightly-knit church community. I was involved and I belted-out the hymns, regardless of any judgement.

Beauty was all around me.

09/18

Excitement grew as I prepared to see my oldest off to high school. It was his first experience with the public system and away from the uniforms and practises he had known for the past 8 years. I so appreciated that the boys now had a faith-based foundation. The structure that came with it and the community we experienced were all beautiful pieces.

However, at this time wrongs to the First Nations' people had been revealed and I began questioning some aspects of the church and past behaviours of its clergy. In addition to this, the first transgender child who graced my youngest children's school was met with immense resistance by faculty members. Shortly after this, the father of one of my son's classmates came into the Grade 2 classroom and announced that the children were now to refer to his daughter as a boy. A shift was occurring, yet the school's administration was unable to adjust their policies. Such traditions are deeply rooted, and it would take time to see a noticeable change.

I valued much of what the Catholic system had to offer, while these issues weighed heavily within me at the same time. I felt a misalignment with that which I believed. My young ones had many years to complete their schooling and, with all that was going on in our lives, leaving the Catholic school would not be a wise decision. Re-evaluate, re-absorb, re-adjust, and sometimes this takes time.

The stress was taking its toll on me. I continued my schooling while being on limited funds and the solo parent of four young boys for the summer. I had become less able to maintain brain clarity. Labour Day was almost upon us and my husband suddenly realized that summer was ending, and he hadn't spent any time with us. We travelled in separate vehicles for a trip to the outdoor pool.[118] Upon arriving, I had gone to the wrong location, and my son and I attempted to find the place. We stumbled through grassy hills on foot. Arriving late and bewildered, I was met with the usual condescension and criticism. Dealing with him had become intolerable.

It was the evening before school started. The three boys would begin new grades, and the oldest prepped for his first high-school day. My husband did not arrive home and was unreachable. When the boys asked his whereabouts the following morning, I covered by saying he had stayed-up in Whistler to work. The kids readied for school and prepared for the annual photo in front of the ivory rhododendron bush, with smiles and poses, off we went, our 3-year-old in tow. Arriving home, I called his cell again; it went straight to voicemail. The chill went up my spine. The next call I made was to the authorities as this time would be different.

The constable attended within the hour, and we sat in the living room. Photos were needed to complete the missing person's file with questions relating to whether this had happened before, what kind of character he is, distinguishing marks, usual places he would go, associates, etc. This time, I was far-removed from the street-combing of days gone by. I had told him the last time, "This was my last time." As I write this, I hear George Michael's "Spinning the Wheel" again:

[118] Three years prior, I had set a boundary to no longer drive with him due to excessive speeds, erratic driving behaviours, and cellphone usage while driving.

> ... I just want you to know I won't go through it again.
> Those clouds are closing in.
> And I will not accept this as a part of my life.
> I will not live in fear of what may be.
> And the lessons I have learned
> I would rather be alone than watch you spinning....[119]

Yes.

I went on with my day and picked-up the kids from school that afternoon with fellow parents asking how our summer was and me likely providing a cheery response. (One truly never knows what is going on in the lives of those they encounter.) As the evening went on, the kids asked of his whereabouts again. Although my experience told me differently, my response was the same as before, he was working in Whistler.

Forty-eight hours of blankness without word. After 2:00 a.m. the ringing telephone woke me, and the sound of an officer on the other end identified himself from a precinct in another area known for its shady ways. He stated they had pulled-over my husband's vehicle and, having identified him from the missing person's report, they had him in front of them. "Would you like to speak with him" he said. "No," I replied. "Is there a message you would like me to give him?" he said. "Tell him we hope for his safe return," I swallowed, not sure whether I truly believed this. The missing person's report would be closed as he had been located. Five more days of him being gone and, on the seventh evening, my mom came over to help-out so I could focus on a pre-scheduled Zoom meeting downstairs.

When I reached the top of the stairs around 9:30 p.m., my eyes met with hers. "He's here" she said in a melancholy tone, motioning to our

[119] Michael, G., & Douglas, J. (Songwriters & Producers). (1996). Spinning the wheel [Song]. On *Older* [Album]. Label: Virgin.

middle son's door. The door closed; I entered to find the room pitch-black. I flipped on the light. He was sitting on the end of the bed, hood pulled up-and-over his head, the hollows of his eyes dark and ashen, like he had seen hell and brought it back with him. "You have *some* nerve," I growled. "What...what?" With his palms up, he motioned shrugging his shoulders upwards. "What are *you* trying to start here?" As always, it was me, not him. *Me* to blame. I let him know that he needed to leave, or I would call the authorities. He started in on me, saying this was his house, and *I* needed to leave. The police arrived, and he was told to get a few personal items together and vacate temporarily, while things cooled. By 7:00 a.m. the following morning, I had the car packed and ready to go with belongings for myself, our four children, and our dog.

Conversations between us confirmed that he "was not going anywhere." "This was [his] house." Seeing as we had decided to keep me off of the home's title, so I "would be able to list the home for sale in the future," he figured this to be true. *His* house—regardless of our years living in it together or my financial contributions, regardless of the fact that I had raised his biological son as my own for the past 9 years along with our other sons—he was "not going anywhere." I couldn't fathom what life would look like in the months to follow.

For the next 5 weeks, my sons and I set-up home at my parent's house. Each day I drove them an hour each way to and from school. Each day, each way, over two bridges and through two tunnels, one travelled under a body of water. Not a leisurely 1-hour drive, but one in city traffic which required considerable concentration. Each day I stayed in town for 7 hours to wait for them to finish. After dropping-off the kids at school, initially I stopped by the house only to find remnants of paraphernalia littered around inside. Each day, new signs and indications—signs that he was not yet done with his destruction. Each day.

Adaptability was also one of the strengths with which I scored high in the strengths test. This was adaptability at its finest. The last few years I had proven I had adapted to many circumstances, and this was the end of him and his addiction being an active part of my life.

Some days when I entered the house, candles were still burning in blackened glass jars on top of my grandparent's heirloom bedroom set. Was this my house—our house? A strange eerie feeling everywhere, the stench of decay all-around. The light of love from children utterly extinguished. In days ahead gear was strewn about with copious amounts of tin foil. What did someone do with so much tin foil? And Brillo pads—What—Why?[120] How had this become my reality? I did not sit in these questions for long. I had work to do, my children to get far away from this, and myself to save.

Days ahead had cutlery from the matching sets I had bought charred and littered throughout. Blackened homemade pipes fashioned from household bottles, medicine bottles, and charred tin-cans. Bottles—so many bottles. Light grey suede stilettos, Size 5, placed *just so* by my side of the bed, and women's belongings with their cheap and dirtied ways. There—in my house. There.

The neighbours began to reach out as neon taxi cabs (which were not from our town) became commonplace. Their fares were not those we had around here. Their patent red thigh-highs glaring starkly with those who visited our quiet farming community. There was so much that I needed to shoulder on my own. There was so much from which I needed

[120] I had to turn to Google for this one.

to shield the children. I prayed and grew much closer to God during this time. I surrendered completely to my faith, not making space for this to take me down.

My suitcase had been packed for a flight to Salt Lake City the following day. I was scheduled to attend a convention for a MLM wellness business I had been involved with for some time. Due to the circumstances, this trip never happened. Rather, I spent the day with a lawyer to obtain legal advice. I had scheduled 3 days to move-out much of our personal belongings and much of the furniture. Days when he would not be inside the house. I frantically packed and boxed all we had built. Memories of my children's childhoods now charred and tarnished. I would do this largely on my own.

One morning, a dear friend of mine came straight from her shift as an emergency room nurse to help. Another day, an RCMP officer friend came to help on her day-off. Women. Such resilience and strength. Far from the woman whose patent-leather boots held her upright as she gave herself to the pull of the pipe. My husband. He had given himself to hard drugs, to alcohol, to her, to all the others.

We women worked, we packed, we disposed of, we put our heads down (the healthy way) and got it done. Three days amidst the degradation of humanity in its vile pull, away from any and all that is love, any and all that is God. Any and all. Each day, new things to view, bloodied hospital gowns mentioned that he had been admitted, swearing and cursing in vulgar volume (I later learned). Only to be released and, again, continue—in my house—in all that *we* had built. Disgusting display of humanity in my newly-renovated house.

I have seen other mothers who have written about their feelings of loss they had felt when their family's home had been uprooted and had moved elsewhere. Time to prepare, to pack, to purge, to ponder. Their family intact; their memories boxed and moved. Often moving to a more spacious and functional layout. There is pain, loss, and transition in this experience. I understand this. My experience was the different—there was deep grief, immense disbelief, and an inconceivable lack of understanding as to how this could be happening. Again though, I did not wade in these thoughts. I did not have the time. I just did it—one box at a time, one move forward in each moment. I did not put my head down or rock in the fetal position. I did not have the desire. I got to it. I moved into the solution in the small ways I was able. I trusted the process. I maintained my H.U.G. position throughout, even in this state. Would scrolling into oblivion have helped? No. I did it, and it was painful in its entirety. Denial and distraction from reality is seldom beneficial.

I recall being downstairs packing a wardrobe box at the front door with boots and shoes in the bottom, all our coats on hangers, baseball bats, and badminton racquets among other possessions. Not knowing my reality, a MLM teammate of mine messaged me. Having stated her symptoms, I provided the recipe for the wellness blend which would assist her ailments. I continued. Then focused on what remained in my tunnel,[121] put my head down and travelled through. I had accepted the generous offer to store some of our cherished belongings in the garage of my precious neighbour who lived kitty-corner from our house. I had limited time and the need to remove our belongings from this house was urgent. With each passing day this became clearer.

I entered our garage and saw lawn chairs between garbage, paraphernalia, bottles, and piles of cigarette butts. Our garage, where I had practised flamenco on the plywood, where our children had run

[121] For more on this topic, see the "Tunnel-Vision" section in the chapter "Further Education".

inside to grab their hockey sticks for the next match out-front, their soccer ball, their bubble wands.

The bubble of my life had now burst.

Though the rats had been removed, the infestation of human detriment had moved-in. I secured one wardrobe box and wheeled it out the door, cigarette burns on the side of it, crack rock and crumbs falling-off the top as I walked. For anyone who truly knows me, my clothing, shoes, accessories are a loved collection from various travels, high-end consignment boutiques, and the individual colourful style that had expressed me. My cherished collection. Had they no conscience whatsoever? It was beyond comprehension.

I wheeled the dolly across the street holding all that was still intact inside. In the centre of the street, the sun shone on my face. I leaned my head back and felt its grace. Within that moment I heard "You are guided, protected, and cared for." A smile from deep within spread across my face. I truly felt this—I was guided, protected, and cared for. Early-on in my recovery I would hear in my head, "Do God's work, and he [she, or they] will do yours." Stay the course, do not falter, and when I do I get back up and continue. No road is without flaws. Some lessons more dangerous than others.

Guided, protected, and cared for was what I deeply felt that day. That day. That detrimental day. Alone, yet fully connected to source, and able to *feel* completely. I was there. In my pain, in my vulnerability. I was there, and I felt it *all*. No selfies, no video blog, no crying on camera. There. Present. Forever ingrained in my memory. There.

The moving truck arrived with the same fellow from the rat infestation/termination, now shining with twinkling eyes of recovering from alcohol and drug addiction. More recently he was diagnosed with cancer, which took his attention but not yet his twinkle. Through the move he remarked about my demeanour, about my leaving pieces of furniture for my husband to be comfortable and having him move a smaller dining set upstairs. He commented that in the past he had moved other women with *far* less a story whose husbands had also wronged them and, who through their anger, had slashed furniture with butcher knives in front of him. Not I. These thoughts had not entered my mind. I had one life to live, and one to get away from. Grace and I would travel together, even through this.

The days ahead brought more challenges. Our house was listed for sale and access to it was paralyzed. I was the listing agent, and one can perhaps imagine how that progressed. My husband called and, in a low growl, demanded that *his* son be brought back as I "have absolutely *zero rights* to that child!" I obliged, begrudgingly, believing that what he said was true. He also wanted the dog brought back too, our beloved St. Bernard-X whom we had had since she was a pup. The two were returned to him and, still to this day, this pains me immensely. I had deeply hoped that this would be the push that was needed to have him begin abstinence once again, but this wasn't the case.

The neighbours' calls and deep concern proved otherwise. Reports of our son being left alone, and with the difficulties he had. Only 10 years old, he was assessed to be the emotional maturity of age 7 and required a full-time aide at school. Alone in the driveway, alone in front of the TV. Alone all hours of the night.

I would see him standing in the field down the street from the school or sitting in a spot where he was instructed to go. After school, waiting, sitting in the reeds, head down. There wasn't anything I could do. Even though I had raised this child as my own for 9 of (almost) 11 years, the ministry also treated me as an outsider who had no rights. Though social workers said otherwise, this would take time prove. It was out of my hands. Painfully, I had to let him be and focus fully on my other three and their well-being and to scrape together what was left of my sanity. My tunnel tightened.

Days later, I entered the house when no-one was home. Going into the kitchen, I saw the unmarked phone number of the local women's shelter still under a fridge magnet, which I had placed there after his last disappearing stint. Living under a gun, under one's thumb,[122] always preparing. Scout's motto, Girl Guide's honour.[123] Me.

I looked around. Mold grew on pots on the stove. Flies encircled the dried-up dog dish. I left, disgusted, and took the dog with me.

I don't clearly recall the timeline of when all this happened, but a week or so later I arrived at the front door to obtain the last of our belongings. I was stunned to find that the locks had been changed—an act that later I would find-out was initiated by my then mother-in-law—the fiercest enabling force behind him over the years and the funder of the previous 11 treatment-centre stays.

I will not speak negatively about treatment centres. They are the way out for many who are blessed to be able to benefit from this helpful and immersive environment. But what I will say is this: Once people have been released from a treatment centre, they must do the required work[124] afterward or there is a high probability they will relapse.

[122] My dad used these sayings. They meant never being at the mercy of anyone else.

[123] For those not familiar, "Be prepared…" is both the Scout's and Girl Guide's motto.

[124] They must find and work with a sponsor, continue to rigorously work the 12 steps, attend daily meetings for a time, and sign-up for a service position.

Work. There, again, I said it. Many areas of my life have required work. Pay attention, let go of old ideals, feel the soul-levelling gut-punching feelings, and do the work required to prevail. Travelling through peeling the onion layers of how I arrived at that point in my life, what the root causes were, and the deficits within that kept me feeling as though I needed something external to feel enough.

Hmmm...

There it is again, some*thing* external.

No road is without flaws.
Stay the course, do not falter and, when you do,
get back up and continue.

The Ministry

As I had previously mentioned, at 8 months old his young son had been taken away from his mother's care, the father's and my involvement began when the child was 18 months old, and he was transferred into his father's and my care at 24 months. Now, days ahead of his eleventh birthday, his son was removed from the care and custody of his birth father. "Absolutely zero rights to that child!" echoed in my mind and the ministry had also nullified my entitlement.

With his addictions, child in his care or not, it did not matter. *Gear* was littered everywhere for the child to see. Gear which I will not speak of further, but a worse sort than I had seen in the house within the first few days of our leaving. It was in the child's best interest to be removed—yes. Yet it did not make it any less painful. "Absolutely zero rights to that child!" He was placed in a foster home—and I continued.

I had secured a rental in town and would do my utmost to keep the kids in our community for the duration of that school year. A move again, out of my mother's home. (I shudder to think what we would have done had she not had the space and the willingness to house us.)

I found support in my first husband, who was astonished at how futile the situation had become. The two husbands had a relationship, and my relationship with my first husband, long since mended with forgiveness on both sides. I was pleased to have a friendship with him. Others commenting on how well we got along, and how good it was to see. He is a good person. Interestingly, he and my mother were there for me during this time of need as I rebuilt once again. We stayed in the community and kept firm to the views in the forefront of my tunnel.

Sobriety first, family next. Meetings, fellowship, close friends, close circle. Chin up, eyes ahead.

I found solace in the songs at our church and wept in the back pew as I sang them. My life. *This* was my life, our lives, eyes focussed forward. I took a financial hit in order to keep my children in their respective schools, which I felt was important in creating as little disturbance as possible for them. I stayed steadfast, focused, and sober. I continued to do the work.

As mentioned, I was kept from details surrounding my second husband's son and his apprehension from his father. Eventually contact was made from his foster family to get the boys in touch and have visits together. I was relieved to meet them and feel the loving safety of their beings. Of all the possibilities, this was a blessing. Time passed and the ministry called asking if I would take our son back, as they were looking for a more permanent placement. The paternal grandmother had been asked first but had declined due to "mental health issues."

Of course I wanted to bring him home with us, but I was beside myself with having to make such a decision about someone with whom I had previously lost all rights. Back on me, my cross to bear. I wanted to once again provide the most *normal* life that he could have and reunite him with his brothers. However, my intuition told me that he would be used as a pawn for his father and grandmother to have recurrent contact with me—he would be used *against* me to continue their lies, and *I* would be their excuse—again. I had truly suffered from being up against these two, unjustifiably so, and I wrestled with being put into this situation again. Prior to our relationship, I had not previously known a dynamic of this nature existed.

After having created some space between us, taking this on would pull me back into the fold. The decision weighed heavily on my being. I prayed about it, meditated, walked with it, spoke to my inner circle about this burden. I needed outside help to evaluate what was best for all involved. I saw my counsellor and did not alleviate any angst or intuit any firm resolve.

I decided to make an appointment with our priest. I had never gone to him individually. The days were numbered as to the time remaining before I had to make the decision. Upon entering, I was greeted by two lovely women who worked in the parish office. Before I went inside, I was certain I knew how the meeting would go. Certain that I would be summoned to put some further effort into saving our marriage, certain that a set of marriage counselling sessions at the parish would be referred.

I sat down and waited in the room amidst the ornate gold and ivory décor—the smell of history, old books, and long-seasoned wood. Shortly after, the priest arrived and sat across the large carved wooden desk which, in the fragile state I was in, caused me to feel smaller. I began to describe the situation briefly, and he pulled out a thick pad of lined white paper. He asked for my full name and wrote it centred at the top of the page and began to question me about recent happenings, and those of days and years gone by. From there he asked my husband's name and wrote it on the left side. Looking at his name, he read aloud "Victor," then "Vitor. He is not victorious. He is a *loser*!"

Stunned, "Wow," I thought, "Perhaps this meeting would be more forward thinking than I had anticipated." Still convinced that he would try to make me see a way to keep the family intact at any and all cost, we continued. He asked me the names of all the children from oldest to youngest and their ages. As he wrote them down the column on the left side of the page, leaving space between each, I started to take notice that he would go to the top and repeatedly circle my full name in a large oval. We continued to talk. Feeling more comfortable, I shared candidly about what had recently occurred, and what had occurred over our last 10 years together. We spoke about sobriety, and the topic of taking-on raising my husband's biological son as my own.

He listened intently as he repeatedly circled my name. At this point he looked knowingly into my eyes, then tapped the pen repeatedly, leaving dots inside the oval. He leaned-in across the desk, his voice deepened, "And what about *her*? Where is *she* in all of this? When are you going to get back to *her*?"

This shook me to my core. A chill travelled from each of my wrists and met at the back of my neck. Yes, her, where was *she* in all of this? *When* would I get back to her?

The truth in his questions and knowing what I needed to do pierced through my being. My clipped wings seemed to stretch-out ever-so-slightly in those moments as though I knew everything and nothing all at once.

Going further he said that, if I took the child into my care, it was his belief that the father and grandmother would use him as a *pawn* against me. Pawn. This was the exact word I received in my contemplations surrounding my desire to rescue this boy. The rescuer once again. It was levelling to accept yet freeing to gain small steps with my internal wisdom, which urged me not to take-on anymore. As for our son, the priest said that his wish was that God would keep him and guide him through his experiences and his pain, and for his life ahead. We prayed aloud about this and the immensity surrounding all involved.

This visit provided the clarity I needed to move through the situation. I wept. With each forward step, I needed to get back to me. Years later, I had an epiphany surrounding this day. I saw with clarity the reason I had not had a daughter was that part of my life's work has been to learn to nurture the daughter I never had—myself. I notified the ministry of my decision. It was gut-wrenching.

Our house was still for sale, but it is not possible to sell a home to which the listing agent does not have access. I met with a local lawyer to discuss my rights, and he assured me that I was equal owner of the property, despite the fact that I was not listed on the land title. He also informed me that my husband had remortgaged our property of which I had no knowledge and the sizable second mortgage had been approved and funds released the day prior. His and his transients' benders would be well-funded for some time.

During this time, he also posed as a minor to open a fraudulent bank account. The bank informed me that, with the assistance of one of the females present in the house, he had forged my signature on my cheques. This was yet another circumstance I would deal with in the years to come for which he would not take responsibility.

My husband's detrimental lifestyle continued over several more months. Our neighbours contacted me with information, emotional support, and to express their shock, disbelief, and distress about the situation. Our neighbourhood became one in which residents did not let their kids play outside. With the blinds closed and curtains drawn, the neon green taxis coming-and-going all hours of the day and night, and my husband parking diagonally across the double-wide driveway as if to say, "Its mine, all mine!" Everything had become a blatant display of his self-degradation.

Later he claimed that *he* had not done *any* of this—it was his addiction. A complete and utter inability to own any of it. I didn't buy into this. I have come from a place of knowing the choice to do the work surrounding staying sober. But his life is his own to live, not mine. My hope is that he will gain the tools to see clearly rather than continue to live in a place of denial believing that we do not look at what has happened in the past. Without clearing-up the wreckage of our pasts,[125] how can we make our way to a better life?

> An epiphany: The reason I had not had a daughter was that part of my life's work has been to learn to nurture the daughter I never had—myself.

[125] Alcoholics Anonymous World Services. (2001). *Alcoholics Anonymous: The story of how many thousands of men and women have recovered from alcoholism* (rev ed.; p. 8). New York, NY: Author. Accessed 2024-06-30, https://anonpress.org/bb/Page_164.htm

Choices

> No one can make me change. No one can stop me from changing. No one really knows how I must change, not even I. Not until I start. I will remember that it only takes a slight shift in direction to begin to change my life.[126]

So here again I insert the phrase "live and let live."[127] Words by which I live. Whether others are addicted to alcohol, drugs, gambling, food, or exercise, etc., their sexual preferences, religions, belief systems, and political affiliations are not for me (or anyone else) to be concerned about. I do, however, have a choice about those who surround me and how I fill my time. I have the choice of what I view with my eyes and hear through my ears (enter lady on phone beside me on the elliptical machine) and, very importantly, what I *choose* to engage with online.

Has *the thing* truly increased connection for you? Do you feel these so-called connection devices fill their original intention? In small ways, perhaps—but they have gone way beyond their usefulness. What was first meant to increase communications with others has plunged many of us into darkness.

> I don't have to tell you that hate and fear are being sown online all across the world....this dark undertow which is connecting us all globally...is flowing via the technology platforms.[128]

[126] Al-Anon Family Group. (1992). *Courage to change: One day at a time in Al-Anon II* (p. 3). New York, NY: Author.

[127] One of the AA slogans that are often posted at the meetings I attend.

[128] Cadwalladr, C. (2019, April). Facebook's role in Brexit—and the threat to democracy [video]. *TED talk.* Accessed 2024-11-15, https://www.ted.com/speakers/carole_cadwalladr

Along with the purpose of social connection, *the thing* is being used to sell to us, to track us, to manipulate our thinking and our way of *being* in the world.

Another disturbing issue is innocent children falling victim to the online luring of predators. Everyone is shocked when they hear about this, and I cannot fathom how devastating this would be. My heart aches for these children and their families. I think of the parents who may have not recognized the need for extensive monitoring device usage. Children and teens being in their rooms with the door closed for hours at a time may contribute to such situations. Or perhaps it happened during school (don't get me started on this topic) or away from home.

Please understand. I am not blaming or condemning parents—or anyone. I feel the fatigue; I hear the voices. "It's the wave of the future." "It's just how it is." "It's not going anywhere." I hear them. "But their friends all have them!" Yes, and time will reveal whether or not any of their friends fall victim to the highly increased teen self-harm and suicide rates, or the muse of an online predator who took the remainder of their childhoods from them. God forbid either. Or maybe it was less glaring. Maybe their grades were sub-par and lacking the needed attention and support to succeed wholly. I dislike having to say these things, but these issues need to be unveiled. Yes, these issues need to be discussed and confronted with honesty and sincerity, with caring and integrity but, at the forefront, with action.

We have somehow bowed down and are lacking in the ability to pinpoint the damaging aspects of this high-level of device reliance in a firm and informed manner. And this spineless approach contributes to the downward pull from *Homo erectus* to jellyfish follows suit. Are you seeing a visual of taking back the reigns and standing-up once again? Amazing. I am right here with you.

This could be the script of your dialogue with those under high-school level which goes something like this. You child arrives home from school with device in hand and you, mighty phone bill payer, say something like, "I need to see your cell phone please." You take it, insert it into your back pocket, and invite them to sit down with you to talk.

> "I have made a mistake. By giving you this cell phone I now realize that, in fact, I have taken away so much more from you. You will get it back in the future, and when you do it will look differently than it does now, but we will talk about it at that time. There will be no further discussion about this."

At this point, you will undoubtedly receive backlash as they have likely come to rely on *the thing* in ways you couldn't have imagined. This is alright. It may be difficult, but you can do this. Float away jellyfish. Float far, far away.

There is a tendency to feel as though we can see the argument that ensues when the grip of said device is pried from their clutches. Perhaps on some occasions we can, and on others we cannot. Regardless, if your device-addicted offspring has this fight response, that is the first indication of how serious a pull *the thing* has on them, and this is how your exchange might sound:

> "But how am I going to text Logan and Emma?!"

> "When you see them tomorrow you can let them know that your parent saw things differently and you no longer have a mobile phone."

Following in his elder brother's footsteps, my middle son will be entering high school in the fall and will bring his previously-deviceless self to school with a cell phone that has no data. We have already had the conversation about him being allowed to have one social media app on his device and we have discussed what this will be. I will have access to his phone and will be the one who installs anything further. As time continues, I will reassess. He will be permitted to have one social media site installed on our home computer, which he already uses and is in a common area of our home. Seems straight-forward to me. *Homo erectus.* Device payer. Simple.

I do not get physical with my kids in any negative ways, I do not yell and, as mentioned before, I do not swear. I discourage my middle son from saying the words "crap" and "hell," as these too I do not use. I will say to them, "We are gifted with a language that has thousands of words from which to choose. Why would you choose such words in order to express yourself?

My father swore from time-to-time, so I grew-up with that. He would swear at the TV when watching the news and seeing the reports of someone who chose to do what they did. He had an Afrikaans accent, which somehow made it sound different to me. Yet, I still chose not to adopt it as my own habit. Am I a saint because of it? Absolutely not. I merely bring forward that we have choices, no matter how big or how small. Choices.

My son showed me a clip of a teenage boy who was sitting amidst his gaming set-up. His Asian mother entered the room. She attempted to get his attention and have him stop gaming. Within seconds he was screaming at her, yelling profanities, and then began trashing the place. He threw his keyboard, then picked-up a chair and threatened her while she cowered in the corner. The whole scenario was filmed and posted on social media for anyone, young or old, who had access to these sites, to observe. How did we arrive here? How have we allowed this to seep-in with such strength that this all-powerful force has become the ruler of so many? What is to come?

There are so many videos of injurious actions that circulate. On the radio[129] this morning, I heard a secondary source report about the footage of the beating death of an African American man. Later, the video recording was posted. Why would I choose to view this? Do I already know the man was killed violently by multiple persons in their positions of authority? Yes. Why would, or should, this footage be made public on social media, and how could this be beneficial? It seems this serves to further fuel the hatred already present. I can only speculate that those last horrific moments of a son's life being exposed for public viewing furthers the trauma endured by the family and, again, how is it helpful—to anyone? Shouldn't this be left to the officials, the courts, and the juries? Our governments need to employ a specialized task force assigned to ensure that, whether it be videos, images, or textual content of a restricted nature, such content not be posted on *any* public forum.

Does this mean that I live in denial of some people, the choices they make, the vile and damaged hate-fuelled systems that exist inside them which they feel they need to unleash on others? No. I am aware. Well-aware. Is it racially-based, sexually-based, religion-based, hate-based, or otherwise? Sometimes some, sometimes all. It is my belief that these all come from lack of love, lack of nurturing, lack of presence, the disconnection from self, others, guidance from source. It is frightening

[129] The format I have chosen to learn about current events since the onset of the pandemic.

for all of us. So, what can be done in the short-term to steer us into a positive direction?

For me, I have made small, yet impactful, changes to how I choose to operate in my life.

- I have stopped watching the news.
- I do not look at the news online either as some of the visuals of the footage are distressing and not for my highest well-being.
- I keep-up on current events by listening to the news on the radio.
- If there is something in particular happening, I can look that up specifically.

I also do not subscribe to video streaming services. Well wait, I did previously. But when *Welcome to Chippendales*[130] mini-series was broadcast on "The Best Place on Earth's" (Disney's platform), that was the final straw for me. While internally reassessing what had become of the pure intentions of Disney's creator in contrast with what it has become, I promptly removed the provider. I must clarify, this is not the two cartoon chipmunks, Chip and Dale. This is a movie about male strippers and the rise of this profession. From time-to-time, I subscribe to one streaming service in order to catch-up on recent documentaries and interest-based programs. This is usually short-lived.

Choice. We have it. "But Timmy down the street has *all three streaming services*!" Great, let him. I'll be over here owning what is right for me, for us. (Insert *Homo erectus.*) Choice.

Has the scroll-flip-scroll between the multitudes of choice taken away from simply being? Watching one show from beginning to end and,

[130] Siegel, R. (Creator). (2022-2023). *Welcome to Chippendales* (Mini-series). Los Angeles, CA: 20th Television.

during the commercials, getting-up to refill our water, grab a snack or take a bathroom break. What about having to *wait* for the next week until the show comes on again?

When other life experiences do not provide that dopamine rush, that quick fix, that instant hit, impatience, irritability, and restlessness intensify. Instant gratification can be highly problematic.

After hearing some of my story, let me ask you, "Has my life been a smooth unfaltering quick-fix of arriving where I would like to be?" In Grade 7, I wrote on the inside front cover of my small red-and-black address book my wish of becoming a household name; has this come to fruition? Did I anticipate being faced with what I encountered through the choices I made in life and the cards I was dealt along the way? Was it instant gratification? Come on. Absolutely not. Instant gratification is seldom reality and, if it is in the short-term for some, is it sustainable?

I am not suggesting that anyone's experiences are the same. We all experience hardships, some illnesses, some disease. Others experience tragedies that are incomprehensible for many of us to understand. I have never lived in a war-ravaged country or escaped a burning building; I have not been affected by slavery or been homeless living on the streets. I have not experienced fertility struggles, have not had to make a decision to give-up a child, nor have I experienced the loss of one. I recognize from the depths of my being that some people's struggles are those that I will not be able to truly comprehend. I do, however, feel deeply for those affected by these sorrows and countless others that I do not know as my own.

I have however waged many wars in my mind, inside my body, in my cells, in order to free myself from the strongholds that kept me from experiencing a life well-lived. Aside from the addiction, I have encountered and endured dire circumstances with a number of destructive individuals. Some I consented to be with, others were a part of situations outside of my control. Those I had a relationship with brought forward generations of conditioning, traumas, and dependencies in an attempt to demoralize and diminish my being in their process. I worked, I saved, and I fought for what was mine, particularly my dignity and self-respect. I still do. But back in those moments at the age of 28 when I had to sell my condo, I said to myself "If not now, in the future, only better." And I believed it. Did it happen the next year, the year after that, or in the following decade. No. I still had much learning to do as I trudged my path, took-on more individuals, their pains, their sufferings, and their indecencies. I learned, and I continued. My faith increased and the amount of toxicity I was absorbing along the way decreased. Over time, I learned the importance of putting my oxygen mask on first.

Would immersion into any device have helped me to get to where I wanted to be? Would my understanding of myself, what ails me, and my shortcomings be improved by swiping through the *feeds?* (Interesting term, "feeds," which generates thoughts of all the unhealthy consumption out there. Remember, boardroom.) Would watching more videos, clips, or profiles truly get me out of the situations that I was in and to recognize my true potential? Does the endless scroll and the pull elsewhere help assist me in moving closer to that which is my creator's will for me? What about you? Does it? What about your children who may already qualify for the unable-to-maintain-eye-contact-for-3-seconds category?[131]

[131] This category may not apply to neurodiverse children.

Enter Robots

Years after having my plane tickets, convention passes, and suitcase in the trunk of my car to leave that day,[132] I was able to attend the convention once it opened-up again after the lockdown. We were thrilled to be able to attend a large-scale in-person event. There were differences that were glaringly apparent since the re-opening of the stadium. We all brought our re-usable water bottles however, mid-day when I arrived at the water-cooler station, the jugs were empty. I circled the various locations of multiple jugs and discovered they too were all empty, at least on this level. I stood at the end of a divider and stared towards the host's counter down the corridor. Behind it, there was a case of bottled water and three young men.

I walked-up and said, "I would like one bottle of water please, and do you have a price list and menu of what else you serve here?" One young man answered, "You need to scan the QR code." That is all he said. Okay, I thought. Begrudgingly, I reached for my phone. Upon scanning the code, I discovered that I would first need to enter my full name, address, birth date, and credit card info in order to proceed. "Sorry," he said, "It's not our choice. It's just the way they do it." Hmmm. Right. *Them* again. How sad I thought. As in the song "Victoria's Secret"[133] about an old man in Ohio making money from girls, this same sort of dude feels the QR code system is an upstanding way to do business.

Aside from the detailed personal information collection required to purchase said bottle of water, I truly felt for those employees. Thankfully,

[132] Refer to middle of chapter "09/2018."

[133] Jax. (2022). "Victoria's secret" [Song]. On *Dear Joe* [Album] (Songwriters: Jackie Miskanic, Mark Nilan Jr, & Dan Henig; Producers: Jesse Siebenberg & Mark Nilan). Label: Atlantic.

it did not require a blood sample or iris scan to complete the registration, however if we continue on this trajectory, this may not be far-off. The young men were not at fault. These systems are defining how we do business and are attempting to take away our freedom of choice. What are we doing to stand up against strategies such as this?

I had a choice. However small, I had a choice. I thanked them and went back to my seat, water-less. We would have to wait. Yes, that's right, wait. I chose not to support this practice as I disagree with all that it represents. As consumers, we fund this human-less experience by participating in it. "The wave of the future—it's not going anywhere." (Oh, how I wish you could hear the tone of the voice I hear saying that.) Enter robots.

Not only are we fostering a generation of H.D.G.'s, but we are decreasing the ability to take and count cash, receive and give change and, most importantly, to have any thoughtful human exchange with customers whatsoever. It is us, the cattle, that make this all possible. (Insert "Moo" sound here.) Walk away. "Don't Believe the Hype!"[134] Sorry in advance, but that dude who thought this was a great idea for database collection and the elimination of employee training will have to re-assess his business model when fewer people fall for this ploy. But this requires discipline!

Think. Think about such things. Think about those young men missing-out on beneficial service-related skills. Keeping cash in our society is important. It is a form of currency that is not digitally connected, and big banks and credit card companies do not obtain a cut.

[134] Public Enemy. (1988). Don't believe the hype [Song]. On *It takes a nation of millions to hold us back* [Album] (Songwriters: Carl Ridenhour, Hank Shocklee, Eric "Vietnam" Sadler, & William Drayton; Producer: The Bomb Squad). Labels: Def Jam, Columbia, CBS Records.

Take your business elsewhere to show your lack of support towards this business model. However please continue to shop in stores, and if you find the customer service is subpar then go elsewhere rather than resort to shopping online. Brick-and-mortar stores strengthen our local economy while adding to human interactions.

There has been much *talk* about the lack of customer service these days. Why? Well, let's talk about that. How many employees are now either holding or glancing down at their phones? Yet for whatever reason, employers do not implement a zero tolerance for cell phone usage during work hours. Jellyfish syndrome again. I suppose with the impending doom of their business' being taken-over by robots, employers all have bowed down to this being the *only* option for employees.

Supply and demand. Supply and demand. If the owners of the QR code-only establishments continue to be supported by all who bow down, they will thrive. On the other hand, if you otherwise decide to shop elsewhere, well, what happens then? Some people feel as though they need to be angry about their stance. Rather, you have the choice to support or quietly go elsewhere. It is not the employees that set-up these systems, it is the employers and large corporations behind them.

At the gym, I glanced towards the TV (see, who needs headphones?) and Pink was on with "Never Gonna Not Dance Again." At that moment in the video she had arrived at the checkout, grabbed the phone from the young cashier's hand, and threw it in the fishbowl. Precisely. Seriously folks, why? How? For all those employers who continue to allow the growing dribble of service, we see you. We notice. It does matter. Jellyfish. "If I could kill *the thing* that makes us all so dumb,"[135] she sings.

[135] Pink. (2022). Never gonna not dance again [Song]. On *Trustfall* [Album] (Songwriters: Alecia Moore, Max Martin, & Shellback; Producers: Max Martin & Shellback). Label: RCA.

Yes. But how do we kill something that a generation does not know how to live without? And the rest of the H.D.G. goes on to support heads down, dribbling away. "We've already wasted enough time!"[136] Yes. Yes. We have, and we continue to do so. Hold the reigns again. "Fight the power!"[137] Let us connect, truly, let us dance and not feel like we have to film it. Let us be together—truly together—again.

Do you want to sit in a rabbit hole watching hours of videos of the shuffle, or do you want to get-up and get going, head-up, connecting rather than spending your time video and "content" watching. Dance, create, read (physical copies) better yourself, live. Life spent with your head down, being sucked away, influenced externally, is not life. My greatest wish is for us to be able to live again. Stand-up and live. *Homo erectus*, remember? What a gift. Precious, priceless.

From the first steps of my children to many moments of entertainment, I was there, present. I did not film them. Several years ago, seeing and hearing the gospel chorus sing "Like a Prayer" at the Madonna concert, their royal blue satin robes flowing to the rhythm. Their souls fused with mine as though I was floating within the melody. These occasions were filmed in my mind and can be replayed this many years later. The lucid recall is ingrained within me. These occasions were vivid and memorable.

Let me ask you: All those events you attended and filmed rather than being truly present at the time, do you watch those videos or are they lost within the volumes of so many others? And for those who do not film

[136] Pink. (2022). Never gonna not dance again [Song]. On *Trustfall* [Album] (Songwriters: Alecia Moore, Max Martin, & Shellback; Producers: Max Martin & Shellback). Label: RCA.

[137] Public Enemy. (1989). Fight the power [Song]. On *Fear of a black planet* [Album] (Songwriters: Carlton Ridenhour, Eric Sadler, Hank Boxley, Keith Boxley; Producer: The Bomb Squad). Label: Motown.

events, how does the sea of upheld phones alter your experience? How does it alter others' experiences? More—*lost* in the abyss of it all. More.

And what about the over-consumption we (Westerners, in particular) engage in, both online and otherwise? I refer to this as A*more*ica,[138] and this is not a positive. "Tread lightly fellow humans," I say. Never assume that anything is ours for the taking. Do not continue to fall victim to the online pull of *the thing*. Time to snap-back into true reality. Many people are scratching their heads as to how we arrived at this place. Look around. H.D.G. members everywhere, regardless of which generation they fall into specifically. We have a responsibility to ourselves (and others) in *everything*. Personal accountability. You have the power of choice. Do not let anyone or any*thing* convince you otherwise.

Please think about these topics and determine ways in which you can make meaningful changes.

Those of us who would like to see change need to do our part. Model what is freely yours to others around you. Some may follow, others may not. We cannot change others—we can only change ourselves. Rather than complain, take action in the ways that you can. Grasp the reigns of your life once again. Close your eyes. Do you see them—the reigns? They are there, and they're yours to hold. Replace the holding of said device with holding the reigns-of-your-life once again. Begin to rearrange the hierarchy of your life in terms of where you have placed your device before yourself, ahead of others, and above your connection with the God of your understanding and our responsibility as inhabitants of this planet.

[138] A play on words to further describe the over-consumption of North Americans as a whole.

Oftentimes people assume that another person has it all. I may be standing beside you in rain boots on a muddy soccer field under an umbrella, or we may be FB *friends.* But do you truly know me? My eyes full with depth and knowing, you might assume that I had arrived there with ease. There may be a mom at school drop-off that you have chatted with in small ways over the years. How about her? Do you know her, her struggles, her achievements? What has she endured through carrying, birthing, and raising those children she is waiting to pick-up? A man, hands clasped, kneeling at a church pew, what are his prayers? You are there with him. This is real. Do you make contact by smiling and offering the first "Hello" and slowly getting to know him over time? It's amazing how such a simple gesture can at times open people up to connect on a different level. Yet from social media posts, we only see snippets of one's being, and often these are the glitz of one's life being presented. Of the hundreds of *friends* on your social networks (or maybe thousands), how many of them do you *truly* know?

What is on the flip-side of the benefits of their glamour shots, family vacays, and the much less-frequent loss of their beloved family pet? I understand how difficult it is to lose a pet. I also understand the devastation of losing a parent. But wouldn't those close to you prefer that you shared this information with them directly rather than through social media avenues? How did we become so disconnected that this is now the way we communicate on difficult emotional issues instead of reaching-out directly to those with whom we are close?

To me, it seems easy to come back from this way of being.

Which makes me wonder, do people actually know themselves and take the time to think whether this is truly the way that they want to be? Are your close connections important to you and what do you do to foster them? Can you *truly* have close connections with *all* the people you are friends with on social media? Do you wish to spend your time torn between living in the present moment and being drained by electronic communications? How does it benefit you to see what a celebrity had for breakfast? Now may be a good time to take a few moments to reflect on your feelings surrounding these topics.

As I've said, everyone has a story, and each and every day that story evolves further. So what are your plans, big or small, and how will you get there? What are your dreams, your aspirations? How do you see yourself having a positive impact in your lifetime? How do you wish to contribute?

I often refer to a small book written by Mother Theresa. This morning, I opened the publication while on the toilet. (Yes, I said it. I have three kids, and space is limited for reading in the morning while they are getting ready for school.) I opened it to a page I had read before, and it said this:

> Dear Lord, the Great Healer, I kneel before You,
> Since every perfect gift must come from You.
> I pray, give skill to my hands, clear vision to my mind,
> kindness and meekness to my heart.
> Give me the singleness of purpose, strength to lift-up a part
> of the burden of my suffering fellow men [people], and a
> true realization of the privilege that is mine....[139]

and it spoke to me once again. A few moments to hear, to be open, to be guided. Yes, a privilege, each and every one of us is gifted with another breath. All of us, privileged with another breath.

[139] Mother Teresa. (1995). "The fruit of faith is love" (p. 82). In *Mother Teresa: A simple path* (compiled by Lucinda Vardey). New York, NY: Ballantine Books.

So how will you choose to use your breaths? Will you choose to tap into the limitless power within you, cast away the master-minded distractions, and arrive in the H.U.G. again? It does not happen overnight and, like any dependence, requires practice and thoughtful restoration.

Heads-Up Strategies

> "The journey of a thousand miles begins
> with a single step."[140]
> ~ Lao-tse ~

So how do we begin to modify our device usage? Here are some straightforward recommendations to connect in the *real* world again.

1. Get back to the basics.

- Be available in-person to each other again.
- Come back to eye contact, heads being held upright again.
- Reintroduce common courtesies, the return of privacy and being considerate of another's preference to not being made privy to your mobile phone conversations.

2. Be mindful of others.

Looking down at a *smart*phone impedes engaging with an individual, a group, or an audience.

Whether with one or more friends, taking attendance, instructing a class, or giving a speech, etc., when *the thing* enters the equation, the atmosphere is altered. If you are delivering a speech, please consider bringing it on paper rather than pulling out your *smart*phone.

[140] Al-Anon Family Group Headquarters. (1992). In *Courage to change: One day at a time in Al-Anon II* (p. 3). New York, NY: Author.

Please be mindful in public spaces when there are others around you. Aside from the social implications, openly sharing your phone conversations with those nearby can invade their space and experience.

Exposing others to Electromagnetic Fields (EMFs) and their effects on our health is a growing concern.[141,142] This is an important area to be mindful of in terms of respect towards others and valuing them.

3. Use a wristwatch.

Get out your (not *smart*)wristwatch and put it on. Don't have one? Get one. Look at it. Good, you have just used a tool in order to eliminate the need for a device to see the time. A functional tool; perhaps a fashion statement as well. The wristwatch—an amazingly quick and easy step.

4. Reinstate a standard alarm clock.

Alarm clock—yes—remember those? They work well and will be another chain-link dropped from the pull towards *the thing*. Many different varieties—yours for the choosing—complete with a snooze feature that eliminates the need to tap–tap–tap your device upon awakening. Ready to go. Reliable. Most offer a battery backup in case of a power failure.

An alarm clock is also better for your health and sleep cycles. It reduces the *need* to have your device in the room in which you're sleeping (a highly recommended goal) and—bonus—it decreases the instant pull towards *the thing* immediately upon awakening.

[141] Naeem, Z. (2014, October). Health risks associated with mobile phones use. *International Journal of Health Sciences, 8*(4), v-vi. PMID: 25780365; PMCID: PMC4350886. Accessed 2024-10-02, https://pubmed.ncbi.nlm.nih.gov/25780365/)

[142] HealthyChildren.org. (2016, June 13). *Cell phone radiation and children's health: What parents need to know.* Accessed 2024-10-02, https://www.healthychildren.org/ English/ safety-prevention/all-around/Pages/Cell-Phone-Radiation-Childrens-Health.aspx

Again, please be aware that major health issues related to EMFs and blue light emissions are a concern.[143],[144] According to a 2020 study,[145] 70% of people still keep their EMF-emitting phone near their pillow while sleeping. (These are informative articles, and I encourage you to research further independently.)

Setting predetermined times in which you are *off-line* without outer distractions taking precedent is also key. Step away from it all. Re-curate your life in a way that brings positive change—and rewards.

You've got this, you are on your way.

5. Install a landline at home if you don't have one.

Many parents will argue that age-specific children need a cell phone when a parent is not home, and they need to contact them. This gives children a way to contact you without the need of a mobile device and all the negative aspects that come with them. Children aside, adults can also benefit from a landline in that they can separate themselves from their cell phones for a while. And there is a bonus—many landlines also work when there is a power outage.

6. Step back into the reality of connection.

Step back into the reality of *your* connection with people, animals, plants, with sights, sounds, touch, and feelings—with living—with being alive.

[143] Fields, R. D. (n.d.). Mind control by cell phone. *Scientific American.* Accessed 2024-10-02, https://www.scientificamerican.com/article/mind-control-by-cell/

[144] There are a variety of products available that claim to reduce EMFs. However, decreasing overall usage of wireless devices is the most effective and successful way of limiting the impact of EMFs.

[145] Rafique, N., Al-Asoom, L. I., Alsunni, A. A., Saudagar, F. N., Almulhim, L., & Alkaltham, G. (2020, June 23). Effects of mobile use on subjective sleep quality. *Nature and Science of Sleep, 12*, 357-364. doi:10.2147/NSS.S253375

> Connection is the energy that exists between people when they feel seen, heard, and valued; when they can give and receive without judgement; and when they derive sustenance and strength from the relationship.[146]

> Some of us fall into the trap of trying to analyze alcoholism [or any addiction, including ODC behaviour]. We don't want to accept the reality of our circumstances because we haven't yet figured out the rhyme and reason of it....we may never fully comprehend it. Nevertheless, *we have an obligation to ourselves to accept the reality in which we live and to act accordingly* [to get ourselves out from under the developer's grip].[147] (author's italics)

Yes. Yes, we do. We have an obligation—to ourselves—to accept the reality of this mess of un-reality to which we have fallen prey, and to arrive back to reality again.

7. Limit social media usage.

Are you feeling the all-consuming, time-draining, downward-pulling vortex into your device? How did it feel before when I mentioned scaling-down from two, three, or more to one platform? Choose one that will remain, or perhaps you will decide you no longer *need* any. Make a quick post to your friends and inform them of your thoughtful departure. You may choose to direct them to your handle on your remaining site and encourage them to find you there if they haven't already. For those you are close to, you may choose to provide your phone number or email address. Then again, if they do not already have these are they truly your

[146] Restrepo, S. (Director). (2019). *Brené Brown: The call to courage* [Documentary film]. Netflix. Accessed 2024-06-30, https://www.youtube.com/watch?v=ykn_uQrCzWQ

[147] Al-Anon Family Group. (1992). *Courage to change: One day at a time in Al-Anon II* (p. 61). New York, NY: Author.

friends? Give yourself a time-limit to keep the post up, and then begin your exit. Some companies have 30-day exit timeframe—another intricately-crafted strategy in which they ask you whether you're *really* sure. Some even say something like, "We will miss you—you know it doesn't have to be this way!" *Be prepared* as they do not make it easy for you to leave, so stay diligent on your mission.

You've got this! Just remember, you are gearing towards holding the reigns of your own life again.

So, what is in your tunnel?[148] Hold only that which nurtures you in creating the life you envision. If you are *truly* intent on getting your life back, realizing your goals, and taking the steps to achieve them, it will be difficult for you to have space inside your tunnel for outer distractions, such as extensive device usage. Remember—this is *your* life. You hold the power to curate and re-create your life experience.

Vision and capacity are yours by which to gain clarity. It will not likely happen overnight. Become clear on what, and who, is in your tunnel. Perhaps you are a 5-social-media being, or a 4. How can you cut that in half to begin? Whittle it down further from there. Also, go through the people and organizations you follow. How does it feel to view their posts? Does the content align with who you are and what you wish to surround yourself with? If it does not, unfollow—be ruthless.

What is it that you *truly* need?

Several years ago, a best girlfriend who is in my tunnel, gave me a wall-hanging which reads:

[148] If you need a refresher on the tunnel, see the "Further Education" chapter, "Tunnel-Vision" section.

Whatever you dream you can do, begin it.
Boldness has genius, power and magic in it.
Begin it now.
~ Johann Wolfgang von Goethe ~

I have never forgotten these words, this encouragement, and its simplicity. What do you dream? What are you doing today to get closer to your dream? How can you better disconnect with that which keeps you further away from your dreams? How can you reconnect with that which brings you closer to their fulfillment? Whom (and what) have you been neglecting? What (and who) has been lost in the belief in "the wave of the future?"

Think about your funeral service and the words spoken. Did you truly connect with others and leave a lasting impact on how you touched their lives? Or were your relationships sub-par and lacking in true connection because, wherever you were, you were not truly there? Wherever you are, be *All* there, or your tombstone may read:

Superior Swiper
Stop sign texter
Devoted their life to *the thing*

Rise-up, awaken. What can you accomplish when you lift your head-up, eyes forward again? Now is the time. No more moments, walking alongside the herd. (Did you hear the Moo again?) The time is now. When you step away from being *under the influence* of some*thing* or someone else, what would you like to be or do?

8. Streamline your other cell phone apps.

Now to the other apps. Let's look at them. How many apps do you actually use? How many of them do you *truly* need? For example, I started on a step-tracker when we had a challenge at work (with prize incentives). I had never used one before. Though I hadn't been monitoring the app, 2 years later I had only 1200 miles to make it to the Earth's core. I know I walk a lot and, really, I don't need an app to tell me that.

> Studies have shown that if our sleep tracker gives us a "bad sleep score" we actually feel worse and even perform worse I our daily tasks....Are we able to listen to what our bodies are telling us [rather than rely on fitness apps to guide us]?[149]

The take-home message: Let intuition guide, rather than tech.

Make a list of the apps you use and work towards cutting that amount in half. You can revisit this in the future to decrease the amount further. To remember to do this, set-up a reminder in your calendar for 30 days from now to further cut down the remaining amount by another half. Each time your device visits the chopping block, it re-aligns with your purpose and serves you better. Then again, perhaps you've already decided you will move towards a basic flip-phone or other models as previously discussed (see chapter, "I Can See It Now")—or go phone-less entirely.

Adjust your phone's settings to silence notifications/ recommendations or turn them off altogether, so you are not bombarded by "just for you" suggestions.

You can do it. I can hear the sounds of the chain-links dropping to the floor. Do not pick them up.

[149] See cycleseeds on Instagram. Accessed 2024-10-02, https://www.instagram.com/reel/C_GRALKo5uz/?igsh=Nzg0amF3YWFpcnhq

As each day passes, you are being liberated.

9. Set-up time-limits on using your device throughout the day.

Schedule times you permit yourself to check your remaining social media sites and emails. Give yourself time limits that you adhere to. As an example, 11am and 8pm for 10 minutes each session—using a timer ensures you stay within these parameters and allows for the temptation of rabbit-hole(ing). Be diligent with yourself. Perhaps you will feel better suited to the rule I have for my one (remaining) social media site in which I permit myself to view the first 5 posts that are on my feed. These days, half of those posts tend to be ads so, at times, those 5 may end up being only 3 or even 1. My belief is that I will see what I am meant to see—and I cast the rest aside—and no cheating. My family and friends know that if it is something important, they best send it to me via text message or let me know via a phone call or in-person. They also know I do not always answer right away, as I am *living* my life rather than being charmed by my phone.

10. Browse the internet confidentially by switching search engines

Replace your current search engine in your browser program on your devices (and computers) to browse the internet with Qwant[150]:

> The search engine where you are the user, not the product!
> …
> Fast, reliable results you can trust

[150] Suggested by a former employee interviewed in *The Social Dilemma* (2020) [Documentary film].

No storage of your search history,
no resale of your data.[151]

Qwant also doesn't "...bias the display of search results."[152]

11. Change settings to ensure all visual and sound notifications are eliminated.

Eliminate all banner notifications and turn off all app notifications with the exception of those that are truly needed—if any.

12. Reduce the number of your personal email addresses.

How many personal email addresses do you have? How many of them do you *truly* need? Depending on your answer, attempt to cut this number in half as well, and let those affected know of your change.

Attending to your email when at home is key to not allowing you to be ruled by it as you move through your day. Allot a certain amount of time to look at and respond to emails. Find what works for you.

13. Consider alternative device styles.

Consider a flip-phone, jelly-phone, or light-phone rather than the current *smart* versions, which are often far from designing your life with *smart* choices. Be a voice for change. Supply and demand. With big tech dominating the market, they wouldn't have it any other way. There are very few not-*smart* phone options currently in the market, particularly in Canada. Upon arriving at the local mobile phone provider to make the switch to a flip-phone, they provided one smaller sub-par 1980s-*esque*

[151] Qwant [Website]. Accessed 2024-12-06, https://about.qwant.com/en

[152] *Wikipedia: The Free Encyclopedia.* (n.d.). Qwant. Accessed 2024-12-02, https://en.wikipedia.org/wiki/Qwant

alternative. With enough users making the switch to non-*smart* phones, it will put pressure on the market which is monopolized by the giants.

14. Incorporate more activities into your life.

Of course, we all have duties to attend to in our homes, workplaces, and lives. Yet incorporating some me-time and down-time into your activities is vitally important as well. Spending time in silence, meditating, or listening to music, reading a good book, interacting with others (see "Believe" chapter), walking, being in nature, spending time with pets, visiting friends and family, tending to our Earth or gardens, exercising, etc.

What is interesting and fun to you? Allow this to be your new focus. Rather than scroll away your life, go after your passion and purpose.[153] Move your body, which stimulates your mind and contributes to your well-being. And do things that bring you joy.

Making effective choices is a process of becoming aware of how we have allowed *the thing* to seep into every facet of our daily lives—in all the places, all the time. We are neglecting our children. We are robbing them of their childhood experiences by placing devices in their hands. We are also neglecting ourselves, each other, and our planet by having allowed *the thing* to take precedence.

With reducing your habitual device usage, you could very well be amazed with the results. The new-found time and space you reclaim from *the thing* will be a blessing. On the other hand, it can make you feel restless or anxious for a time. This is not unusual. Go easy on yourself and breathe into the feelings as, with any new habit, it takes time to feel at ease.

[153] Abraham-hicks.com speaks of "purpose and passion" and offer myriad insightful information surrounding these topics, among others.

Where Were We?

So, would you like to hear what happened next? Remember, everyone has a story. You do, I do, the man on the corner with no shoes, dirty feet, and a cup for change does. Of course he does. I hazard to guess that oftentimes these people have more to their stories than many of us. How did he get there, what pain has he endured, what has he lost along the way aside from what you presume is in front of you? At this point, will you have arrived enough to look-up and make eye contact, perhaps give him a smile? Do this with people. Connect again. Send them love, which increases the collective of positive energy.

Remember, *everyone* has a story.

Our house (I no longer referred to it as a home) remained for sale without my access to it for several months until eventually becoming listed with a different realtor from an area outside ours. He said he had run into a neighbour who had told him "You will be hard-pressed to sell this house for $800,000 after what has been going on in there for the last 6 months." Not only was the house down $250,000 from our original list price, but there were also multiple liens and charges against its title. Crushing.

Yet I continued—continued to make plans to move out of the community once the school year ended. Continued to accumulate debt in doing so. One person would not leave and we five were uprooted because of this. One sober mother who continued to navigate the next steps methodically to safeguard the interests of those I had in my care (including myself). I had few options during this next rebuilding phase.

My parent's home was offered as a solution to house us, and I was so grateful for this. I moved back in with my mom, three sons in tow. It would be for 1 year. Grateful. Entirely grateful. Not at all what I had imagined for this stage in life, but completely grateful. My mom already had our St. Bernard-X in her care since I had first rented the place with "no pets" as a bylaw. So we were together again, and we made it work.

In time, our house sold, and my husband was forced to leave. I was unsure what his level of sobriety was at this point. Eventually, he became *clean* again and was able to get his son back out of foster care. I will always be grateful to this family who took our son into their care, and it is my belief God played a large part in his placement.

This makes me think of a time when my husband had arranged to meet at a local big box store (which I loathe). It was obvious he was not yet sober. The meeting was organized for him to purchase a birthday gift for our middle son, who was also present. He looked at his phone incessantly while filling his shopping basket with multiple bottles of aerosol air fresheners and Live Clean® brand shampoo and bodywash bottles. Through my grief, I laughed inside thinking: "He is going to need a lot more than that to live clean."

My husband had not seen our other boys for over 2 years. It was a long road of slowly rebuilding trust—and it was a *very* tedious process. As part of the ministry's ongoing involvement, he scheduled his visits with the boys, and *he* choose those who would supervise the visits (ludicrous). Due to their questionable character, I needed to step-in to screen these people. Next was the ongoing issue of his dangerous cell phone use, excessive speeding, and blaring music antics while driving. He was not permitted to transport the children for several months, which meant that I had to do the driving an hour each way to facilitate his visits with them. None of it was easy.

There was also the ongoing impression he had been giving his son—that *I* had rejected the child in his time of need. As always, laying the blame on anyone but himself. Someone else was responsible—deflection away from themselves in any and all circumstances—this is the addict's way. Words spoken freely in front of my other two sons, which I attempted to untangle in a diplomatic way. Grace, dignity, humility, work. It was apparent that I had become the scapegoat again—the pawn in his game of life. I suffered greatly during this time. I asked God to assist him and his son in finding their way to honesty, integrity, and a peaceful resolve.

As for me, it has been a long road of learning forgiveness. I once attended a seminar of a sizable group, mostly women, coming together to share safe space, led by a world-renowned facilitator. She guided us in the use and application of essential oils to assist in releasing stagnant and stuck emotions, along with deep breathing, movement, mindfulness, and journalling. While there, the topic for the day's events was brought forward. Forgiveness. I shuddered going straight to a place of "I will *never* forgive him (or his mother)!"

I was angry, depleted and, even with the program that I hold dear to me, I did not feel as though I would ever forgive them. But I would never give-up on this prospect. We journalled as instructed, we were asked questions, the light dimmed, and Zen music played. I sobbed and found it difficult to be silent. At one point the facilitator stood near me, I felt her directing the negative energy away from me. Though the process was deep, I did not leave that day with any feeling of forgiveness—it would take a lot more unravelling to peel away the levels of wounding.

I continued. We moved into my parent's home, and shortly thereafter the pandemic hit. Lockdown, shutdown; my energetic sons, me, my mother, and our St. Bernard-X. It was difficult, we were patient, and we made the best of it. We practised online yoga together in the living room. We took walks in the forest with our gentle giant.[154] We coloured hearts and taped them to the windows. We banged pots and pans in support of frontline workers. After having left our beloved community, all the boys started at their new schools with those they did not know. It was most difficult for my oldest who left his lifelong friendships, transitioning into Grade 9 where he knew one student in the entire school. All we had built and all that was familiar had changed for us. It was difficult, but we had each other, and that was beautiful.

Not long after the first full lockdown, our beautiful dog became ill. Her hind legs completely seized. They were not able to support her any longer. It was devastating as I could see she wasn't ready to go. Her eyes did not speak as if to say, "I am ready, it is my time, I thank you for all that we have shared." She panted, like laughter with each breath, clear eyes which looked to us as they always had. Like horses do, they seem to look inside of you—intuitive, knowing—as if to say, "but we really just got back together, and I love you, and can we have more time, please?"

The blood work and x-rays were inconclusive, not revealing anything abnormal. Yet she was unable to walk. Transporting her was close to impossible. Using a camp blanket, my slight mom and I tried to hoist-up her hindquarters. Our veterinarian working only a couple of days a week with strict rules of one masked family member being allowed in at a time. She was 8½ years old, born on my birthday. Even though this giant breed only had a lifespan of 5 to 8 years, I was not ready to let *her* go.

[154] Our St. Bernard-X.

Our dear Rocha—the name had hit me in the side of the head, the left side, behind my ear, when she came to us at 8 weeks old. "What does it mean?" I wondered, as I held her on my lap coming back from the farm that rainy night where she had been born with 14 other siblings. When we arrived home, I looked-up it's meaning. Rocha, a Portuguese word meaning "The Rock." (Though my father had taught us some Afrikaans, I did not know any Portuguese.) Of course. She would be the rock of our family from that day onward.

We said goodbye, and the pain and the loss of so much that had been imbedded within deepened. What was once our family unit had dissolved, beam-by-beam, tile-by-tile, up in smoke, lost to the shadows. The loss of our dog was the final piece, yet somehow a strong and functional unit remained. There was *still* a rock at its centre. Proven time-and-time again, one who had travelled many roads at this point resilient, determined, and unshakable. I was patient, I waited, and I had faith. I continued to continue.

Life does not always happen the way we would like. Those who have grown-up in the *instant world* seem to have less patience in general. They have become accustomed to things happening instantly with the click of a button. This is not how life is for many, perhaps most, in the *real* world. When they do not experience instant gratification, they can feel irritable, restless, and unsatisfied. As for me, I needed to learn to be patient, to wait and rest in the faith that had grown within me since first finding it "inside the rooms."[155] Some might say this is a peculiar place to find God, but this is where it began for me. Though many find other ways, this organization

155 "Inside the rooms" is a term used to describe AA meetings.

saved me. It gave me back my life while showing me the way to live without alcohol—a poison to my mind, body, and spirit.

In the years to follow, I began to perceive how *smart*phones were poisoning our minds, bodies, and spirits, yet the symptoms from *the thing*'s usage are not as obvious as those from drugs and alcohol—a slow burn, not as glaring.

During this time, I had begun working in the field of special education for which I had re-schooled. My cap and gown ceremony scheduled, I had my diploma and could progress into something steady that was void of the peaks and valleys my previous job as a realtor at times encountered. I accepted employment in a local elementary school and was assigned a student who had previously lost four education assistants due to his extreme and difficult nature. If anyone could stay and make a change, it was me—or so I thought.

We live in a province where inclusive education means that any student can attend schools in regular age-appropriate classes with a supportive environment. I was aware that this student could become physical, and I felt I was prepared to face him head-on with my training and life experience. After all, he was a child. The beginning brought about some positive exchanges and an inside view of what some of the traits of autism could include. He was highly intelligent and had an acute ability to recall minute facts and details. His preferred activity was to hold interview sessions with school staff. Each session was granted as a reward for completion of unpreferred schoolwork.

It was a big change from the work I had done in years past. I enjoyed the overall school atmosphere, the beauty of the fish tank in the front entranceway, and most staff members were upbeat and enthusiastic.

Months later another lockdown had us unable to be in schools, and we began Zoom sessions along with my kids being at home for theirs. Once we were able to return to school, there was another brief honeymoon phase, and then the extreme behaviours emerged more frequently. On one occasion, I suffered a fall down an embankment and my pants were ripped resulting in a bloodied knee and a permanent scar on my foot. I was offered the remainder of the day off.

It became more apparent what I had gotten myself into with this child. I met another woman who had previously liaised with this student and had a 1-inch patch of hair ripped from her head. Both of us were spat-on, kicked, slapped in the face, and criticized about our clothing. Though this student was an immigrant, he shouted at others saying, "Go back to your own country!" which made me shudder.

As the instances became more extreme at the workplace, each time the student yanked my hair, I would have a sudden reaction in which my eyes would fill with tears. It was not necessarily the pain, but rather a sensation that would run through my body. It had become highly apparent that I would need Ukeru Systems defence pads to be able to work with this student, and I enrolled in a full-day training for their effective usage.

During the training, I saw the link to my past assault when one man grabbed the hair on the back of my head, while another swiftly kicked me in the jaw with his steel-toed boot. We had been asked to share what came-up for us during the training, so it felt safe to share this story with fellow participants. As I spoke, the room quieted to a pin-drop silence. When I had finished the story, the facilitator said the account was so intense that she needed some time to be able to continue. It had never occurred to me that this story would so greatly affect them. For me, it had happened 20 years ago, and I had worked through many of the emotions surrounding this event.

I knew then *why* the strikes to the right side of my face, the hair pulling, the verbal attacks, and the anxiety I felt when around this student were affecting me so greatly. With continuing to work with him and witnessing the impact of his actions on the school community, I recognized that he was brought into my life to help me address the residual distresses from my previous traumas. It had become apparent to me that I had further work to do in this area.

No-one should ever have to tolerate and/or witness such extreme behaviour—anywhere—let alone day-after-day in the school system.

I am all for inclusive education and inclusivity in general, however the current inclusivity policies appear to be greatly flawed. They lack equal consideration being given to special needs students and those who care for these students. Behavioural issues vary greatly from student to student and are on the rise; special education assistants are at risk in working with volatile students. Those who are assessing complaints need to be professionals with the specialized training in evaluating such situations. Regular in-person assessments may be required and, in some cases, placement in an alternative school environment may be necessary for the safety and well-being of all involved.

At times I had visions of carrying a neon poster-board up-and-down the steep highly trafficked street that read: "I have just dropped my kids off at school, and I am now headed to work to be punched, kicked, slapped and spit-on in support of Inclusion BC's Inclusive Education Program." But this is the current system's mandate.

I was chosen for this role, and signed-up for it, willingly. I stepped into this placement with the best of intentions but was unaware of the system's deficiencies—that is, endangering employees and other students in the process.

After 23 more attacks and the detailed reporting process that goes along with each one, there was a final assault which would come to be my last. I won't divulge all the details, but I was cornered beside a filing cabinet in the back of the room while the defence pads were at the front of the room. I had touched my student's binder. He became irate and struck me in the face. He hit me in the face again, kicked, and lunged at me, and spit directly into my eye—we had just arrived back in school after the COVID-19 lockdown. In that moment, I was done and, although in my heart I truly wanted to be a stable person for this student, this time I had to again choose myself.

I finally took a firm stand. Once I became vocal, things happened quickly. The occupational health and safety representative came and listened attentively. But in the days that followed, union reps became involved and claimed this kind of behaviour was commonplace. Their attitude was that one "best get used to it." I questioned how is it appropriate for a class of Grade 1 students to be walking down the hall witnessing a student screaming and swearing, which echoed through the school, while assaulting his care workers and lying on the staircase kicking his legs wildly? This certainly wasn't what I wanted my children to witness at school.

The human resources representative said this is a good opportunity for students to be aware of what they may face while out in their communities as grown adults. "Really?" I vocalized. "I am grown woman, and I have *never* encountered behaviours like this in my community" thankfully. Yet this was their standpoint, and so it was. Please don't misunderstand, as I've said, I am all for inclusion—however this student's behaviour was not only unpredictable, it was also violent. And at the cost of the employees and fellow students' well-being and safety, I question such school board policies.

The incidents with this student triggered deep wounds and injustices to resurface, which drove me to revisit the feelings I had buried since I was assaulted many years ago. I created the time and space to dive deeper into the depths of traumas past.

Where Is the Love?

Black Eyed Peas released a song in 2003:

> Father, Father, father help us
> Send some guidance from above
> 'cause people got me, got me questioning
> Where is the love?....
>
> Wrong information always shown by the media
> Negative images is the main criteria
> Infecting the young minds faster than bacteria....
>
> That's the reason why sometimes I'm feelin' under
> That's the reason why sometimes I'm feelin' down[156]

Yes—and that was then. That was before—before the full infiltration. That was when media was on televisions and in movies. Now we are being barraged constantly, unendingly, full-time, all the time, in all the ways. Pummelling our senses, our eyes, our minds, our ears. But one question remains: Where is the love? Does the moment of love that you feel from the photos you see from Jimmy's Tae Kwon Do tournament protect you from the other negativity you ingest on all the other avenues along the way? Ask yourself.

Like anything important, we must take inventory, create a pros and cons list, and make a conscious choice as to whether this is the direction we want for ourselves and those who depend on us.

[156] Black Eyed Peas. (2003). Where is the love [Song]. On *Elephunk* [Album] (Songwriters: will.i.am, Justin Timberlake, Taboo, apl.de.ap, Printz Board, Michael Fratantuno, & George Pajon Jr.; Producers: will.i.am & Ron Fair). Labels: A&M, will.i.am, Interscope. Accessed 2024-06-30, https://www.azlyrics.com/lyrics/blackeyedpeas/whereisthelove.html

> We only got (One world, one world)....
> ....And something's wrong with it (Yeah)
> something's wrong with it (Yeah)...[157]

2003. Check your calendar. We aren't there anymore. We are here now, in this time, 20+ years later. And where are we? Are we farther ahead, or further behind. Is this truly progress? Ask yourself: Is *the thing* truly advancing our species? I'll wager that you already knew the answer before I asked you.

I mentioned before that my Number 2 personality trait is positivity, and that is precisely the direction in which I would like to see humanity moving. My dad used to always say, "I'm on your side," and I would like to say to you, dear reader, "I am on your side, too."

I urge you to ask yourself, "Where is the love?" Is it on TikTok? How about Twitter?[158] Is the love truly on Facebook? Really, is it? How about Instagram, Reddit,...? (You continue the list.) Are these where the love is? Next ask yourself: Is our attachment to these devices actually "leading us *away* from unity?"[159] Take a look out there. Sit on a bench (head-up) and watch people for awhile. Do this a few times in different locations, if able. "Instead of spreading love, we're spreading [and generating] animosity."[160] Listen to the song. Now, multiply its concepts by 100, or 1,000, or perhaps even 10,000. That is where we are now. Why? Because we have *allowed* this to be. We, the people.

[157] Black Eyed Peas. (2003). Where is the love [Song]. On *Elephunk* [Album] (Songwriters: will.i.am, Justin Timberlake, Taboo, apl.de.ap, Printz Board, Michael Fratantuno, & George Pajon Jr.; Producers: will.i.am & Ron Fair). Labels: A&M, will.i.am, Interscope. Accessed 2024-06-30, https://www.azlyrics.com/lyrics/blackeyedpeas/ whereisthelove.html

[158] At the time of this writing, Twitter had changed its name to X.

[159] Black Eyed Peas. (2003). Where is the love [Song]. On *Elephunk* [Album].

[160] Black Eyed Peas. (2003). Where is the love [Song]. On *Elephunk* [Album].

We have come to "*believe* the hype [author's italics]"[161] and we have willfully consented to being consumed by it. We may have intended to increase our connections with people, yet we have failed to recognize the resulting negativity—that is, what *the thing* actually *takes* from us.

Dramatic? Look around.

> In this world that we('re) living in, people keep on giving in....
> [Yes. Listen to it. Yes, they do.]
> Not respecting each other, deny thy brother....
> If you never know truth then you never know love.... [Yes.]
> Selfishness got us followin' the *wrong direction*....
> Gotta keep my faith alive 'til love is found....[162] [Yes. Yes.]

I'm not saying there isn't value in some of what is viewed. But how can we know truth when we rely on *fake* news and the media's spin, deceptiveness and manipulation, others' inflated opinions, advertisements and propaganda, influencers, etcetera? How?

> It is as though we have less and less control over who we are and what we believe.[163]

> Imagine a world where no one believes anything [that is] true.... That's where all this is heading.[164]

[161] Public Enemy. (1988). Don't believe the hype [Song]. On *It takes a nation of millions to hold us back* [Album] (Songwriters: Carl Ridenhour, Hank Shocklee, Eric "Vietnam" Sadler, & William Drayton; Producer: The Bomb Squad). Labels: Def Jam, Columbia, CBS Records.

[162] Black Eyed Peas. (2003). Where is the love [Song]. On *Elephunk* [Album] (Songwriters: will.i.am, Justin Timberlake, Taboo, apl.de.ap, Printz Board, Michael Fratantuno, & George Pajon Jr.; Producers: will.i.am & Ron Fair). Labels: A&M, will.i.am, Interscope. Accessed 2024-06-30, https://www.azlyrics.com/lyrics/blackeyedpeas/ whereisthelove.html

[163] Justin Rosenstein (inventor of Google Drive, Gmail Chat, Facebook Pages, and the Facebook Like button) interview in Orlowski, J. (2020). *The social dilemma* [Documentary film] (Writers: Davis Coombe, Vickie Curtis, Jeff Orlowski; Producer: Larissa Rhodes). Exposure Labs, Argent Pictures, The Space Program; Netflix.

[164] Tristan Harris interview in *The Social Dilemma* (2020) [Documentary film].

After a time, alcoholics "can not...differentiate the true from the false."[165] This is what alcohol does to the human brain after repeated exposure. Excessive device usage appears to follow suit. With repeated exposure to the falsifications and fake news, the user is unable to differentiate the true from the false.

> ...We [will] probably destroy our civilization through willful ignorance, through some sort of bizarre autocratic dysfunction. We [will] probably fail to meet the challenge of climate change. We [will] probably degrade the world's democracies so that they fall into some sort of bizarre autocratic dysfunction. We [will] probably ruin the global economy. Uh, we probably, um, don't survive.... I really do view it as existential.[166]

"Father father"[167] (mother mother, or whatever or whomever you believe in) created you, which created this planet that we are incredibly blessed to walk upon (or roll or crawl upon), "send some guidance from above, 'cause people got me, got me questioning where is the love?"[168]

"Can you practise what you preach [or will] you turn the other cheek?"[169] Can you see *the thing* in a different way and put it away, put it down, discipline yourself to come back? Can you, or—more importantly—will you? Are you able to gain clarity on how you neglect

[165] Alcoholics Anonymous World Services. (2001). *Alcoholics Anonymous: The story of how many thousands of men and women have recovered from alcoholism* (rev ed.; p. 8). New York, NY: Author.

[166] Jaron Lanier (computer scientist, computer philosophy writer, and technologist) interview in Orlowski, J. (2020). *The social dilemma* [Documentary film] (Writers: Davis Coombe, Vickie Curtis, Jeff Orlowski; Producer: Larissa Rhodes). Exposure Labs, Argent Pictures, The Space Program; Netflix.

[167] Black Eyed Peas. (2003). Where is the love [Song]. On *Elephunk* [Album] (Songwriters: will.i.am, Justin Timberlake, Taboo, apl.de.ap, Printz Board, Michael Fratantuno, & George Pajon Jr.; Producers: will.i.am & Ron Fair). Labels: A&M, will.i.am, Interscope. Accessed 2024-06-30, https://www.azlyrics.com/lyrics/blackeyedpeas/ whereisthelove.html

[168] Black Eyed Peas. (2003). Where is the love [Song]. On *Elephunk* [Album].

[169] Black Eyed Peas. (2003). Where is the love [Song]. On *Elephunk* [Album].

those around you in its presence? Start by making small changes, or perhaps you already *feel* that it doesn't need to be that slow. Put the song on. Dance. You've got this. Twenty years ago, and here we are now. A devolution of our species. *The thing* has become the dictator. We have set-up ourselves for *the absence of presence* that has never been experienced by any generation that has come before.

I think many people know, they feel *it*, but cannot quite put their finger on what *it* is. They resign themselves (Moo) to the-wave-of-the-future justification, "It's not going anywhere." I am not saying it has to "go anywhere" (well, maybe on silent in your purse or murse[170]), just that its usage needs to be examined and, subsequently, modified.

Then recently, I was on a nature walk and saw this sticker on a garbage can.

"Wake-up before we all live in a digital hell!!!"

It spoke to me with strength.

I am not alone in this—there are others who feel this way too—and are (perhaps) *seeing* the signs as well. But it's not enough to just feel and/or see the signs—action must be taken as well. We can begin to view this as a *fascinating* social experiment that has reached the failure stage and, as we know better, we choose better.

There have been many cultural norms made in our society today: For example, the "mommy wine culture" being glorified as something that is needed in order for moms to cope with the stresses of all that we encounter in this modern era. I saw a mom walking with her teenage daughter on a sunny yet cool weekend afternoon. Her heather-grey

[170] A man's purse or a "man purse."

sweatshirt read "This wine is making me awesome." I have seen this shirt several times before. What came to mind immediately were a few things. First, something like, "It is so unfortunate you feel like you need wine to make you awesome." Second, hmmm, "It's noon on a Saturday." It's 5 o'clock somewhere—right? Next, of course, I thought about the message that this sends to her daughter. "Mommy is not awesome but, if she adds wine, then she is…." And lastly, I thought, "Well perhaps she just didn't have any other clean clothes."

Now swap-over to your device and ask yourself this question: "Are you in denial or, like so many others, are you okay with your life being drained away by the outer pull towards *the thing*?" All the messaging, in all the places, all the time. My thought is that we are each individually created to be awesome without the use of mood- or mind-influencing substances, including devices. And if you are struggling to find *your* "awesome" without crutches to assist, then it may be time to uncover how those *needs* came to be and how you can get back to being your naturally awesome self. It may take time, but it is well worth discovering. It may also require a new set of *compadres* to journey alongside.

God knows that, when I first began my passage into sobriety, it required a full re-vamp of those with which I spent my time. Like my friend who claimed, "But you are so fun when you are drinking!" What? I had projectile-vomited on her CD tower from top to bottom.[171] Just pause for a moment and visualize the number of crevices, boxes, cracks, metal, flooring that was involved in this clean-up. Fun. Fun to be stumbling around, unable to see, others telling me my eyes were "just

[171] A CD tower is a tall slender CD storage shelf unit.

gone," shoe-less, hiccupping for 18 hours, which went away while being driven to the hospital. Fun. If *this* is fun then....

My point is that changing our ways will often be met with resistance. It has been said, "misery loves company," and so do cattle. Cattle love company. Who else would they be able to stand around with chewing their cud all day and defecating on the ground? Think about all the people walking blindly down the street with their heads down or FaceTiming very loudly in front of you. Consider the openly public cud-chewing conversations and the numerous other bystanders who are subjected to them. The defecation that exists on the internet is vast. Not much different if you ask me. Moo.

The other day I sat at a stoplight beside a transit bus and saw through the window a woman sitting flailing one arm around while holding her phone in her other hand, talking to the screen. No rules. Free for all. I thought, "Oh, I can only imagine what the other passengers are having to listen to!" Judgemental, yes, but I would say that regardless of its nature, such conversations should be scheduled during private time. To me, its simple. We need "No Phone Zone" areas or policies put in place where calls and videos are not permitted. Rules could easily be posted to help people to become more conscious and ultimately behave differently.

I get it—*the thing* has brainwashed our society at a rate that many have not been able to fully grasp. Those in charge rely on keeping us on their apps to build their platforms further while ensuring they hit the top spots of the Forbes List.[172] And who am I to call attention to this issue?

[172] Forbes List. *The world's real-time billionaires.* Accessed 2024-06-30, https://www.forbes.com/lists/list-directory/#17691018b274 and https://www.forbes.com/real-time-billionaires/#347a032a3d78

Well, I am an individual who has seen and experienced the revolting side to human nature and the effects that hiding and masking can have, which proves to be harmful in the long run. This is not sustainable without serious repercussions. I am a woman who knew life before *smart*phones and social media and who lived and breathed in a world of real-life connections with others. A smile, a gesture, a good morning, a greeting, eye contact, a phone call to a friend—time spent together. Such small interactions are vital, they help us thrive.

I am also a woman who sees the potential in all that we humans can do. We have the opportunity to truly come together and achieve amazing progress, yet most of us have resigned ourselves to the vortex into which we have been sucked. So much hope and promise yet we lack individual and collective action.

I also believe in our ability to lift-up one another and the domino effect of doing things differently. I believe in our capability to produce lasting positive change.

System Reboot

In my view, the only one capable of rebooting your system is you. As with alcoholism or drug addiction (or addiction to porn, sex, gambling, food, shopping, etc.), the first step is admitting there is a problem. Admitting that you have developed a habit of picking-up your little buddy upon awakening in the morning, or shortly thereafter. From there, you begin to check-in on all *the things*. Keeping it near you throughout the remainder of the day and into the evening; responding to its chimes, dings, pings, red alerts to ensure you keep checking, keep using. Picking-up, checking, picking-up, using, checking, picking-up. Last thing at night, just one more time—just one more hit. Some people may even fall asleep with *the thing* cradled in their hand. Like the red-wine glass my ex-husband fell asleep with on the couch, only to awaken when he lost hold of it, and it smashed on the floor. Are you rolling your eyes right now thinking, "But it's not the same!" And why do you think it's not the same, or *what* makes you think it's not the same?

Something that hijacks your focus and takes your attention elsewhere with every scroll—a significant issue to explore. Do you obsessively think about *the thing*? You may not even be aware of it as a conscious thought. Remember, carefully crafted, designed in such a way that you don't *consciously* think about it. It does that for you, which is why it is so insidious. It's there for you, always. It will not *allow* you to forget.

Time lost, so much time lost.

There are those who have said, "Okay. I admit that I am addicted to it, but I am okay with that." This is one of my favourites. Alright, so let me get this straight. You are fine with years of your life being wasted, lost to *the thing*, no replacement of the time? You're okay with our collective human race being moulded towards the inability to walk with our heads up and countless people losing touch with their true selves? You are at peace with the resulting decrease of self-esteem due to many things, including the often-false comparison of others, alarming rates of suicides, and funding and support of extremist and separatist groups? I understand you have become accustomed to the ease of viewing your distant uncle's birthday pics. Yet at the same time, such platforms also connect insane wingnuts across the globe (who likely otherwise would not have found each other) to band together, train, and further mass destruction.[173] You are okay with astronomical rates of predatory behaviour, luring of children, people falsely impersonating others, scams, and outlets for the sickest of the sick to get away with things we had never known possible previously?

At this point, it is foolish to not see the bigger picture, to live in a bubble and not see how our individual involvement contributes to these platforms thriving. Allow yourself to see it for *all* that it is.

When are we going to get back to living and stop the obsession with scrolling others' lives—the mockery of memes, misogyny, anger, hatred, jealousy, righteousness—with their underlying tones so well-disguised. Though most of the world's people are good people, with the continuing advancement of technologies, caustic individuals are able to locate and access like-minded people who wish to engage in malicious and horrific practices. Through supporting these platforms, we enable the trolls of the world to keep their belittling comments and toxic spew alive. The range

[173] Cynthia M. Wong (Human Rights Watch senior internet researcher) interview in Orlowski, J. (2020). *The social dilemma* [Documentary film] (Writers: Davis Coombe, Vickie Curtis, Jeff Orlowski; Producer: Larissa Rhodes). Exposure Labs, Argent Pictures, The Space Program; Netflix.

of dangerousness is vast. When asked the question "What are you most worried about?" Tim Kendall's response was "In the shortest time horizon—civil war."[174]

We are moving further away from ourselves, from our *true* selves, and adding another addiction which has become a more socially acceptable and glaring dependency.

When are we going to get back to living in real time?

> I don't have to tell you that hate and fear are being sown online all across the world....This dark undertow which is connecting us all globally...is flowing via the technology platforms.[175]

As each individual moves away from these platforms, one-by-one we will take a stand against the devastating side of these social media apps. If we stop engaging with these people, if we don't reinforce their behaviour, we are not giving them the attention they seek and there will be less opportunity for such destructiveness to multiply.

> It is foolish to not see the bigger picture, to live in a bubble and not see how our individual involvement contributes to these platforms thriving.

Trolls aside, there are all the advertisements we see on *the thing*. Think about all the items you have purchased that you did not intend to buy prior to picking up your *smart*phone. How many items have you ordered that were promoted by either a celebrity or a young beautiful

[174] Tim Kendall (former director of monetization at Facebook, former president of Pinterest) interview in Orlowski, J. (2020). *The social dilemma* [Documentary film] (Writers: Davis Coombe, Vickie Curtis, Jeff Orlowski; Producer: Larissa Rhodes). Exposure Labs, Argent Pictures, The Space Program; Netflix.

[175] Carole Cadwalladr interview in Amer, K., & Noujaim, J. (Directors). (2019). *The great hack* [Documentary film] (Producers: Karim Amer, Geralyn White Dreyfous, Judy Korin, & Pedro Kos; Writers: Karim Amer, Erin Barnett, & Pedro Kos). The Othrs; Netflix.

person? Once in your hand, did you discover the product(s) didn't contain the advertised ingredients, or contained carcinogenic or other components you would have never purchased had you been able to see them in the first place? The bombardment of all *the thing*s—all the pop-ups, the notifications, the algorithms—all of it from all the angles.

But you can get your life back. If you don't know what it is to have a *real* life, you too can arrive back on this planet with the collective others who take back the reigns and decide to live once again. H.U.G. people unite! If you have not yet noticed, Earth and all its inhabitants desperately need this. We are the only species that is actively destroying life on our planet. There is more at stake than ever in our human existence, and with much of the world's population having succumbed to pull of their devices, they are not left with the time and energy to do what is needed. We need to ask ourselves, "What is the priority?" It is truly an urgent choice we must make.

The world needs you—now. As we have already established, it is next to impossible to focus on what is required when our attention is turned downward towards a material object (really, that is all it is). Technology developers continue working to drive the messaging beyond the current targeted pathways deeper into the brain stem to achieve a more lasting impact than ever before.[176] We have allowed *the thing* to become the dictator, big tech plays the part of puppeteers, and we are the marionettes. We have given *the thing* our power.

[176] Zafar, A. (2023, November 17). *Social media gets teens hooked while feeding aggression and impulsivity, and researchers think they know why.* Accessed 2024-06-30, https://www.cbc.ca/news/health/smartphone-brain-nov14-1.7029406 In particular, see the "Struggle to focus" section "Watch | *Brain activity changes when scrolling social media" video.*

But in light of what you now know, you can stop this consequence if you so choose. If you subscribe to the "I am okay with that" school of thought, then Namaste.[177] I wish you nothing but the best. On the other hand, if you desire to live otherwise, then I invite you to begin your transformation:

Begin Your Transformation

- Close your eyes.
- Inhale…Exhale…
- Inhale…Exhale…
- Continue to breathe normally and comfortably.
- With your palms open and facing upwards on your lap, breathe, relax into your body, and breathe again.
- Breathe-in the thought of what it is you wish to bring to the world.
- Sit within the peace of an inhale and ponder:
  How is it that I wish to be in this lifetime?
- Ask yourself:
  How can I start today to adjust the relationship I have developed with my mobile device?
  (Remind yourself, this is a material item which, time-after-time, causes your attention to be pulled-away from being present.)
- Sit and breathe-in this question.
  See what answer percolates into your consciousness.

[177] "Namaste is an expression of appreciation and respect towards another person, entity or deity. It can be used as a hello greeting and even as a goodbye, so you might say Namaste upon meeting someone, or before parting ways." In Corozza, M. (2018, December 5). *The Definition of namaste* (para. 1). Thrive Yoga & Wellness website. Accessed 2024-03-17, https://thriveyogawellness.com/thrive-blog/the-meaning-of-namaste-why-do-we-say-namaste-in-yoga

- After some time, ask yourself:
  How do I ensure that, wherever I am, I am all there?
  What small changes can I begin to do today?
  How do I see my relationships evolving once I release my grip on the thing*?*
- Continue to breathe comfortably.
- When you are ready, gently move your hands and feet around in circles, then open your eyes.
- If you keep a journal, now is a good time to write down what came-up for you and develop a plan as to next steps in your voyage of freeing yourself from *the thing*.

A reminder that discipline and practice are required to instill a new way of thinking, and being and setting gauges will help. A useful tactic is scheduling time-limits for using your device throughout your day. See "Heads-Up Strategies" section in the "Choices" chapter for other helpful suggestions.

Now let us be mindful that it is one thing to make changes in our own lives, but what about those with whom we spend our time?

If it feels sufficient to dine with your spouse, sit across the table while they, and possibly you, are also glued to your respective devices, then fill your boots. For me, I choose otherwise. A few years ago, I had informed my sons and my (then) husband that when we were out for a meal, if they chose to be on their devices, I would leave. A few months later when we were dining-out, they all sat glued to the big screen TVs. I calmly stated that "We are not here to watch screens. If you are unable to devote 1 hour of your time to having a conversation together while sharing food, then I am not interested in staying." Now I do take ownership of agreeing to go to this "big screen" restaurant that evening, however they knew my standpoint on screen-time prior to that (whether it be mobile device or

TV-screen). I did end-up leaving, and I have declined offers of going to that establishment since. I share this story in order to illustrate that we do have a choice. It was my choice—and their choices too.

What about you? Do you need to be in a relationship so desperately that you would rather sit across the table from someone who spends the entire time staring into their device? You might want to think about that. Then again, if you are also doing that, I suppose it is a match made in (unconnected) heaven.

Speaking of being desperate (or not), I extended my initial 1-month dating app rule to a total of 3 months. Again, developers of these platforms are skilled at keeping you on them—see, they even got me. ;) Due to the significant differences between those I met in-person and their online profiles, I went against my 1-site rule and tried a second that claimed to cater to high-end professionals. I attempted a total of eight dates. Of those, one resulted in subsequent dates. Overall, this was actually a good experience for me as I had never really dated before. (This was the positive.)

One of my dates was obsessed with trying to arrange further time together, pushing me to meet him at his home, and sweetening his pitch with the fact that his building had free parking outside. Wow. He also complained about the cost of parking outside the restaurant repeatedly while we were dining. High end professional—really? Another date must have been 25 years older than his online profile picture. He spoke the whole time about the business we were both in as he was new and wanted "some pointers...." Snore. Upon moving toward the other site that was said to have a strict identity-screening process and catered to more sophisticated daters (pay parking anyone?), I was promptly catfished.[178] I was not familiar with this term until one of my in-person dates had taught me the word, saying he had much experience in this department since online dating.

I was highly romanced by this individual for several weeks, who had a large portfolio of himself, including video clips, which I later traced to YouTube where I assume he had found them. Perhaps the same method he used to scam the initial identity-proving system. Crafty. After some relationship-building time, he asked me for money to replace his pilot's licence he had apparently lost with his wallet when he left it in a taxi in Argentina between flights. (This was when my alarm bells rang loudly—thankfully.) The depths to which some people will stoop.

Another of my dates was a tall successful multi-lingual university professor and father, who ended our date by masturbating in the front seat of his car as he claimed that he couldn't control himself because I was "so hot." Cheque please. Wow—just wow.

Though my brief time spent with online dating came to a quick close, the experiences delivered a plethora of insights. For the stories one hears about so-and-so who met online and is now blissfully married, I am so happy for them. I, on the other hand, will find love organically, or not at all. In the meantime, I feed myself love, and I truly enjoy my own company. God's plan. Thy will—not mine—be done.

"Let go and let God."[179]

[178] He was using someone else's identity. "Catfishing is a deceptive activity in which a person creates a fictional persona or fake identity on a social networking service, usually targeting a specific victim." *Wikipedia: The Free Encyclopedia.* (n.d.). Catfishing. Accessed 2024-06-30, https://en.wikipedia.org/wiki/Catfishing

[179] A Christian teaching, author unknown.

Believe

A framed quotation that sits on my bedside table reads:

> believe nothing,
> no matter where you read it,
> or who has said it,
> not even if I have said it,
> unless it agrees with your own reason
> and your own common sense.
>
> Buddha

Yes—Yes.

But we are losing these abilities. The tech giants and the influencers would have us believe that mobile technology is the way to increase connections. Do you truly believe in your heart that what has been happening with this technology is moving the human race in a positive direction? Has *the thing* increased connections and heightened unity for humankind as a collective?

Enter robots.

Even some seniors, who lived most of their lives long before the existence of these devices, are now bowing down to this as the way to connect with people. I see grandparents out with toddlers and kids (assumingly grandchildren) and the children have a device in their hand. Why have they succumbed to the lie of how children connect these days? Why is it that they cannot simply be present with each other? They too have been sucked into this ODC. These irreplaceable times and relationships are missed when in the presence of *the thing*, which can never be equated to a Fisher-Price® talking telephone[180]—they are galaxies apart.

Being present during time spent. "Love and time" is the message that South African rugby team captain Siya Kolisi spoke about—the importance of the gifts his grandmother gave him.[181] Against all adversity, it was the love and time his grandmother provided that stayed with him through it all. Let me ask you: Are you truly attentive? Does the love and time you give those around you differ due to the presence of *the thing*?

We do want to arrive back again, we do. People *are* craving true connection. At this point, many are too bewitched to know they can release the shackles that are gripping them so tightly. I often listen to an inspirational radio station while I drive. I find it an uplifting surround of music and positive messages. While listening one day, I heard a lovely woman share a short prayer, which I loved. She said:

> "God, give me the eyes to see what I have missed."[182]

Yes. So many of us have been clouded and can not clearly see how we have been infiltrated and what we have, and are, becoming.

I saw the title of this book stream across my forebrain. There was a clear communication that I am to bring light in darkened times: to encourage others to step into their authenticity; to inspire them share their

[180] Now referred to as the Fisher-Price® Chatter Telephone.

[181] Blackwell, G. (Director). (2022). Episode 5: Siya Kolisi. In *Live to lead* [Documentary series] (Executive Producers: Prince Harry Duke of Sussex, Meghan Duchess of Sussex, Ben Browning, Chanel Pysnik, Geoff Blackwell, Ruth Hobday John Sloss; Producer: Ruth Hobday). Blackwell & Ruth, Nelson Mandela Foundation, Archewell Productions, Cinetic Media. Accessed 2026-06-30, https://quotefancy.com/quote/819185/Gloria-Steinem-I-think-if-we-could-raise-one-generation-of-kids-without-violence-and

[182] I heard this on a program on Praise 106.5 FM sometime in late 2022 or early 2023.

stories, courage, and strength; to urge them to step into action and support each other during these tumultuous times. I was prompted to provide a head-shaking wake-up call directed towards those whose reason and common sense causes them to aspire to a different way of existing and anyone committed to becoming who they wish to be in the world. People are already feeling the backlash that is coming from *the thing* with strength. So consider casting aside the bonds that bind you; move into the H.U.G.; "back to life, back to reality."[183]

After dropping-off my kids at school one day, I saw a lovely woman pushing her infant uphill in a stroller, her toddler walking beside them with a cell phone in her hand. She looked-up at her mom and they shared the most beautiful smile with each other. I thought, *there* is the connection, and what is in her young daughter's hand is the lie.

The grip is powerful. "God, give me the eyes to see what I have missed." We as a society, a population, a nation, have allowed ourselves to be taken over. We have been made to believe that this is how we connect—simply put, this is a fallacy. How has this worked so far?

Take a few moments to sit with this question. Do not wait until things are *different* or *perfect* to start. Don't wait for the creators of *the thing* to hold that press conference and admit to the tangled mess this has become. This will *never* happen. Money and greed powers it all. Money, money, money—another good song, "For the Love of Money."[184] Put it on.

[183] Soul II Soul featuring Caron Wheeler. (1989). Back to life (however do you want me) [Song] (Songwriters: Jazzie B, Caron Weaver, Nellie Hooper, & Simon Law; Producers: Jazzie B & Nellie Hooper). Label: Virgin.

[184] Gamble, K., Huff, L., & Jackson, A. (Songwriters). (1974). For the love of money [Song]. On *For the love of money* [Album] (Producers: Kenneth Gamble and Leon Huff). Labels: Philadelphia International, 3544. In particular, I'm referring to the 1991 *New Jack City* [Film] arrangement of this song sung by Queen Latifah, Lavert, and Troop.

God knows if I had waited until I had a stunning office with an ocean view and quill pen accent piece "placed just so" on my desk, the time to share this message may never have arrived.

Instead, I swept my arm across our family's shared desk to clear away the Lego mini-figures and melty-beads[185] and allowed space for the process. Near me, our guinea pig was repeatedly tapping the ball-bearing on her water bottle in her large cage. On my desk I keep a 2"x3" photo of 6-year-old me. Of all the things that could have surfaced in my storage locker, out of the corner of my eye I spotted what looked like a small piece of paper on the ground. Half-lodged under the locker casing, I bent down, picked it up, turned it over, and dusted it off. Though with scratches on the sheen, she sits on my desk as I write—full of sparkle and shine, the daughter I never had. She too, had dreams, yet the woman she would become has more. Nay-sayers scoffed claiming, "Ha! I have wanted to write a book for like 10 years, and you—a single parent of three sons with a fulltime job—*you* are writing a book? Ha!" I did it anyway. Yes—me.

> Social media won't have a true challenger until a counter-culture emerges, one where fruitful people can join and belong. [The joining begins automatically when you *choose* to separate your existence from *the thing*].[186]
>
> The movement of course will need a leader. A new dictatorship of sorts, led by a benevolent ruler, a self-care tyrant who takes away social media and leaves us alone by ourselves [in the presence of all others who collectively revolt

185 "...melty beads, are small, plastic beads. You arrange them on a special pegboard to form a design. Then, using an iron and wax paper, you melt the beads together. When they cool off, you have a solid piece of plastic in your design." Rendina, D. (2016, August 8). *Three reasons why perler beads are awesome for makerspaces.* Renovated Learning website. Accessed 2024-06-30, https://www.renovatedlearning.com/2016/08/08/perler-beads-makerspaces/ para. 2

186 David, C. (2020). *No one asked for this* (p. 41). New York, NY: Mariner Books.

against it, grasping the reigns of their lives in a beautiful powerful alternative].[187]

It's the critics that drive improvement. It's the critics that are the true optimists.[188]

> Darkness cannot drive out darkness.
> Only light can do that.
> Hate cannot drive out hate;
> only love can do that.[189]
> ~ Martin Luther King, Jr ~

It is important for people to realize they do not need to follow the herd. We can to stand-up *against* what's behind *the thing*. We the people[190]—one-by-one. We the people.

This story is not just about me; it is about all of us. It's about the extreme *phonedemic* proportions that have abducted us from what it is to be human. In our day-to-day lives, we are not flawless, and we are not Photoshopped. The number of "Likes" we receive doesn't have anything to do with who we *truly* are.

Moreso, this book is about addiction, loss of authenticity, and how we have become increasingly distant and shallow in our lives. It is about the outer stimuli and preoccupations that take us away from ourselves, that take us away from others, from facing toxic home situations and

[187] David, C. (2020). *No one asked for this* (p. 41). New York, NY: Mariner Books.

[188] Jaron Lanier (computer scientist, computer philosophy writer, and technologist) interview in Orlowski, J. (2020). *The social dilemma* [Documentary film] (Writers: Davis Coombe, Vickie Curtis, Jeff Orlowski; Producer: Larissa Rhodes). Exposure Labs, Argent Pictures, The Space Program; Netflix.

[189] King, M. L. Jr. (1991). *A testament of hope quotes.* goodreads website. Accessed 2024-08-19, https://www.goodreads.com/work/quotes/52037 [From *A testament of hope: The essential writings and speeches of Martin Luther King, Jr.* (J. M. Washington, Ed.). New York, NY: Harper One.]

[190] *National Archives.* (1787). "The preamble." In The constitution of the United States: A transcription. Accessed 2024-07-24, https://www.archives.gov/founding-docs/constitution-transcript

relationships, from how we're truly feeling, and the neglect that stems from excessive phone, alcohol, and drug usage. If not addressed, all the justifications and excuses that detach us from the reality of *what is* will continue to keep us separated from our natural instinct to connect, to thrive, to create.

Everyone has a story and who we truly are becomes lost in the midst of extensive online sharing and social media absorption.

With worldwide mobile phone subscriptions at a whopping 8.9 billion in 2023,[191] this story is about the possibility of you, too, dropping the crutch that pulls you downward—the fixation that takes time away from you truly connecting and engaging with others, which ultimately diverts and distracts you from reaching your full potential. No matter what generation you are born into, you too have the power to be part of the H.U.G.—to rise again, to bring respect for others into your everyday life again. To show those around you that you are present, you are here, you will no longer disengage.

> The way sometimes seems long and weary. The weariness of others must often be shared by me. The weary and the heavy-laden, when they come to me, should be helped to find the rest that I have found. There is only one sure cure for world-weariness and that is turning to spiritual things. In order to help bring about the weary world to God, I must dare to suffer, dare to conquer selfishness in myself, and dare to be filled with spiritual peace in the face of all the weariness in the world.
> I pray that I may be a help to discouraged people. I pray that

[191] Taylor, P. (2024, February 7). *Number of global mobile subscriptions 1993-2023 in millions.* statistica website. Accessed 2024-06-30, https://www.statista.com/statistics/262950/global-mobile-subscriptions-since-1993

I may have the courage to help bring about what the weary world needs, but does not know how to get.[192]

If there are more mobile phone subscriptions than there are people on the planet and there is ongoing proof of people feeling less connected to other people than ever before, does that not that illustrate the magnitude of the situation?

Michelle Obama said, "I think we need to be with each other. We really do. I think when we gather, and we mix our togetherness, we feel better."[193] But are we doing this with our devices in hand? More and more we hear about each other from our feeds which, typically, are inaccurate and only a portion of our realities—a distortion of the *truth* of who we are. Oftentimes sensitive exchanges are not appropriate for online forums, and yet so many individuals choose social media as a channel for communication.

Through sharing in-person we are able to get to know each other more and to gradually uncover the truths about one another.

It is as though many of us emerged out of the global pandemic forgetting who we are with an added layer of withdrawing further from true connection. Many of us had been bombarded from all sides: hammered by media newscasts on television and social media sites, overwhelmed by excessive Zoom calls, and overdosed on information all while isolating from reality deeper into a black hole of misinformation. Though our society was entrenched in the H.D.G. prior to this, coming

192 Hazelden Foundation. (1975). May 6. In *Twenty-four hours a day.* Center City, MN: Author.

193 Mendoza, L. (Director). (2023). *The light we carry: Michelle Obama and Oprah Winfrey* [Documentary film]. Diversified Production Services, Higher Ground Productions, Jesse Collins Entertainment; Netflix.

out the other side of COVID-19, reliance on outward stimulus was considerably more glaring. *The thing* had pulled us further downward.

Layers of conspiracy theories began to surface and were felt by many. Some believed that we were being locked inside in order for tech companies to install 5G towers while polluting the Earth's atmosphere further.[194] During the lockdown, other theories materialized including the stand opposing vaccinations. This time period "became a fertile ground for the bloom of [several] conspiracy theories already existing but struggling for…global attention."[195] The pandemic's anti-vaccination movement initiated mainstream social media sites actively censoring their users' posts while "the United Nations painted a sobering picture of how the pandemic has fuelled terrorism and violent extremism."[196,197] This mushroomed into conspiracy theorists being pushed underground onto less mainstream sites, thereby giving them the traction they sought while expanding their prospective audiences and followings.

> Terrorists and violent extremists have also sought to exploit pandemic-related sociocultural restrictions that have led people around the world to spend increasing time online, by strengthening their efforts to spread propaganda, recruit, and

194 Knowledge Nile. (n.d.). *Is 5g an issue for the environment and human health.* Accessed 2024-12-03, https://www.knowledgenile.com/blogs/is-5g-an-issue-for-the-environment-and-human-health

195 Kużelewska, E., & Tomaszuk, M. (2022, July 1). Rise of conspiracy theories in the pandemic times. *International Journal for the Semiotics of Law, 35*(6), 2373-2389. doi:10.1007/s11196-022-09910-9

196 Morris, R. (2022, December 30). *Researchers warn of rise in extremism online after Covid* (para. 1). *BBC.* Accessed 2024-10-03, https://www.bbc.com/news/uk-politics-61106191

197 United Nations Security Council. (2021, December). *Update December 2021.* Accessed 2024-05-19, https://www.un.org/securitycouncil/ctc/sites/www.un.org.securitycouncil.ctc/files/files/documents/2021/Dec/cted_covid19_paper_dec_2021.pdf

> radicalize via virtual platforms (including gaming platforms).[198]

Where do we draw the line—and how? Where are our governing bodies and what attention are they giving to the restriction of misinformation? Why is our government not blocking access to extremist websites? Conceivably, a specialized task force to monitor, escalate, and intervene in serious situations is necessary.

It appears that many of us, however, have surfaced from the pandemic with another harmful pollutant in hand. Zapped into a deeper relationship with our now dearest friend (*the thing*), we resurfaced unable to break this bond that now binds so many of us.

Just stop. Put it down. Put it away. Come back. Breathe. Feel. Drop the cradling of *the thing* and allow yourself to be cradled. Be supported by nature. Be held in eye contact with others. Be cradled in getting to know yourself. Be nurtured in the love of whoever or whatever you believe created this planet and all its inhabitants—it longs to hold you. Be present, be here. Be *all* here; with head up, eyes focused ahead, one heartbeat, one breath, at a time. Feast on the glorious connections that are yours to have and build in real-time—Right here, right now.

> Take her hand, she will lead you through the fire
> Oh and give you back hope
>   and hope that you won't take too much
> Respecting what is left she cradled us,
>   oh she held us in her arms
> Unselfish in her suffering she could not understand

[198] United Nations Security Council. (2021, December). "Key Trends." In *Update December 2021* (para. 2). Accessed 2024-05-19, https://www.un.org/securitycouncil/ctc/sites/www.un.org.securitycouncil.ctc/files/files/documents/2021/Dec/cted_covid19_paper_dec_2021.pdf

> that no one seemed to have the time
> to cherish what was given.[199]

You see, this writing is about humanity being depleted of the trueness of connections and replacing that realness with something fabricated, something external. Some claim that this is the wave of the future, but I say your personal future is whatever *you* envision it can be. Ask yourself this question: Have you *found* yourself in *the thing* yet? The longer we spend hidden behind the screen, the further away we move from reality. How many of us truly recognize the amount of attention and focus we give away to *the thing*? Why *choose* to squander so much of your time? Time is so precious.

> "Time is the big, precious, unrenewable resource."[200]

Sitting behind a device and submerging ourselves in its content (or lack thereof) can be used as a dissociative[201] technique to keep us away from ourselves and others. Will you continue to bury your head in fake news, false information, and the narrative of others' lives to avoid facing yourself? "Busy" can also be a drug of choice. Many of us keep *so busy* we can't truly be known, by ourselves or by others.

As mentioned previously, *The Social Dilemma* is a behind-the-scenes exposé that dives into "the psychological underpinnings and manipulation

[199] McLachlan, S. (Songwriter). (1993). Mary [Song]. On *Fumbling Towards Ecstasy* [Album]. (Producer: Pierre Marchand). Labels: Nettwerk & Arista.

[200] Brown, B. (2019). *The call to courage* (Movie script, p. 100). Accessed 2024-06-30, https://www.stockq.org/moviescript/B/brene-brown-the-call-to-courage.php

[201] Dissociation is "a mental process of disconnecting from one's thoughts, feelings, memories or sense of identity." Better Health Channel. (n.d.). "Dissociation and dissociative disorders." In *Mental Health and Wellbeing* (Bullet 1). Accessed 2024-06-30, https://www.betterhealth.vic.gov.au/health/conditionsandtreatments/dissociation-and-dissociative-disorders

techniques by which…social media and technology companies addict users."[202] It is a Netflix documentary that won a pair of Emmy's with five additional nominations. Many of the people interviewed in this documentary are those who worked to develop apps and platforms for *the thing*. Their in-depth discussions about how they were hired, instructed, and/or trained to repeatedly attract their users with the idea of increasing their dependency and usage.

If you haven't seen this film, please do. If you did take the time to watch it, what happened? Did you change your usage? In all likelihood, you simply continued in your previously patterned way: programmed inside the abyss, sucked downward, without any *action* to make change in your *own* life.

> We were naïve about the flipside of the coin.[203]
>
> If technology creates mass chaos, loneliness, more polarization, more election hacking, more inability to focus on the real issues, we're toast.[204]

Yes. Please read that quote again. We are completely clueless about what is happening to us. We have less awareness about who we *truly* are and what we *truly* believe. Along with the onslaught of these new technologies we, particularly the younger generations, have become highly influenced by propaganda and what *others* think and believe.

It may well be time to consider people who continuously stare into their phones as addicts feeding their ODC addictions. Rather than seeing

[202] *Wikipedia: The Free Encyclopedia.* (n.d.). *The social dilemma* (2020) [Documentary film]. Accessed 2024-06-30, https://en.wikipedia.org/wiki/The_Social_Dilemma

[203] Said by a former employee interviewed in Orlowski, J. (2020). *The social dilemma* [Documentary film] (Writers: Davis Coombe, Vickie Curtis, Jeff Orlowski; Producer: Larissa Rhodes). Exposure Labs, Argent Pictures, The Space Program; Netflix.

[204] YouTube summarized. (n.d.). *Tech companies' control and responsibility (sec:113).* Accessed 2024-06-30, https://app.youtubesummarized.com/r/s3Q4159tJxAguODwiEirY

this as *normal*, we best shift our perspectives. The world has been overturned by tech companies preying on our drives, our weaknesses and emotions, our need to be liked, to be given attention. The user taking hits first thing in the morning, all through the day, last thing at night. Addiction. Addicts.

> "There are only two industries that call
> their customers 'users':
> illegal drugs and software."[205]

And now, we allow our children to become addicts in childhood—dopamine rush, quick fix, instant hit—because why? Because Robbie down the street has one and…and…and…(I'm seeing jellyfish again) and babies in strollers are being handed *the thing* as a parental coping mechanism. How? Why?

"Modern advertising was created with the innovative techniques used in tobacco advertising beginning in the 1920s"[206] and, while men were already in the throws of this addiction, in the 1950s to 1970s women and children were targeted by advertising on TV shows, movies, print ads, billboards, etc.[207] Though the West has awakened considerably to tobacco risks and has implemented rigorous limits, other countries in the world are still entrenched in past marketing strategies.

Technology has brought us to a whole new level of impairment. No external advertising necessary (although we get a fair amount of that too).

[205] Edward Tufte (statistician and political science professor emeritus) interview in *The Social Dilemma* (2020) [Documentary film].

[206] *Wikipedia: The Free Encyclopedia.* (n.d.). History of nicotine marketing ("1914-1950: Interwar"). Accessed 2024-10-25, https://en.wikipedia.org/wiki/History_of_nicotine_marketing

[207] *Wikipedia: The Free Encyclopedia.* (n.d.). History of nicotine marketing ("1914-1950: Interwar"). Accessed 2024-10-25, https://en.wikipedia.org/wiki/History_of_nicotine_marketing

The thing comes fully-equipped with everything necessary to develop a solid dependence. We are being warped by a highly addictive technology that distorts our way of thinking, feeling, and being. Fundamentally, this is:

> …not a fair fight….
>
> Super computers and thousands of engineers who have goals that are different than your goals….So who's going to win that game? Who's going to win?...
>
> We have created a system that biases toward false information. It is a disinformation-for-profit business model….
>
> We are more profitable to a corporation if we're spending time staring at a screen, staring at an ad, than if we're spending that time living our lives in a rich way….
>
> How do you wake-up from the matrix, when you don't know you're in the matrix.[208]

> I put a spell on you, 'cause you're mine
> …
> You better stop the things you do
> I ain't lyin'
> No, I ain't lyin'
> …
> I can't stand it 'cause you put me down...
> I put a spell on you, because you're mine…[209]

We are more profitable to a corporation if we're spending time staring at a screen, staring at an ad, than if we're spending that time living our lives in a rich way….

[208] Tristan Harris interview in Orlowski, J. (2020). *The social dilemma* [Documentary film] (Writers: Davis Coombe, Vickie Curtis, Jeff Orlowski; Producer: Larissa Rhodes). Exposure Labs, Argent Pictures, The Space Program; Netflix.

[209] Screamin' Jay Hawkins, & Slotkin, H. (Songwriters). (1956). I put a spell on you [Song] (Producer: Arnold Maxin). Label: Okeh. Accessed 2024-06-30, https://genius.com/Nina-simone-i-put-a-spell-on-you-lyrics

From teens to senior citizens and anyone in between, people report feelings of loneliness which they fill with device use.[210] From the *Live to 100* documentary:

> in the United States we have a loneliness epidemic. A population that is increasingly lonely, increasingly isolated, and increasingly needs human connection more than ever….Now we're discovering in America that loneliness can cost 15 years of life expectancy.[211]

The centenarians interviewed and discussed in this film did not have devices in their lives. Yet immersed in our urban societies, we somehow feel powerless to see living our lives any other way. We see the problems of the whole world through social and news media—and we absorb it into our being.

Whether you *choose* to continue this absorption is up to you.

> We are being warped by a highly addictive technology that distorts our way of thinking, feeling, and being.

Does increased time spent on your device truly make you feel less lonely, or would your time be better spent getting out there, meeting others, being active, getting involved, reading a good book, or spending time immersed in other joyful or productive avenues? Perhaps you keep your life so busy on social media (or other avenues) that you don't risk connecting with others in person. Or maybe you have the discipline to watch video clips for only 15 or 30 minutes and are able to stay in your

[210] Office of the U.S. Surgeon General. (2023). *Our epidemic of loneliness and isolation: The U.S. General's advisory on the healing effects of social connection and community.* Accessed 2024-10-24, https://www.hhs.gov/sites/default/files/surgeon-general-social-connection-advisory.pdf

[211] *Live to 100: Secrets of the Blue Zone* [Documentary series]. Season 1 Episode 1: "The Journey Begins."

pre-determined parameters. More often than not, hours are dribbled away. Over the period of a year, the daily dribble accrues into an enormous amount. Think of the accumulated time lost over one's lifespan. The wasted time is staggering.

Another all-consuming hazard teenagers and adults may fall into is spending countless hours on online gaming platforms—particularly those who lack social skills and real-life connections.

> We have engineered most of the physical activity out of our lives with mechanical gadgetry. And now we live this environment of ease [is it ease?] and excess. We are mostly victims [or products] of our environment.
>
> The casual social interactions that you have throughout the day with the postman, with the person you meet at the bus stop, with the baristas, are actually a better predictor of longevity than diet and exercise.[212]

All the small interactions (that we actually show up for) help to improve our lives, while lengthening our time here.[213] In this technological age, perhaps our biggest challenge in our relationships is to take the time to savour each other and those around us, to savour our human experience.

Music plays such a vital role in my existence. I value it greatly. I grew-up around it and receive freedom, inspiration, and comfort from it—not plugged in my ears taking me away from real exchange, but hearing it all around me, feeling it resonating through my being, touching my soul. Me amidst the music running through my mind—without headphones—embedded in my memory for access anytime. I have mentioned some of

[212] *Live to 100: Secrets of the Blue Zone* [Documentary series]. Season 1 Episode 4: "The future of longevity."

[213] *Live to 100: Secrets of the Blue Zone* [Documentary series]. Season 1 Episode 4: "The future of longevity."

the music that has inspired me within the pages of this book.[214] For example, in her song, "Elsewhere,"[215] Sarah McLachlan sang "Peace in the struggle to find peace."[216] She is a talented artist, a woman of depth.

Music aside, be in silence completely. Just be. Do you remember how space, time, and silence feel? They are amazing—extraordinary gifts—and they are yours to behold. A fellow Canadian, Alanis Morissette, in her song "Thank You"[217] sings:

> Thank you, thank you silence.
> ....
> How 'bout me enjoying the moment for once.
> ....
> The moment I let go of it
> was the moment I got more....
> The moment I jumped off of it
> was the moment I touched down.
> ....
> Thank you nothingness,
> thank you clarity,
> thank you, thank you silence.
> ....

Yes. Thank you silence.

And if you are struggling with the transition away from *the thing*, use this publication as well as other books and readings for guidance and support. At the back of this book, I have included lists of readings, resources, and songs that I have found enlightening.

214 I've included a song list at the end of the book and more extensive playlists on my website (www.phondemic.com).

215 McLachlan, S. (Songwriter). (1993). Elsewhere [Song]. On *Fumbling Towards Ecstasy* [Album]. (Producer: Pierre Marchand). Labels: Nettwerk & Arista. Accessed 2024-09-25, https://www.sarahmclachlan.com/track/elsewhere

216 I elaborate further on this song in this chapter.

217 In 1998, before device infiltration.

Also welcomed are friends sending each other inspiration, such as short sayings, quotes, and affirmations. Today I was sent an excerpt, which reads:

> Until you heal the wounds of your past, you are going to bleed. You can bandage the bleeding with food, with alcohol, with drugs, with work, with cigarettes, with sex [or with excessive mindless device scrolling]. But eventually, it will ooze through and stain your life. You must find the strength to open your wounds, stick your hands inside, pull out the core of your pain that is holding you in your past, the memories, and make peace with them.[218]

Too radical? Perhaps. But what is it that causes the pull away from oneself, from *your* self? Why the need to fill the loneliness, or to pick-up *the thing* repeatedly again and again? Does this substitution have you feeling *truly* connected? If so, then you may need to re-evaluate what connection *really* is. Dwell on these questions for awhile. Mull them over in your mind and see what surfaces. Depending on your response, this is where effort will be required to establish lasting change.

Applying practices that distance ourselves from dependencies builds depth of character while teaching us not to cling to something external.

[218] An Iyanla Vanzant quote.

Carpé

It felt as though I was the only one who was able to distinguish the true source of our disconnect. Others feeling that something is off-kilter and out-of-balance seem unable to pinpoint *why* that is. Or if they could discern what *it* is, they were not able to take a next step in breaking-free from this modern-day addiction that has gripped us so tightly that we are resigned to it being the "wave of the future." Put it down, whether in bed all hours of the day or night or landing in a seat in a coffee shop with *the thing* grasped in your hand. Put it away.

I hear the whisper of the late Robin Williams in the scene in *Dead Poets' Society*.[219] As he and his students viewed the black and white photos of images of:

> …those who are now pushing-up daisies….They have a message to share with you….If you listen real close, you can hear them whisper their legacy to you. Go on—lean in. Listen. You hear it?
> Carpé—hear it?—Carpé.
> Carpé diem.
> Seize the day, make your lives extraordinary.

Rise-up—Awaken. Rise-up from your seat or your bed. Heads up when you're walking (and driving) from where you are to where you are headed. Just put *the thing* away and enjoy the moments—the beautiful moments. The world is waiting for you. *You* are waiting for *you*. Our

[219] Weir, P. (Director), & Schulman, T. (Writer). (1989). *Dead poets society* [Film] (Producers: Steven Haft, Paul Junger Witt, & Tony Thomas). Touchstone Pictures, Silver Screen Partners IV; Buena Vista Pictures Distribution.

creator is waiting for you. And at the very same time, no-one is waiting for you—everything continues whether you rise-up or not.

The choice is yours.

"Gather ye rosebuds while ye may."[220]

This life is now, and it will not be fulfilled through dribbling it away into another video, another reel. The *real* is here—it is yours to have.

Real. Right now. Here. Now.

Yours—Now.

Choice. Carpé—Hear the whispers of *truth* growing louder. University dorm-room plans take a different turn; boardroom ideas are dissolved. *The thing* has morphed into something other than initially planned. Even those involved in its creation have admitted this: the interns, Chief Executive Officers (CEOs), developers, creators of *the thing*.

Evolve away from it. The truth to be had is right here, right now, with the awakening that lies within you to live it. We the people. Social media ads be gone—"I see it too often;" "It's irrelevant;" "It's offensive;" "It's inappropriate." Yes, yes—words to live by. We have all seen *the thing* all too often. It has taken our species over and now we wish to live differently than that, which is not truly living. And yes, *the thing* is irrelevant in *truly* living a life. Yes. Yes. We crave something more, something genuine. In my mind, I saw flowers blooming from tightly-closed buds. Yes. Bloom again, walk freely again.

Heads held high. The movement begins. The movement of first repositioning your head in an upright position, stable, on top of your

[220] Herrick, R. (1648). To the virgins, to make much of time [Poem]. *Wikipedia: The Free Encyclopedia.* Accessed 2024-10-12, https://en.wikipedia.org/wiki/To_the_Virgins,_to_Make_Much_of_Time

neck, like the upheld human you were designed to be. This can be the wave, the wave of *your* future. We have all been out of synchronization for some time now. Allowing the sync of our computers and devices to over-rule the sync of our selves. I am not a robot. I will swiftly identify all of the traffic lights, crosswalks, and motorcycles within the provided squares in order to prove that. Yet at the end of the day, we have allowed our brains, hearts, minds, bodies, and spirits to fall prey to short-changing the *true* gifts of our human nature.

I deeply value Sarah McLaughlin's album *Fumbling Towards Ecstasy* and her song "Elsewhere":

> I love the time and in between
> The calm inside me
> In the space where I can breathe
> I believe there is a distance I have wandered...
> Reaching out and reaching in
> Holding out, holding in
> I believe
> This is heaven to no-one else but me
> And I'll defend it as long as I can be
> Left here to linger in silence
> If I choose to.[221]

Love, real connection, touch, intimacy, gestures, and togetherness—these cannot be substituted. I do not choose to "linger in silence"[222] in opposition towards big tech, their infiltration of our society, and their overt overwhelming of our existence. Nor do I wish to stay silent about what I have overcome in my life in contrast to what one may think they see on the surface. However at times, I do choose to be silent when I feel

[221] McLachlan, S. (Songwriter). (1993). Elsewhere [Song]. On *Fumbling Towards Ecstasy* [Album]. (Producer: Pierre Marchand). Labels: Nettwerk & Arista. Accessed 2024-09-25, https://www.sarahmclachlan.com/track/elsewhere

[222] McLachlan, S. (Songwriter). (1993). Elsewhere [Song]. On *Fumbling towards ecstasy* [Album].

the need to centre, to connect to source and detach from outer distractions.

Who and what we are must *not* be defined by an algorithm. What fuels us, drives us, saddens us, touches us, plagues us? We best not rely on super computers and a panel of employees, who target us to work against ourselves while feeding us more nonsense, pursuing us further, pulling our heads downward. This is not what we were meant for.

If you believe that we are meant for more, are you able to choose differently?

Addiction. Brain centres, brainstem targeting. What is it that *you* truly believe? Time is so precious. We never get a misspent moment back. Pandemic aside, we are heavily immersed into an ever-intensifying *phonedemic*. Boardroom. Targeting. Further, more. Massive corporations, more. Stockholders, more. Higher stakes, more. Shareholders pressure, more. More—More—*you* fund the more.

> This should scare you—at least a little....these powerful corps have seized control without us even realizing it happened. Big tech also remains largely unaccountable for their actions...hiding behind secret algorithms. They also took over the world so easily, and with such style and finesse, that we willingly came along for the ride.
>
> We signed up to use their free software, downloaded their free apps, used their free maps and free email, clicked on their tricky links, and sent them all our photos, videos and contact numbers....even our passwords and credit card numbers can now be easily hacked. We didn't see it coming. We were so

> naïve. And they all sat back and laughed—all the way to the bank.[223]

More—More. Stop more.
Now—You.

You *can* stop more, breathe more, notice more, arrive more, be present more, put *the thing* down more. Drop the chains more, free your mind more. Wherever you are, be *all* there more.

Lean in. Do you hear them, their voices? "Carpé." Can you hear them? If you can, do you *believe* their message? Or does the *pull* run so deep that you wish to waste some more, you would rather scroll more, compare some more, look at ads some more? More.

I just heard the words my elementary school principal said years ago, which cross my mind from time-to-time.

"Be the best that you can be."

It's quite something that someone can leave such a lasting impression on a person with such a seemingly simple phrase. He passed away suddenly of a heart attack in his early 50s, which was a shock and great loss to our community. Out of hundreds of students, I was chosen to write and deliver the speech at our school's memorial. Now many years later, I still remember the first lines I had written, which I delivered from the podium.

> Mr. Truman shared a special feeling with children in our community. He wanted people to be the best that they could be. That's what he was to me. He never let people down. When he said he would do something, he always did....

[223] Barr, C. (2023, September). *Easy ways to rule the world* (para. 2 and 3). *Page Six.* NorthVancouver.com or PageSix.com

I was also given the additional honour of presenting his wife and children with a bouquet of balloons and attached messages that we released to the skies. I must add that this was the 1980s and the threat of pollution (atmosphere, ocean, and land) was not as well-known as it is today. What goes up must come down—when we know better, we do better.

Accountable, present, trustworthy, encouraging. Aren't these some of the traits that people deeply value? As I have stated before, I am not looking for things to go back to how they were. This is not realistic, or possible. We evolve. I have endeavoured to show you some of the ways in which I have evolved, and now I invite you to ask yourself: "Am I the *best* person that I can be?" Or in returning to our topic, "Have I signed-over my existence to the downward pull of technology, claiming my spot amongst the cattle along with the others?" "Am I truly bringing my best self forward—or have I, too, succumbed to my device's insistent grasp on my attention?"

One life—here, now. Inhabitants on a planet, right here, right now. If we do not give our downcast heads a shake and choose differently, as a species, we may cease to exist living on Earth. Choose to be present again. *Choose* to be the best that you can be.

I know fellow humans that where we currently are is far from our best selves. Remember, carefully curated, designed to fire-on and target the momentary dopamine rush that stimulates the craving centres—the same craving phenomenon that motivates alcoholics and those addicted to drugs to use again. Yes, I realize this may be difficult to digest. Many of you will find all the ways in which this does not apply to you as I first did with the prospect of being classified as an alcoholic. I understand the pain that this may cause. Each and every click and swipe funds its continuation and further development. This is not a fair playing field.

These *smart* devices have been designed for us to unknowingly fall prey. You have not been aware it has been intensifying its clutches over you, over time, as any addiction does. I have first-hand experience with this—I understand.

One life—and this is the part where you get to look at yours. What do you want from your existence? How deeply do you wish to arrive? Arrive in the feelings, arrive in each relationship, the emotions, the seasons, the moments, the hardships, the triumphs. Arrive in the fact that we have all been given a life on this planet that exists in a galaxy with billions of other stars and planets in a mind-blowing jaw-dropping array of real-time astonishment to be witnessed daily. Are you the best that *you* can be? And does the time spent on your device *in any way* hinder you from fully showing-up. Does *the thing* take you away from being your *best* self today? The world and its people need you, and *you* need you to arrive and be present in life's *bona fide* experience.

Role call please: Rachel, present; Talia, here present; David, here; Zoe present; Bill here present; (insert your name here—are you here, and *actually* present? Are you?).

I was blessed to hear Charlotte Cardin's "Phoenix" live at a music festival this past summer.

> I had to burn everything that I was,
> just to come back like a phoenix.
> [Yes, I know this one well. Powerful lyrics.]
> I'm building it up slowly. [Yes.]
> And we can rise from the ashes just like a phoenix.
> [Yes. Yes, we can.][224]

[224] Cardin, C., Brando, J., & Stebbings, P. (Lubalin). (Songwriters). (2021). Phoenix [Song] (Producers: Jason Brando, Marc-André Gilbert). Label: Cult Nation.

Rise-up again without reliance on this crutch that takes you elsewhere so frequently. It is entirely possible.

One of the most frequent phrases I've heard in the last 10 years is: "I don't know how you do it." I understand this statement, wholeheartedly. At times, I do not really know how I've done it either. I approach my life and what I do each day as a unique gift and blessing. I suppose it is our outlook and attitudes that determine the scope of our capacity.

I have been given so much: the opportunity to raise three sons with distinctive personalities, each in a different stage of life, and being able to raise them while living in sobriety after having previously been gripped by a powerful pull elsewhere. My life, my existence, and who I am today has been shaped by both the struggles I have endured and the faith I have gained along the way. I have prevailed with grace and dignity, and I am immensely grateful. I feel so blessed to have the relationship I do with the God of my understanding and to feel this presence and closeness in all aspects of my life. I genuinely feel in tune with the living, breathing, and feeling mechanisms of my body and mind. I truly feel connected. It is remarkable.

I once shared my approach to parenting with a Grade 2 teacher. She was overwhelmed with her students' behaviours and was wading in strong feelings around this. I expressed my approach—that each personality is a gift—that we can all learn something from one another. She came to me the following day, beaming, and let me know that by making this shift in her attitude, she was able to completely turn-around her approach with her students.

Our perceptions are important in shifting our attitudes and patterns. Modifying our approach has an impact on others' reactions. Are shifts like this lasting? They can be, yet oftentimes require thoughtful practice, especially if this feels foreign to you.

If we continue to use our mobile devices as the way we humans connect with each other, we will surely undermine and lose-out on real and true exchanges in life. If we are spending time with people and just staring at our phones while doing so, then why get together at all? If movies like *The Mitchells vs. the Machines*,[225] which clearly illustrate the discomfort of a family sharing a meal and having to talk to each other in the absence of their devices as a seemingly impossible task, this further glorifies *the thing* as the norm for today's *modern* family. *Diary of a Wimpy Kid: The Long Haul*[226] film is another glaring example of device over-usage that normalizes the extent to which we have lowered our standards.

There are many other films and series today that glorify disconnection in relationships and families and device dysfunction in full force. For example, a bratty little daughter glued to her mobile device selfie-posing and scrolling her way through her days. People support these shows by continuing to watch them, which lends to standardizing such behaviours. This aside, if parents are ODC addicts themselves, their children naturally pattern themselves after their closest role models.

Seize the day. Seize your life. Rise-up from the ashes just like a phoenix. The power is *within* you to set a different precedent for your life

225 Rianda, M. (2021). *The Mitchells vs the machines* (Producers: Phil Lord, Christopher Miller, Kurt Albrecht; Writers: Mike Rianda, Jeff Rowe). Columbia Pictures, Sony Pictures Animation, Lord Miller Productions, One Cool Films; Netflix.

226 Bowers, D. (2017). *Diary of a wimpy kid: The long haul* (Producers: Nina Jacobson, Brad Simpson). Fox 2000 Pictures, Color Force, TSG Entertainment; 20th Century Fox.

and how you choose to show-up in the world. Do not let yourself continue to be fooled. You are more intelligent than that. One can go on vacation, see other parts of the world, and watch the waves; or we can walk down the street or attend a symphony or art gallery. But if while you are there you are glued to your mobile device, then are you really there? And in terms of being present, was your experience more like 30%, or 20%, or perhaps 10. Although physically you were there, much of your time was spent elsewhere.

Do not let yourself continue to be fooled.
You are more intelligent than that.

The Only Way from Here Is (Heads) Up

While writing this book, on my desk were two cross-border Powerball® lottery tickets for a billion-some-odd dollars that I had purchased months prior. I would look at them from time-to-time, but I didn't check their numbers, and so they sat. I do not often purchase lottery tickets, and it occurred to me that whether I was the winner or not, I would continue writing. I guess this is what Oprah meant when she said, "Find a job that you love, and you will never work," which I would now translate to:

> Love of one's life, love of one's craft,
> love of one's process.

The process is the unmasking of oneself to show-up more fully, to love oneself and, in turn, have the ability to love others—wholly.

One day, I intend to create a wall of my childhood photos, high contrast black-and-white, mostly taken by my dad—the talented photographer with whom I grew-up in front of his camera. Though I didn't end-up having a daughter, those photos will pay tribute to the little girl inside—the daughter I never had, who lives within me.

Through loss and struggle, I have prevailed, and I now feel closer to my true self. If you, too, feel as though you have been lost and have allowed the FoMO mentality sweep you away, the return to your authentic self may feel that much more freeing.

I believe in love, and I believe in humanity. I choose to be my best, to lead my life with light, and to see the light in others whenever humanly possible. I love love, young love, elder love, the way eyes meet to share love; love between a parent and child; the holding of hands walking in front of me expressing love.

I once sat in a theatre production, and I could *feel* the love between a couple two rows in front of me. The man moved the hair away from the eyes of his love, her loving response, the way they looked into each other's eyes, their small gestures. Is this not the fullness of experience for which we yearn? Isn't this closeness what we're meant for in life's journey? The beauty and fullness of love in these exchanges is beyond words.

Regardless of my life's path, I continue unjaded. I feel others in love, and I smile. Beautifully connected miracles. I am content. This is an immense gift.

After living in the light for some time now, it has become a far more natural state in which to exist. As for what comes next, I am not certain, yet I continue to expand my heart and hold space for others. I would enjoy acting and dancing again, and possibly singing as well. (Broadway anyone? Don't put it past me.) I am drawn to politics having grown-up around it. Yet, with the recent political climate, I am unsure as to whether I would become involved in a public forum. Shoe designer? Writer? I have many ideas.

"The trouble is, you think you have time."[227]

This life is for living, for savouring, to "suck out all the marrow...,"[228]—to live deeply—one breath, one experience at a time.

Each and every one of us has a story, and each day it evolves to include more. I chose to allow an intuitive thought to guide me. One

[227] Kornfield, J. (1994). *Buddha's little instruction book* (n.p.). New York, NY: Bantam Books.

[228] Thoreau, H. D. (1854). *I wanted to live....* Walden Woods Project website. Accessed 2024-10-23, https://www.walden.org/?quotation=i-wanted-to-live

single word flashed across my mind—*phonedemic*—followed by the funnelling of information. I did not bow down to adversity. I continued forward.

How would you like your life to evolve? How would you like your focus to shift? How will your life unfold if you create the space for flow?

We can all make the conscious choice to be part of the H.U.Generation. Just by arriving, you hold space for others. Live intentionally, show respect for humankind—and be, here, now. We need each others' *true* attention again—this is what is missing.

> Look to this day,
> For it is life,
> The very life of life.
> In its brief course lie all
> The realities and verities of existence,
> The bliss of growth,
> The glory of power—
> For yesterday is but a dream,
> And tomorrow is only a vision,
> But today, well lived,
> Makes every day a dream of happiness
> And every tomorrow a vision of hope.
> Look well, therefore, to this day.[229]

And just as important (if not most important), if we are to continue inhabiting our planet, it is in dire need of our attention. Earth is approaching irreversible damage, and we are pushing it past the breaking point. To put it bluntly, with the world's population staring into their

[229] Kālidasā. (1975). Sanskrit proverb 5th Century A.D. In *Twenty-four hours a day.* Center City, MN: Hazelden Foundation.

*smart*phones an average of 2190 hours each per year, if we do not make the necessary changes to ourselves and our way of living, *we* will cease to exist.

If you are unsure of where to begin, simply begin to let go of *the thing*.

> "There is only one time when it is essential to awaken. That time is now."[230]

[230] Kornfield, J. (1994). *Buddha's little instruction book* (p. 83). New York, NY: Bantam Books.

Afterword

> This life is for living
> —for living deeply, for experiencing, for savouring—
> one breath, one heartbeat at a time.

Some time has passed since the ink first dried on the pages of this book. I successfully met my personal deadline of its completion[231] on the day of my 15th year of continuous sobriety. The real estate market had once again picked-up, so it was timely that the space created from its lull began to dwindle. Having three children 5 years apart (sequentially) and the youngest two in the Catholic education system, meant that first communion, confirmation, and high school graduation all occurred in the end-portion of that school year. I knew this cycle would be more involved than was typical, so I embraced the time ahead, breathed deeply, and moved toward all that was to be.

Shortly after the first communion event, I was walking a steep trail with my small dog, whom I had rescued from Chile late the year prior. Though this was several years after the loss of our gentle giant, I was still grieving that loss and was not prepared to take on another. I identified with her story: pregnant and shunned by her *owner* and left to fend for herself and her puppies on the street. Upon seeing her face and hearing her story…well…arrangements quickly ensued for her to come to us.

Our walk began as usual, but when crossing a shallow stream, I lost my footing and fell backward. As I went down, my leg kicked-up high above my head while my dog's plastic bag holder smashed against the

[231] The final before-editor draft.

rocks underneath my body. The sharp sound was like shattering glass against a bolder. By the time I was up, my dog was gone.

With four ways out to the trailhead, I rushed to get to the centre and frantically asked others along the way if they had seen her. Early-on, a dog walker reported that my dog had "attached to her pack," and when they realized she was without her owner and tried to secure her, she bolted.

Dogs, and animals in general, have played an important part in my life. As a child, I faithfully wore a 1980s button that said "I ♥ Otters." My very first recollection in life dates back to when I was 2 years old and went with my family to pick out our puppy from the White Strath-Robin Kennels in Ontario. The sheer excitement of the puppies running in front of my young eyes, their sweet smells and their endless unconditional love hooked me in the most beautiful way.

The initial day was spent combing nearby trails with two sightings by my oldest son and his friends. In the search for this vulnerable pet, we quickly arranged a group of volunteers in the mountains and streets which are frequented by coyotes and bears, among other wildlife. When met by people who raised their eyebrows and muttered about predators, I quickly squelched their views and grandly stated, "Oh, we are connected, and she is coming back to me. I know this." "No, my dog is a survivor. She is coming back to us."

I share this story because this was a rare occasion when—yes—I did need my mobile phone on hand at all times. I did post to as many social media *lost dog* sites as I could muster the energy from my average of 2 to 4 hours sleep per night. Along the way, amazing caring heart-centered individuals and organizations presented themselves. Within the first 3 days, we had a team of 17 volunteers who routinely hit the ground, with one in particular leading the way. We had posters made and hung and we worked tirelessly without the help of any professionals, aside from the amazing and generous drone operator who combed the thick peaks of the mountainous areas surrounding us.

Each day, new tips. Each day, more sightings. Through this process, I learned that after the first couple of days a dog is lost, their pre-frontal cortex shuts-down. They move into survival mode and are transported back to some 33,000 years ago when their ancestors existed prior to their introduction to domestication.[232,233] Due to her traumatic start in life and adding to her skittish nature towards unknown humans, we quickly realized that it would be an ordeal to locate and subsequently secure her.

My days and nights became entirely focused on her safe return. A 5:00 a.m. wake-up call to comb the areas in which she was last spotted, I returned home to awaken my boys, make their breakfasts and lunches, and drop them off at school before resuming the search. My devoted team lobbied around me to scour the areas in which she was sighted. Many exhaustive up-hill searches were achieved with the hope of reaching her before night fell once again. During this time, I became acutely aware of dawn and dusk and the hours of light that were available until darkness set-in again.

Around Day 4, I received a message. This was not a DM or a PM,[234] it was a communication sent from source to my mind—it said, "Your faith is being up-levelled." Shortly after, the messenger clearly stated, "This is not a test." Moments later the voice reiterated "Please understand, you are *not* being tested. Your faith is being up-levelled." It was profound. I

[232] Lost Dogs of America. (2023, May 6). *What does survival mean?* Accessed 2024-10-25, https://lostdogsofamerica.org/what-does-survival-mode-mean

[233] *Wikipedia: The Free Encyclopedia.* (n.d.). Domestication of the dog. Accessed 2024-10-25, https://en.wikipedia.org/wiki/Domestication_of_the_dog

[234] A direct message or personal message.

needed to surrender, to let go entirely while having complete faith in source to bestow a positive outcome.

In the past, the potential for happy endings had often eluded me. I was relentless and so was my team. The days and nights became gruelling; at times my confidence was shaken. The certainty of early days faded with the glaring eyes of coyote packs and their nearby night-time howls, which permeated my being and intensified my drive to find her. As the days passed, my kids began complaining. "You're just never here anymore!" echoed in my mind as though I had taken-up late-night bar-hoping as in days long gone. I soothed them and their sorrows and assured them that I was working hard to bring our girl back home to us. "This was not part of the plan!" I would say to people when describing my desire to provide a new life filled with love and security to our sweet-soul canine, who had already endured so much in her brief life.

As previously mentioned, at times our highest learning can come from the struggles we have navigated—or are navigating. Some of our best plans are not seen as suitable in the "Sunlight of the Spirit."[235]

I did not wish to learn this lesson, yet it was presented to me. I did not desire to drive around with a large dog-catching net and snare in the back of my car, nor did I wish to speak of setting humane traps for her potential capture. But I did these things anyway—and many more. I did not want to look at the remains of a deceased dog in our area that had been found and to feel the dread that it might be my dog.

> At times, our best learning comes from the struggles we have navigated—or are navigating.

[235] An AA phrase that means: Once we have been able to clear away the wreckage of our pasts, we can dwell in the newfound sunlight that is present in our lives, which is produced by our creator.

I slept (or rather didn't sleep) in the parking lot of my children's school as our dog had been spotted in this area several times, which is not close to our residence or the trails where she was lost. After our dog repeatedly came-up on a specific video camera, I stayed in complete blackness in the backyard of that home, hearing distant rustles in the ravine from which we thought she might be getting water. With flashes from the sensor-light, I was twice confronted by a large skunk that was 2 feet from me while I sat cross-legged on my yoga mat.

Early-on in our process, on three occasions a dear man and his wife had seen our wee dog on their security system, which had thought her stature was synonymous with an otter—and you know "I ♥ Otters." Beautiful people a-plenty presented themselves in a community-wide search to bring our sweet pup home, which was far from the negative news and human disconnect we witness constantly at this time in our development. There *are* truly hard-working full-hearted humans who join together for a common purpose in real-time love and connection.

Several days in, I exited my search to go home and dress in a floral frock and a pair of heels. I tucked the two dog leashes I had worn clasped around me from the start under the church pew and watched my middle son's confirmation ceremony. One of the kids said, "Oh, you are still looking for that dog? I thought she was dead a long time ago!" "No," I assured her in my gracious tone. "We have several sightings each day, which we go to immediately. I swallowed. "She is coming back to us soon."

Our dog was on the upper-levels highway three times, reportedly "travelling against the traffic" and "running scared." While some pulled-over attempting to help, others blared their horns (please do not do this—it makes the situation worse for the animal). Sirens and honking became a trigger to my senses, and prayer in those moments lightened my wearied soul. The heat of the season increased; the days had turned into weeks. For the first time, there had not been a sighting in 3 days. Sitting at the kitchen island with my soul sister—my wing-woman who had travelled to be with me through many days and several nights—I finally broke-down. In an attempt to draw her out of the woods late at night, we had weenie roasts in the field near where she had first gone missing, together with another saviour I had met in the early days of this process.

It was daytime, 2 days short of 3 weeks, and within 10 minutes, I received four calls of sightings in the area where she had first been lost. This was the first time in all the days that she had been seen in the original area. The locations were close to each other, which made us feel we would be able to get close to her. Then night fell and my faith rose-up to face the darkness once again and the accompanying angst.

The following morning, I did my usual routine with the kids and headed to the park once again. Shortly after 9:00 a.m. a call came in and another, then two others. Within minutes, five of us were in the area along with the most beautiful rescue dog couple with whom I had worked through much of this process. These gentle warriors were pivotal in the rescue and re-homing of over 150 dogs from Kabul. I felt their presence in my time of need was provided by God. That day our dog had gone into a townhome complex which led to another forest system I had not known about during my 30+ years of living in this area. On the advanced mountain-biking trail, I did not see one brave biker during our 6 hours there.

For the first time in 20 days, I had sighted her, twice. My heart leaped. Still, I was just another predator to her survival-mode eyes. She turned and bolted in the opposite direction. I crept through a thicket of brambles trying to avoid breaking the branches beneath me. I spotted her drinking water from a punctured garden hose. The husband of the couple directed me to stay where I was—that he was going up. I stayed as advised. From there, I had the intuitive thought that I just needed to stop. I needed to stand still. I sat down off the beaten trail. As I laid back on the slope, the sunlight beamed from the clear blue sky above through a large evergreen's branches. I stayed there and was present. A bag of treats on the left side of me, another bag on my right. Leashes crossbody in the same position they had been for weeks. I waited. Silently, I talked to my dad. As I had throughout, I thanked him for teaching me to walk in the forest, to breath in the air, to savour their gifts. I spoke to all of the dogs of mine who had gone before. I asked them to guide my dog back to me. I communed with our creator.

Twenty minutes later I heard a branch break above my head. I looked up to the left and saw nothing, apart from the lush vegetation and the warm glow of the sunlight above. Before I could bring my head back, my small 20-pound dog was on top of my torso, licking my face and whimpering in my ears, while she vibrated on top of me like a bee in a hive. Laughing I said, "Oh my gosh, are you real!?" "You look so small!" Not skinny, but small; her fur seemed pale in colour. I quickly clasped the leash onto her collar and slipped the other over her head. In her excitement, she jumped-up kissing my chin repeatedly and, while turning around and around, she became entangled within the leashes.

I quickly called my teammates to let them know I had her. "What do you mean you have her? Do you need us to come?" "No, I have her, two leashes on—I have her! Stay where you are, I will come to you." I was able to walk down the trail with her held securely in my arms to their crying joyous eyes. The cuddles and love that surrounded us all in those moments—a journey of faith and healing, previously complete strangers brought together by one common bond. Love.

This experience strengthened my love for humanity. Together-ness, connection, positivity, rallying together in what makes us human. Love, true exchanges, helping and embracing each other in times of need. Strength, perseverance, and working towards what is right, coming together against that which drags us downward. And at the end of the day, some might say, "What are you going on about? It's just a dog." And yet, it was so much more. The entire experience represented 20 days of individuals uniting, strengthening, community-building, many near misses, and *faith at the centre* of it all for her safe return.

And where was *the thing* during all this? Yes. I used my mobile phone—it was a lifeline for communication during these days of need. This was a circumstance out of the norm—an isolated incident. So, yes, I walked around with *the thing* in my pocket. In times of crises, cell phones can be helpful and timely modes of communication, and this was one of those times. It was important to receive the calls from the 120 posters we put up in the vast spread of locations our dog was spotted—and we needed to receive those calls in real-time.

> Cell phones can be helpful and timely modes of communication in times of crises.

When it comes to usage of *the thing* however, (just like with *anything*) it is important to differentiate between necessity and dependency (habit), a behaviour we may need to relearn.

> Heavy dependence upon anything outside of myself is addiction. I can be addicted to drugs and alcohol, to sex and tobacco; and I can also be addicted to blaming people, to illness, to debt, to being a victim, to being rejected. Yet I can

move beyond these things. Being addicted is giving up my power to a substance or a habit. I can always take my power back. This is the moment I take my power back!...I have an external spirit that has always been with me, and it is here with me now. I relax and let go, and I remember to breathe as I release old habits and practice positive new ones.[236]

Since first beginning this manuscript in the latter half of 2022, much has developed surrounding the topic of *smart*phones and their impact on individuals. Curiously, over the course of the editing process some webpages that addressed the connection between cell phone app development and dependency may no longer be accessible via the web. I invite you to continue-on and do your own research. Be diligent and beware.

Many facts are concealed, perhaps in an effort to continue to drive *the thing* deeper into our lives. With the dark web continuing without government regulation and intervention, more individuals and groups are continuing to gain traction in their pursuits toward pulling society downward. As with *the thing* and its applications, artificial intelligence (AI) advancements claim to be a tool for the betterment of our species and more billionaires have been produced with its development. Though this technology may have some positive attributes, there are strong indications that it may mutate into something detrimental and outside of the scope of human control.

What will the harmful repercussions to this *advancement* be? Are we standing-up to lobby against the damaging effects that AI may bring? Where do we the people stand on this?

[236] Hay, L. (2018). August 4th: In *Trust life: Love yourself every day with wisdom* [A daily devotional]. Carlsbad, CA: Hay House.

From pediatrics to geriatrics, overuse of mobile devices can have an adverse effect on emotional, mental, and physical well-being, self-esteem, and loneliness. These health issues are plaguing our society at all-time highs. Though greater attention is now being focussed on the detriment *the thing* is having on us, more lives have been lost, and many of them young.

As the new school year commences in my area, mobile devices will not be permitted in high schools, which is a positive. Yet when the bell tolls, those same young people make-up for lost time, satisfying their habit, continuing their streaks,[237] and absorbing it all. These devices are a *socializing repellant* for, particularly but not limited to, young people. Rather than true socialization, people have resorted to bowing their heads down in a twisted attempt to come together.

Though awareness of *the thing's* impact on us grows, many will continue ceasing to take hold of the reins of their lives. Tech companies persist in having us surrounded by a full-scale assault on our senses, attacking our dopamine centres in a push/pull bout on our meek defenses. Outlandish conspiracy theories continue to plague societies; most recently, groups claiming hurricanes have been orchestrated by the US government[238]—a powerful example of how some people have reached the next level of insanity, mistrust, and reliance on false information.

Parents continue to give-in to the ease of providing a screen as a short-term solution to behavioural issues that often augments these

[237] A tactic in Snapchat to keep users active.

[238] Gollom, M. (2024, October 9). Rampant conspiracy theories are hindering hurricane relief efforts, say officials. *CBC News: The National.* Accessed 2024-10-25, https://www.cbc.ca/news/world/hurricane-helene-misinformation-1.7346969

behaviours once the "digital pacifier"[239] has been removed. As ADHD and other behavioural issues have skyrocketed, they will likely continue to do so with the needs of young people being more than our systems are able to address. Hoax posts are becoming the norm:

> Police have noted an influx of hoax posts, primarily on Facebook, that involve missing children, wandering seniors, children found with no identification or injured pets. The posts include photos intended to elicit an emotional response, indicate the event occurred in [the event's location] and ask people to share or "bump" the post to help spread the word in the hopes of a successful resolution. In most cases comments are turned off, there is no contact information and the only request is to share the post.[240]

This is now another level of havoc we can accredit to *the thing*. Many are responsive and get involved under the ruse of good intentions. Further to this, people are posting their personal issues from cheating husbands to suicidal teenagers, and more. It seems that everyone has become a counsellor, chiming-in with their opinions surrounding other people's posts. Though some responses might be helpful, others can be ill-informed and toxic. These are serious issues, which require professional guidance and support rather than seeking opinions on social media.

We need to take a closer look at ourselves. Rather than bring these concerns to social media, why not convey them to your inner circle of confidents and ask for their feedback? This increases intimacy and bonds

[239] A term referred to in Orlowski, J. (2020). *The social dilemma* [Documentary film] (Writers: Davis Coombe, Vickie Curtis, Jeff Orlowski; Producer: Larissa Rhodes). Exposure Labs, Argent Pictures, The Space Program; Netflix.

[240] Lethbridge Police Service. (2024, July 9). *Police advise residents to verify posts before sharing on social media.* Accessed 2024-09-30, https://www.lethbridgepolice.ca/news/posts/police-advise-residents-to-verify-posts-before-sharing-on-social-media

with your *real* friends. Sitting in stillness and mediation can also help the answers to come.

The "wrong information…shown by the media"[241] continues at full throttle, infecting "young minds faster than *bacteria.*"[242] "Kids wanna act like what they see"[243] on social media. TikTok videos replace the needed books, togetherness, love, and time that are vital for success. Rather than parents raising their children with the help of their village, we are allowing YouTubers to take-over child-raising instead. "Instead of spreading love,"[244] animosity is now swelling at light speed and affecting us with such a force that many are continually lost to the grip of *the thing.*

What has "happened to the values of humanity?"[245]
Where do we go from here?

We must see *the thing* for *all* that it is and choose differently.
We the people.

Though the *phonedemic* continues to surge, it can still be derailed. Many movements including "Wait Until 8th"[246] groups which encourage parents to "delay the *smart*phone" until Grade 8 (hmmm, why didn't I think of that?), "delay social media" (typically until age 16), and "establish

241 Black Eyed Peas. (2003). Where is the love [Song]. On *Elephunk* [Album] (Songwriters: will.i.am, Justin Timberlake, Taboo, apl.de.ap, Printz Board, Michael Fratantuno, & George Pajon Jr.; Producers: will.i.am & Ron Fair). Labels: A&M, will-i.am, Interscope. Accessed 2024-06-30, https://www.azlyrics.com/lyrics/blackeyedpeas/ whereisthelove.html

242 Black Eyed Peas. (2003). Where is the love [Song]. On *Elephunk* [Album].

243 Black Eyed Peas. (2003). Where is the love [Song]. On *Elephunk* [Album].

244 Black Eyed Peas. (2003). Where is the love [Song]. On *Elephunk* [Album] (Songwriters: will.i.am, Justin Timberlake, Taboo, apl.de.ap, Printz Board, Michael Fratantuno, & George Pajon Jr.; Producers: will.i.am & Ron Fair). Labels: A&M, will-i.am, Interscope. Accessed 2024-06-30, https://www.azlyrics.com/lyrics/blackeyedpeas/ whereisthelove.html

245 Black Eyed Peas. (2003). Where is the love [Song]. On *Elephunk* [Album].

246 Wait until 8th: Let kids be kids a little longer [Homepage]. Accessed 2024-09-30, http://www.waituntil8th.org

good tech boundaries."[247] Offline and unplugged clubs are popping-up throughout European countries and are now beginning to take shape in Australia and parts of the US with waitlist spaces for other areas. Users relinquish their cell phones at check-in to enjoy a day of device-free connection with other like-minded surrenderers. A prominent producer who holds electronic dance music sets is also heading in the right direction. He does not allow devices present at his events and presents those gatherings as "This Never Happened." His philosophy is that removing phones and pictures from the mix brings back the overall experience that accompanies such events.[248] But these events *did* happen. So I am moved to ask, "Why do we require a cellphone to acknowledge that the event happened?" In my view, using this language diminishes what is gained in not having our devices present. Our human abilities of memory and recall are far more attuned without the distraction of a device in hand. By not having access to their devices, chances are that people were far more *present* than they would have been otherwise. It *did* happen.

I wonder whether attendees think of their phones during these events. I wonder whether, afterwards, they realized they had a fuller experience without their devices, if they appreciated the show more and, in turn, if this caused them to want to duplicate this feeling and not bring their devices to other events. I wonder if they visualized themselves arriving at the check-in desk to relinquish their phones, and rather cheerfully announced to the attendant that they do not have one. I wonder whether they may have had a glimpse of wanting more in life and less of *the thing*.

[247] From bio on Wait Until 8th's Facebook page. Accessed 2024-09-30, https://www.facebook.com/search/top?q=wait%20until%208th

[248] *Wikipedia: The Free Encyclopedia.* (n.d.). Lane 8. Accessed 2024-12-02, https://en.wikipedia.org/wiki/Lane_8

I wonder.

Though I, personally, have not attended any of these events, I routinely leave my device at home or lock it in the center console of my car. My device does not rule me. I often have extended time away from it. Through dealing with my own addiction and the accompanying experiences, it is apparent to me that tactics such as these often serve to only temporarily pause our usage. Without fully recognizing and understanding the depths to which our dependencies permeate, first we need to admit we have a problem, then we must take action in making the *necessary, and lasting,* changes.

Weekly I have the opportunity to watch my youngest son during his swimming lesson. As always, I sit amidst the crowd, each in their disconnected EMF-filled bubbles. I feel surrounded. And yet, I watch attentively. On that day, I witnessed my son descend underwater in a cross-legged meditation pose, complete with both hands in mudra position. In this peaceful poised posture, he endeavoured to bring his body weight to the bottom of the pool. Brilliant I thought. I smiled. I was present for this, and many other beautiful displays, which so many others missed while possibly looking at reels on how Gen Z's can pinpoint one's age based on the height of their socks or whether (or not) their hair is parted down the centre. I have heard about this but have never spent (and will *not* spend) my time viewing such materials. Actually people, variety is the spice of life and, as such, I vary my sock height and, at times, (gasp) even go without. Also, my hair is blessed with two cowlicks in the front (Cindy Crawford anyone? She is a timeless beauty), and so my center part may not be possible for those mindless enough to truly believe this: a) is in any way meaningful, and b) allows one's age to be ascertained. Such superficial hollowness can be sickening. No matter whether we're answering emails, scrolling Facebook, messaging or otherwise, why has it become so hard to be all there, where-ever we are. Again:

Wherever you are, be *All* there.

As you know, everyone has a story—not to be confused with a social media story, which I feel would be better termed as a snippet, a fragment, or a drop (in the bucket of life).

The purpose of this story is to help us awaken, to reclaim our attention from *the thing* and step into uncovering our true and authentic selves—away from the masks and falsehoods that we have grasped onto so tightly.

As for my story, I have stepped away from the external ties that had bound me for a significant period of time. The resulting effect is I have grown to develop more fully, to know myself, and to accept myself lovingly. The little things don't bother me anymore. Larger incidents and setbacks typically do not destabilize my serenity like they have in the past. It is a wonderful place to exist.

> The most beautiful people we have known are those who have known defeat, known suffering, known struggle, known loss, and have found their way out of the depths….Beautiful people do not just happen.[249,250] Elizabeth Kübler-Ross

Anyone who chooses can also arrive in this place. I must say the grass is lush and vivid over here, even on the cloudiest of days. Let go of that which takes you elsewhere and step into that which is. It may not be

[249] *Goodreads.* (n.d.). *Elisabeth Kübler-Ross: Quotable quote.* Accessed 2024-06-30, https://www.goodreads.com/quotes/202404-the-most-beautiful-people-we-have-known-are-those-who

[250] Years ago, a dear friend gave me a card with this quote on it. I hold it dearly as I do her.

all sunshine and flowers along the way, but the journey will be well worth the effort. You are *so* worth the commitment.

Be relentless in the pursuit of following your dreams as the developers of *the thing* and its applications are distancing you away from them. And know that each day your story changes, it expands and evolves. Do not be fooled by anything otherwise for another moment. Step into the right here, right now. It can be the most beautiful place, even in times when it is not. And that, in and of itself, is *the* most beautiful *thing*.

Arrive. I am right here with you.

I continue to walk with my head held high, unruffled (for the most part) by that which attempts to call my attention elsewhere. I still help people-in-need, though I have stepped away from attempting to save them as it has proven futile at best. I continue to rescue animals, to save worms on the pavement and gently reposition snails in danger of being stepped-on, and to give a hand-up to anything else in need. You may see me. I'll be the one dancing in coffee shop line-ups or grocery-store aisles or, pulled-over, dancing in my car.

Recently, I caught a man standing in the mall, moving his body to the overhead music. He was taken aback in the most beautiful way when I went and started dancing with him. A stranger, *per se*, yet living and breathing right here, right now—a beautiful H.U.G. exchange.

Life is here to fully experience. Life is for loving. Be involved. Contribute.

A 5-time homeowner, since my last divorce we live in a rented basement suite. In the final editing stages of this publication, an atmospheric river travelled through our area and our flat was flooded. Regardless, I did not allow it to deter me. While completing the last phase of editing, the restorers tumbled the walls down around me, and literally pulled the rugs out from under me.

Yet I continued.

I continue to be inspired, to share the good word, to bring light in darkened times, and to urge you, too, to continue to prevail—in all circumstances.

Share your light, rise above that which pulls you downward, believe you have the power to release yourself and to make your life, and the lives of those around you, better.

With each passing breath, my intuition tells me I am growing closer to my true self. I continue to show up, to listen, to do the work, and to expand my faith. While the pursuit of finding myself is not without flaws and faltering, there is one point of which I am certain—the longer I stare into *any* screen, the further away I will be from recognizing my true potential and fulfilling my purpose.

So let me ask you: Where are *you* in all of this?

When are you going to get back to *you*—
undistracted—and away from being *under the influence*?

> There is only one time when it is
> essential to awaken.
> That time is now.[251]
> ~ Buddha ~

[251] Kornfield, J. (1994). *Buddha's little instruction book* (p. 83). New York, NY: Bantam Books.

Appendices

Abbreviations & Acronyms

AA: Alcoholics Anonymous

ad: advertisement

ADHD: attention-deficit/ hyperactivity disorder

AI: artificial intelligence

Al-Anon: organization that supports families and friends of alcoholics and addicts

aka: also known as

app: application/program downloaded by the user and used on a cellphone or portable device

BFF: best friend forever

BTW: by the way

CEOs: chief executive officers

DJ: disc jockey

DM: direct message

EA: education assistant

EMFs: electromagnetic fields

execs: executives

FB: Facebook

FoMaRL: fear of missing a real life

FoMO: fear of missing out

Heads-Down Generation: H.D.G

Heads-Up Generation: H.U.G.

HTF: How the fuck?

IEP: individual education plan

IG: Instagram

IPV: Intimate Partner Violence

IV: intravenous

LPs: long-playing (phonograph) records

MLM: multi-level marketing

MP: member of parliament

ODC: obsessive device compulsion

ODD: oppositional defiance disorder

QR code: quick response

phonedemic: widespread technological device addiction, which continues to spread globally—the result being the loss of humanity's ability to *truly* connect

PM: private message

RCMP: Royal Canadian Mounted Police

rehab: rehabilitation

Rep: representative

Streaks: a Snapchat tactic to keep users active

Socializing repellant: something that deters one from true social interactions

TV: television

the thing: any mobile device onto which the user can install apps

UN: United Nations

US: United States

WTF: What the fuck?

Suggested Readings and Documentaries

Alcoholics Anonymous World Services. (2001). *Alcoholics Anonymous: The story of how many thousands of men and women have recovered from alcoholism* (rev ed.). New York, NY: Author.[252] (Also referred to as *The Big Book*)

Alexander, B. K. (2008). *The globalization of addiction: A study in poverty of the spirit.* Oxford, England: Oxford University Press.

Amer, K., & Noujaim, J. (Directors). (2019). *The great hack* [Documentary film] (Producers: Karim Amer, Geralyn White Dreyfous, Judy Korin, & Pedro Kos; Writers: Karim Amer, Erin Barnett, & Pedro Kos). The Othrs; Netflix.

Carr, N. (2011). *The Shallows: What the Internet is doing to our brains.* New York, NY: W. W. Norton.

Cooper, A. (2018, December 9). Groundbreaking study examines effects of screen time on kids. *CBC: 60 Minutes.* Accessed 2024-06-20, https://www.cbsnews.com/news/groundbreaking-study-examines-effects-of-screen-time-on-kids-60-minutes/

Doyle, G. (2020). *Untamed.* New York, NY: The Dial Press.

Fincher, D. (Director). (2010). *The social network* [Documentary film] (Producers: Scott Rudin, Dana Brunetti, Michael De Luca, Ceán Caffin). Columbia Pictures, Relativity Media, Scott Rudin Productions, Michael De Luca Productions, Trigger Street Productions; Sony Pictures Releasing.

Johnson Martinko, K. (2023). *Childhood unplugged: Practical guide to get kids off screens and find balance.* Gabriola Island, BC: New Society Publishers.

[252] *The Big Book* has assisted millions of people in recovery from alcoholism. As of 2009, it had sold over 30 million copies. It is available online at https://www.aa.org/the-big-book and https://anonpress.org/bb

Mercola, J. (2023, July 5). *Heavy screen time changes children's brains.* Cape Coral, FL: Author.

Orlowski, J. (2020). *The social dilemma* [Documentary film] (Writers: Davis Coombe, Vickie Curtis, Jeff Orlowski; Producer: Larissa Rhodes). Exposure Labs, Argent Pictures, The Space Program; Netflix.

Peck, M. S. (1978). *The road less travelled: A new psychology of love, traditional values and spiritual growth.* New York, NY: Touchstone.

Pineault, N. (n.d.). *Smarter tech podcast.* Accessed 2024-12-02, https://theemfguy.com/smarter-tech

Ram Dass. (1978). *Be here now.* Santa Fe, NM: Hanuman Foundation.

Ruiz, D. M. (1997). *The four agreements: A practical guide to personal freedom.* San Rafael, CA: Amber-Allen.

1. Be impeccable with your word.
2. Don't take anything personally.
3. Don't make assumptions.
4. Always do your best.

Singer, M. A. (2007). *The untethered soul: The journey beyond yourself* (p. 177). Oakland, CA: New Harbinger Publications.

Tutu, D., Dali Lama, & Abrams, D. C. (2016). *The book of joy: Lasting happiness in a changing world.* New York, NY: Viking Press.

Weir, P. (Director), & Schulman, T. (Writer). (1989). *Dead poets society* [Film] (Producers: Steven Haft, Paul Junger Witt, & Tony Thomas). Touchstone Pictures, Silver Screen Partners IV; Buena Vista Pictures Distribution.

Suggested Songs

Alanis Morissette, "Thank you"

Black Eyed Peas, "Where is the love?"

Blessing Offor, "Brighter days" (2022)

Blessing Offor, "Your love" (2023)

Charlotte Cardin, "Phoenix"

Everything but The Girl, *Walking Wounded* [Album] and *Amplified Heart* [Album]

George Michael,[253] *Older* album (1996)

Jax ,"Victoria's secret"

John Lennon, "Imagine"

Lauren Daigle, "Losing my religion" (2018)

Madonna, "Like a prayer"

Pink, "Never gonna not dance again"

Queen Latifah, Lavert, and Troop's arrangement "For the love of money"[254]

Sarah McLaughlin, "Elsewhere", "Mary", "Fumbling towards ecstasy" on *Fumbling Towards Ecstasy* [Album] (1993)

Shawn Mendes, "Something big" (2014)

Three Doors Down, "Here without you"

TLC, Unpretty (1999)

Upon completion of this book, please listen to the playlists on my website which broadens the significance of the messages within:

www.phonedemic.com

253 Geroge Michael's songs were my anthems.

254 The arrangement was in the 1991 film *New Jack City* and is on the soundtrack. The song was written by Gamble, K., Huff, L., & Jackson, A. (Songwriters). (1974). For the love of money [Song]. On *For the love of money* [Album] (Producers: Kenneth Gamble and Leon Huff). Labels: Philadelphia International, 3544.

Our tears become holy in the form of ink on a page. Once we have spoken our saddest story, we can be free of it.

Taylor Swift[255]

[255] Tate, S. (2024, April 19). *On air with Ryan Seacrest.* Accessed 2024-06-30, https://onairwithryan.iheart.com/content/2024-04-19-taylor-swift-reveals-secret-double-album-with-extra-ttpd-songs

Acknowledgements

First and foremost, always, thanks be to God, who I believe placed the people, space, and time in front of me to bring this work to fruition. I am eternally grateful for the journey that brought me to intimacy with you.

To my dear friends and family, who either supported my aspirations or did not, you all helped to inspire me and propel me further in achieving this writing.

Immense gratitude to my sons, for being their unique selves, and for their broad range of ages and stages that allowed for a natural younger generation field study on this topic. As *the thing* was introduced into my two eldest son's lives, I witnessed a dimming of their attention and spirits, along with a defiance to let go of its grasp.

I would like to send a large accolade to my editor, Joanie Wolfe who, through a series of synchronicities, was placed in my path by another author. We quickly found common ground and became kindred spirits. We laughed, I cried, we felt, and as we continued forward much expanded in the technological world around us.

Lastly, to the public who glaringly illustrated the addictive tendencies associated with device usage—that is, all those riding in elevators, standing at bus stops, and walking blindly into traffic with their heads down—you have provided more insight to this project than you will ever know.

About the Author

Ana Miranda is a human *being,* a mother, a daughter, a sister. She is a friend to those who have earned the designation, and also to many who have not. She is an observer who feels deeply and is an advocate for positive change. Though Ana is not a researcher, she has done her utmost to backup her statements.

> I am not a rocket scientist, a philosopher, or a wizard. Even if I were all three, I would still find myself looking off the edge of my understanding into a vast unknown. As I recognize my own limitations, I am more grateful than ever for a Higher Power who is free from such restrictions.[256]

The author humbly requests readers to encourage others to purchase this book rather than pass their copies forward. As with many artists, the author's livelihood depends on repeat purchases.

Share love, spread love, heads up.

Be here—Present—Now.

[256] Al-Anon Family Group. (1992). *Courage to change: One day at a time in Al-Anon II* (p. 225). New York, NY: Author.

Manufactured by Amazon.ca
Acheson, AB

16327354R00159